I'm Gonna Teach

The Early Years

By

Kenneth S. Karcinell

Contents

Acknowledgments

Dr. Lionel E. McMurren, who had the faith and the courage...

Dr. Hill Brindle, for the patience and the polish...

Ellen, Sarah, Joey, and Greg for their love and encouragement!

To my parents, Mildred and Carl who did their best!

Preface

As you read through the ensuing pages, the intended message is not about the ineptness of our schools or the treachery of our school boards, but rather about the successes, which can be realized in our schools in spite of these existing circumstances.

To whet your appetite I submit the following two anecdotes for your consideration: Throughout the '60's and '70's educational pontificators were obsessed with finding "role models" for students, particularly minority students. Very often such emphasis resulted in near catastrophic results. I can readily recall two such incidents. In 1966, I was a second-year teacher in a school located in North Central Harlem. The climate of the times was such that race relations between blacks and whites were to say the least strained. Nevertheless, here I was conducting the proceedings of a seventh grade assembly program, when I noticed our principal in the rear of the auditorium. Although there was poor lighting there, I did see a tall black male dressed in warrior like garb complete with spear and loincloth standing next to him. The principal, a short balding man, who was on the verge of retirement and had on more than one occasion shared his views of Florida with me, sent a monitor to me with a note. The note simply said that I was to introduce the guest as a hero of the "Mau Mau Movement," who had just completed a twenty-year prison sentence. As I did so, all of the students rose from their seats and cheered the man. Quietly my white colleagues departed from the auditorium, as did the principal. The warrior began his remarks by teaching the audience how to say "death to all whites" in his native tongue.

To say that the audience enthusiastically followed his lead doesn't truly capture the moment. Undaunted, I sat in my front-row assembly leaders seat and waited for the bell to ring. At that time I initiated an auditorium dismissal routine. "Hell no, we won't go!" the audience began to chant. Grabbing the microphone, I announced, there are four classes in this auditorium who have me for math. Your report card grades are coming out in one week. I would like you to be the first classes to leave. Now! Continuing the chant under their breaths, they exited from the auditorium. Soon after, the others followed. For the next several weeks, there were reported a number of incidents involving the hurling of racial epithets by black students at some of their white teachers. While this type of misbehavior was not uncommon, its occurrences had become more frequent. Additionally there were instances of property damage to the automobiles of white teachers. Neither the principal nor any other school official protested. Surprisingly some parents did. Their position being that in order to present their children with controversy, the school needs to teach them how to first treat such matters in an understanding way. As a result of the parent protest, the school board was obligated to investigate—and it did. When the investigator interviewed me, she inquired as to my impressions. "Why do you ask? Neither you nor your board will ever take the tact of consulting with schools on the presentation of controversy. What do you want to know? Was there tension?" "Yes. Was I afraid? No. You'll have to send more than one warrior when you come for me!"

The search for role models at any cost continued. Early on a Monday morning in '71, the principal convened an emergency meeting of the Executive Cabinet to discuss the implementation of a directive he'd just received from the local school district office. The directive read:

> To: All JHS Principals
> From: District Superintendent
> RE: Role Modeling

Ladies and Gentlemen:

As we continue our quest to furnish our students with opportunities to become exposed to successful role models, we have been presented with a unique opportunity to fulfill this quest en masse. Accordingly, you are directed to make arrangements to transport your seventh and eighth graders to Madison Square Garden this coming Friday for a pre-arranged viewing of a public workout training session by heavyweight boxing contender Brian Miller. (Brian Miller, you see, had recently been released from prison, where he had served in excess of ten years for conviction of a murder he had committed. His message was that while in prison he had seen the light, was reformed, and dedicated to leading a productive life, legally pummeling his opponents.).

For the most part the prime criterion for role model was that one had to have a story, which when revealed would contain some hard luck experiences suffered by that individual early in life but did not stand in the way of his rise to stardom. What would your reaction be to a school board that decided it was necessary to cancel your child's classes so that he/she could attend the boxing workout of a convicted killer because it was supposed to be an uplifting experience for your child who so desperately needed a role model? Talk about highlighting the negative! The superintendent who signed off on the letter was approached by protesting parents, to whom he replied, that he was a very busy man "in bondage to his calendar" and not given to the habit of reversing his decisions. Curious language for a black Administrator, I thought. After all it was the '60's, a decade that had already witnessed countless sacrifices in the name of civil rights gains, gains, which were intended in large part to rid blacks of the last vestiges of dehumanizing bondage.

Given the intransigence of the superintendent, each school in the district made plans to supervise the outing.

Their teachers would supervise all classes. The deans and assistant principals would go along as well. Accordingly, the trip to the Garden, or more accurately the search for Mr. Role Model, would proceed as scheduled.

In the witness accounts given to police later, such words as mayhem, chaos, confusion, carnage, destruction, and lunacy appeared repeatedly. The subway system it was said incurred in excess of $50,000 worth of damage. Six students were arrested for riotous behavior. Two teachers had to be given first aid care for cuts and bruises they had received while trying to break up pupil skirmishes. Several students were reported missing. It turned out that these students had made their own assessment of the situation and decided to spend the day in the movies. I hope that they grew up to become teachers.

Of course the school board closed ranks and, invoking the doctrine of blamelessness, condemned the school principals for not supplying sufficient supervision for the pupils.

For a period of thirty-two years, I and countless others would function in such a climate. To be sure, we held the system, the school boards, and decentralization, (which instead of empowering parents empowered politicians) beneath contempt. Nothing much has changed. What, therefore, is my message? In spite of all that I've described, there are successes to be realized. There are schools—students, parents, teachers, and administrators—that are making a difference. There are just not enough of them. "We need you!"

Part I

The Harlem Years

Kenneth S. Karcinell

Chapter I

The Siege

April 1973. The day prior to any extended school vacation is customarily one fraught with anxiety and gleeful anticipation. Fun-loving students and their stressed-out teachers share these emotions equally. The day before Easter recess would prove no exception. It was late in the morning; I was in my office trying to bring closure to a mountain of paper work, when my attention was seized by my peripheral vision. It reported that a student was roller-skating down the hall corridor. Initially, I rejected this message, as such an overt act of pupil misbehavior simply could not happen on my floor. Comforting as that thought was, I quickly came to my senses and realized that anything that could happen would happen. With this in mind I got up from my chair, went out to the hallway just in time to catch a glimpse of "the skater" making it around the bend into the adjacent hallway. I followed in hot pursuit. When I rounded the corner an empty and quiet hallway confronted me. I began a systematic inspection of bathrooms and nearby vestibules. To no avail. It now remained to do a room-to-room search. This act would not serve to distract the nearby classroom activities. The reason was that from early in the term both teachers and pupils under my supervision had become accustomed to my daily visits. My first two stops revealed nothing unusual. The third stop would bear fruit. The classroom was one in which vocal music was being taught. As I entered the room, I noted that the teacher was seated behind an upright piano well hidden from the view of his pupils. Impervious to my arrival or anything else for that matter, he methodically played a tune on his piano, which I recognized as "My Old Kentucky Home." The students who were variously engaged in such alternative activities as card

3

playing, comic book reading, drawing, or making idle conversation became aware of my presence and ceased from their engagement in the illicit activities. They tried in vain to give the impression that they were into "My Old Kentucky Home." As I walked about the room, my attention was attracted by two obvious violations of school rules and regulations governing safety. The first was that the rear classroom door was wide open. The second was that a window in the rear of the room was open from the bottom up as opposed to the top down. Several students seated near the open window feverishly beckoned to me to come to them, pointing towards the open window. Doing so, I peered out just in time to see my skater take off down the alleyway below. I asked the students to accompany me out into the hallway to tell me their story. To his credit, the music teacher never lost a beat. He continued playing musical accompaniment for the class, which was now fully compliant with the requirement of singing "My Old Kentucky Home."

In the corridor the students told me the name of the skater and incredibly, added that she had burst into the classroom through the unlocked rear door, skated over to the rear window, opened it, and instead of being confronted by a protective window guard, was able to remove her skates, cast them to the sidewalk below, and then perform the olympian feat of jumping down, a distance of approximately twelve feet. Finding some solace in the thought that God protected fools and children, I returned to my office, called the principal and reported the incident to him. I was directed to write it up in detail—Additionally, I was to contact the student's parents and inform them that their child would be suspended from school for engaging in "reckless endangerment to pupil safety and leaving school without permission." I was to further inform them that a "suspension conference" would take place at 9 a.m. on the first day of school following the Easter recess. Immediately,

I called the skater's home to convey the principal's directive. After several rings, to my amazement my skater answered the phone. In response to my request to speak with her mother or father, she told me that they were not home but that her older brother was. I asked her to put him on. After identifying myself I related the morning's events as they pertained to his sister's behavior. Of course I also told him of the principal's judgment and decision. The brother who had identified himself as "Stone," said, "Thanks," and hung up.

At approximately 11:55 a.m. I left my office and made my way down to the pupil cafeteria to monitor my grade's lunch hour routines. While circulating about, I was joined by the principal, Dr. McNaughton. He was a hardnosed former Navy commander, who believed in following procedures in all instances. He also had a reputation as a leader who did not suffer foolishness readily, especially from his subordinates. Standing about 5'9", he was in reasonably good physical shape and was well liked by most of the staff and parents. He was also well respected by the student body. I felt particularly loyal to him because he had made the racially unpopular decision in 1971 to assign me as acting assistant principal of the eighth grade. A position to which I would ultimately be permanently appointed. Dr. McNaughton asked me if I had "followed up" (a trendy educational phrase of the '70's) on the suspension notification to the family of the child who had left school without permission. He seemed to take great pains not to mention the means by which the child had exited the school. When I told him that I had informed the family of the date and time of the suspension conference, he commended me for acting so promptly. Dr. McNaughton then went on to say that he was about to leave to attend a district principals conference and that Mr. Lindle, the administrative assistant, would be in charge (as per the "chain of command"). Little did I know how valuable this information would prove as the day's events unfolded.

Mr. Lindle was a physically imposing man standing about 6'2" and weighing about 240 lbs. His educational background was such that he had expertise in the Language Arts and Social Studies curriculum. He also possessed certain God given skills, particularly the ability to use his natural voice without a microphone when addressing students in the lunchroom or auditorium. I would find out later that Mr. Lindle had also served in the military as a Master Sergeant.

I have purposely tried to provide as complete a profile of the two school leaders as possible. It is important when you consider the time between 1965-73. The political and social climate was in complete upheaval. Race relations among blacks and whites were strained almost to the point of open civil warfare. Indeed this climate would persevere throughout the '60's and well into the '70's. To compound matters, the staff was variously made up of several distinct groups, all of whom thought that they knew what was best for the students. There were a cadre of older and veteran black teachers who kept their politics to themselves, while they taught the old fashioned way. There were a handful of radical whites, who sympathized with the Black Power movement. There was to be sure a fair representation of this movement on staff as well. They made no secret of their disdain for whites. Then there was a group of individuals of black and white ethnicity, who like myself, were born and raised in NYC and made their bones in such notable institutions as DeWitt Clinton, Benjamin Franklin, and Morris HS, just to mention a few. Many of us were products of project living. We had experienced multiculturalism long before the NYC Board of Education inserted it as a mandated study approach in the humanities. These teachers for the most part wore no labels and simply tried as best they could to ply their trade. For many it was a hit or miss

proposition. They were fresh out of college, not having had the benefit of student teaching or theoretical training. But they did want to teach. In later years, Mr. Lindle would say that these teachers were the most receptive to on-the-job training, as opposed to those who had gone to a Teacher's College and had become resisters to change.

Often these groups would come into conflict with one another. It was at this point that law and order could be restored only by the skilled and intimidating negotiating style of Mr. Lindle, who was making people offers they couldn't refuse long before we heard of this practice in "Godfather Part I." So regardless of which group you were influenced by, you knew that once Mr. Lindle got wind of your conflict, it simply had to end. The tragedy to this image, however, was that the individual was so much more. As I would come to realize, he was extremely devoted and dedicated to the well being of the students. He would if asked spend countless hours after school with you, pointing out ways by which you could better hone your teaching skills. His office was a giant room of resource files covering almost every topic in social studies and language arts. He understood that one of the keys to successful instructional delivery was via the "multi-vehicular" approach particularly emphasizing the use of visual aides as a primary teaching tool. Teachers under his supervision were expected to avail themselves of such state of the art equipment as the overhead projector, opaque projector, rexo dittos, slide projectors, record players, and various teaching kits that were "hands-on" oriented. There were map study kits galore. There was a plethora of subject texts on different reading levels. Finally, there was the "trophy case" always under lock and key. The display was a reminder of the many challenges presented by the students. Of note were the varied selection of knives and box cutters. Additionally, one could find several types of zip guns, brass knuckles, spiked helmets, two-inch-wide black garrison belts adorned with

7

furniture tacks, an assortment of fire crackers and cherry bombs, and the centerpiece to the showcase, a glistening machete. No one, to my knowledge, ever asked Mr. Lindle as to how he had come by this collection. The sobering thought was that he had.

In later years, teachers recounting their early interactions with the man would rarely speak of his academic qualities, choosing instead to revisit some altercation they had had with a recalcitrant student or an unruly parent and how Mr. Lindle had saved their asses.

It was 1 p.m. when I returned to my office. I'd stopped in the cafeteria and picked up a sandwich and coke, in anticipation of a quiet working lunch. As I approached my office door, I was greeted first by Mr. Taylor, the senior teacher in the math department, who asked me if I wouldn't mind if he used the rexo machine in my office in order to run off some last minute copies of his Easter break homework assignments. I told him to "be my guest." Two students who had taken time from their Easter party to bring me some ice cream and cake then greeted me. I opened the office door and invited all to come in. Mr. Taylor declined my offer to share in the "goodies" deciding to begin the task of running off his rexo sheets. Of course, I had no choice but to trash the tuna and have the entire Carvel ice cream cake slice and coke as my lunch. The next few moments would see this atmosphere of joy and sharing change to one of shock and despair.

Within seconds of sampling my treats and saying thank you to the students who were preparing to return to their classrooms, there appeared at my doorway a rather fearsome looking contingent of individuals, dressed variably in army fatigues, open fish net tops, and calf length "super fly" style outerwear accompanied by the obligatory wide brimmed hat. There were four such individuals, three men and a woman. Upon closer examination there was a

8

fifth person...my skater, who had a smirk on her face that said, "watch."

The woman appeared to be the leader. I perceived this as she gave the others hand directions as to the positions she wanted them to take. The gentleman in the super fly garb took up a position just outside my office door, closing it behind himself as he left the room. Each of the remaining two adults simply "posted up" on either side of my office, while my skater sat down on one of my guest chairs.

The woman walked over to my desk, where I was seated and had stopped eating, so that I could fully absorb the act of being placed under siege. With her left hand she placed her forefinger over her lips signifying that I was not to speak. With her right hand she produced a snip and proceeded to cut my phone line. As I looked about, I saw that Mr. Taylor and the children who had brought the Easter treats were motionless in their places.

In appearance, the woman was short of height; her hair was tightly drawn back and braided. She bore a body odor, which reeked from alcohol and camels. As I sat at my desk taking it all in, my training told me to stay calm. My years of confrontational behavioral development acquired in the projects told me not to cave but to be equally confrontational. I chose a middle road. I would maintain a professional air and not do anything to put my other guests in jeopardy. Not one to be easily intimidated, I opened my mouth to speak. My attempt to initiate the conversation was pre-empted when the woman produced a hand gun, pointed it in my face and said, "ain't no mother-fuckin' white honkey bastard gonna suspend her child." In one magnificent statement, she had managed to convey not only her purpose for visiting but also what it would take to resolve the crisis. She then lowered her gun, an action that I interpreted as a cue to speak. I began by saying that I would be pleased to review her daughter's conduct that led to the decision to suspend her. I also pointed out that this decision was not one that could be made by me but rather by the Principal. The woman responded by saying, "You're all the same." At that point I suggested to the woman that the things we had to talk about didn't concern the children seated at the conference table. She agreed, and with a motion of her head one of the "guards" she had posted earlier, opened the door and beckoned the children to leave. As the door closed behind the exiting children, Mr. Taylor, who had been standing frozen like at the rexograph machine near the door giving the impression that he was a part of the office décor, sensed an opportunity to make his escape. In an instant he lunged for the door handle and then stood in amazement as the knob fell off into his hand. Seemingly resigned to what he surely attributed to an act of fate, Mr. Taylor resumed his posture of standing statue-like next to the rexograph machine, holding the doorknob in his hand and staring blankly into space.

Returning to reality, I was again confronted by the short woman who was once again waving her gun from side to side and repeating the refrain, "What you gonna do honkey; what you gonna do?" Before I could say anything, the outside guard opened the office door. The interruption this time stemmed from the fact that Ms. Pilson, an English teacher and dear friend, and a fellow patron of Yonkers Raceway, was seeking a consultation with me. As she entered, Mr. Taylor sensing I suspect what could be the last opportunity to escape the siege, lunged out the door and "made it" down the hallway in what could best be described as "God's speed." The guard stood motionless and exclaimed, "Damn!"

As Ms. Pilson entered the room, I was amazed at the fact that she seemed to know my captors. This was evidenced by the fact that she greeted each by their first name. They in turn returned her greeting with obvious respect in their manner. After exchanging greetings, she approached my desk stating that she was going to Yonkers that evening and would I mind marking some picks for her in *The Daily News*, which she placed on my desk. The paper was opened to the Yonkers entries. Sensing an opportunity to communicate the gravity of my situation, I grabbed my red pen and noted across the racing form the following message: these people have guns. They have cut my telephone wires. Get help! To my shock and consternation Ms. Pilson looked at what I had written, then looked at each of the intruders and looking back at me exclaimed, "Don't be ridiculous, there's nothing to be worried about." She then insisted that I make my selections, as she had a class coming up in a few moments. Reluctantly and resigned to the hand fate had dealt me, I took my pen and arbitrarily marked the numbers 10 and 3 for the Daily Double races. These numbers were my birthdate, which I was beginning to wonder if I'd be around for again. Having accomplished the purpose of her visit, Ms. Pilson picked up the newspaper, turned to leave, and in so doing, she bid everyone to have a nice day and left the office as she had arrived, in style.

Once again I was confronted by the gun-toting woman, who was now hurling vindictive after vindictive at me, garnered of course with promises of retaliatory action to my person should the decision to suspend her child go unchanged. Shortly our attention was again diverted by the arrival of visitors. Their presence was marked by the fact that they were engaged in some loud verbal exchange with the outside guard. The conversation went something like this: a gentleman who served as the school security guard by day, and an owner of several bars in the neighborhood by night, and an individual who had performed as a kick returner/running back in the old AFL was clearly heard to say to the "guard" who had obviously displayed the gun tucked into his waistband, "I don't give a fuck what you have, this is a school, take your goddam hat off before I knock it off."

My spirits immediately rose when the "outside guard," the school security guard, and Mr. Lindle came into my office. I assumed that they had been alerted to the crisis by Ms. Pilson, Mr. Taylor, or the children who had been allowed to leave earlier. I found out later that I was right on all accounts. Once again, I looked on in amazement, for just as Ms. Pilson knew the intruders, so too did Mr. Lindle, as evidenced by the cordial manner by which he exchanged greetings with the woman and her accomplices. In the course of their dialogue, Mr. Lindle asked after the fortunes of one of the woman's children who had several years earlier graduated from the school while under Mr. Lindle's supervision. This seemed to break the ice and ease the tension for a moment. The woman smiled, and said, "Mr. Lindle you kept him on the straight and narrow. If it wasn't for you, he'd be in jail or dead." Seizing the moment, he asked her if it wasn't true that whenever there was a problem with her children in the school, wasn't she always able to see him, and get it straightened out. She responded affirmatively with a nod of her head. Mr. Lindle then said that whatever the problem was today, that he could not begin to discuss it with her while she had her gun out. She put the gun back into her bag, and proceeded to tell Mr. Lindle "that this no good honkey cocksucker was trying to get her child suspended for nothin'." Mr. Lindle asked her to sit down. He then checked his watch, went over to confer with the school security guard, and after a few seconds returned where the woman was seated and said he was sure that the police would be arriving soon, as he had called them when informed of the presence of intruders in the school. He suggested that unless everyone wanted to be on the 11 o'clock news that she should give her gun to her sons and that they should clear out. He would continue the discussion with her after explaining to the police that a mistake had been made. Again with a nod of her head, one of her guards took her gun, turned, and with the other two guards as well as the skater left my office. The siege had been lifted. Mr. Lindle then escorted the woman down the hall to an empty classroom, where he assured her that he would listen to the whole story. The outcome of these negotiations would of course be subject to Dr. McNaughton's approval, upon our return from the Easter spring vacation. This was a formality, asserted Mr. Lindle, as the principal usually accepted his recommendations in matters such as these. Before leaving the second floor Mr. Lindle escorted the woman back to my office, whereupon she offered out her hand and said, "I wasn't gonna do nothin'." I shook her hand and led everyone to the door, as I shut off the light and instinctively tried to lock the office door, I allowed myself a chuckle, recalling the utter look of despair on Mr. Taylor's face when the knob fell into his hand. As I held the door open for all to leave, the woman said, "Hey, you need a doorknob." Yeah, I know.

We said our goodbyes at the main entrance to the school. At this point Mr. Lindle checked his wristwatch proclaiming that it was 4:30. He asked me if I'd like to join him for some supper. I thanked him for the invite and told him that I was really of the mind that could best find solace in some type of imbibement. We exchanged holiday wishes and walked off—Mr. Lindle towards his car and me directly across the street to The Flash Inn. Sitting alone, I lit up a Marlboro and while savoring my bourbon, I asked myself, why?

Chapter II

Why?

It was a typically hot and humid August day in NYC in 1965. I had returned home after having spent the day hauling hardware in my non-air conditioned truck. My territory included the greater NYC metropolitan area.

As I let myself into the apartment I shared with my mother, all I could think of was the "cold one" waiting for me in the fridge. Opening the apartment door, there stood my mother with a smile and at the same time a look that bespoke her disappointment. After all, I had graduated college just three months earlier, and truck driving was not what she had envisioned as a career for her son. To make matters worse, when speaking to family relatives who were all too eager to inform her that their college grads were either involved in or pursuing careers in such esteemed fields as medicine, law or business, in answer to their queries about me she would say that I was examining various possibilities.

Not having a family business to join or an aptitude for figures or an inclination to practice law or medicine, I began to look at the various civil service fields. I continued truck driving while informing my boss Mr. Hersh of my plans. He gave me his blessing and asked only that I give him a week's notice prior to my leaving. Mr. Hersh, who had hired me as a part-time driver during my college days, had been a lifelong friend to my mother. He knew how desperately she wanted me to become a "white shirt and tie" professional.

Gaining entrée into a civil service field was dependent upon test taking, pass ranking, and appointment lists. Of course, where there were high demand, lists would continuously be promulgated and tests given on a more frequent rate. The city would pay for this folly during the 1975 budget crunch and near bankrupt condition brought about by the negotiations of the inexperienced Lindsay Administration with the various civil service labor unions. Contracts given out to the uniform service providers, and the teacher's unions in 1968/69 would contain benefits and salary increases that previously and afterward would take the expiration and renegotiation of at least two contracts to achieve.

One agency, which seemed to constantly announce exams, was the Department of Social Services. I took their exam in September 1965. True to present day form, when people contact this agency I never heard from them again. Of course I did re-contact them after a month, so as to ascertain my pass/fail status. I was informed that there was no record of my having taken the exam. The clerk went on to tell me that I was welcome to file an application and pay a fee for the next test offering in two weeks. I informed him that I was looking at my cancelled check used for the fee charges for the test I had taken. Later that day I told my mother of the test-taking fiasco conversation I had had with social services. Nonplussed, she asked me if I'd given thought to teaching as a career pursuit. I asked her how she could think that I could be a teacher. Had she forgotten the math and science tutors? Had she forgotten the four year 75% overall academic average? Had she forgotten the college "C" cumulative average? Her response was that she believed that more important than all that I had mentioned was the fact that I had a big heart. Of course, she went on to explain how noble and proud the teaching profession was. After all, she reasoned, some of our greatest thinkers, men like Socrates, Aristotle, Plato, all the prophets, Ghandi, Confucious, and of late Dr. Martin Luther King Jr., were all teachers, and now you! You should know my mother said, teachers have excellent health coverage and dental plans, two month summer vacations, not to mention a fine pension to look forward to in their retirement years. As she spoke, I conjured up an image, featuring myself in the front of a classroom and speaking to a group of youngsters who were literally hanging on my every word. What a power trip. It was quite a rush! Right then I decided to go for it. The very next day I trekked down to the NYC Board of Education and filed to take the Substitute Teacher's Exam. As luck would have it I would be able to take the test the next day. I was "pumped." To my further astonishment, I received a telegram within two weeks advising me that I had passed the exam and was to report to the Medical Division for a physical, as soon as possible upon receipt of the Pass Notification I was holding. This series of rapid responses from the Board of Education would be the first and last time over the next thirty-two years that I would ever be so favorably impressed with any aspect of their modus operandi. The next day I went to see Mr. Hersh. As soon as I did, I exclaimed excitedly, "Mr. Hersh, I'm gonna teach!" He put both his hands around me, gave me the "Russian" bear hug, and with a tear in his eye and slight hesitation in his voice, told me that he would miss me.

Chapter III

The First Day

Having passed my medical exam, I received a telegram directing me to report to a JHS in uptown Manhattan located in the community known as Harlem, on October 31st. I awoke that morning after having had perhaps one hour of sleep throughout a night filled with anxiety and enthusiasm for the day ahead. After all, I was gonna teach! I finally got out of bed at 6 a.m., showered, shaved, and picked out a white shirt, blue tie, and a charcoal grey cotton suit. My choice was somewhat limited because of the fact that truck driving did not warrant the maintenance of a "white collar" wardrobe. The white shirt readily stuck out in its environs of plaid flannels and sweatshirt apparel. The suit was unchallenged by any like outfit, and my red tie had a stain. Of course, the entire outfit was complemented with a pair of Tom McAnn's black loafers worn on feet adorned with grey woolen socks. There were obviously some wardrobe issues that would have to be addressed in the very near future.

My mother had prepared an elaborate breakfast, which given my nervous state I partook solely of the orange juice, toast, and coffee. As I left the apartment she sent me off with a hug and the exclamation to have a great day! With her sendoff, I went downstairs and got into my '58 stick-shift Impala and set off for my destination. The weather forecast was for rain. I prayed that it would hold off until late in the day. You see, when it rained, my gearshift would get stuck in 1st gear. When that happened, I would have to get out of the car, lift the hood, and move the gear linkage manually. Invariably, my hand would come back caked in grease. I could not have this happen today.

The ride from Rego Park to the school took about forty-five minutes. I had arrived at approximately 8 a.m. While my prayers to the "Rain God" had been answered, I had not thought to pray to the "Parking God." Having circled the block twice, I was about to do so for a third time when in the middle of the block a tall African-American man stood blocking my path. With one hand he was holding what I believed to be a portable radio and with the other he was gesturing for me to park my car in a spot that was clearly vacant because of a hydrant in its place. I rolled down my window and asked the man if he would please move so that I could continue my search. It occurred to me that as I was speaking, so too was he into his portable radio. Not having moved from in front of my car, he again motioned more emphatically that I park in the spot taken by the fire hydrant. He then came over to my window and asked if I was a teacher at the "Fortress." I replied that this was to be my first day, and I wanted to arrive early to create a favorable impression. He strode a few paces away from the car and definitely spoke into his radio. I assumed that he was some type of plain-clothes officer, and accordingly, when he again directed me to park in the fire hydrant spot I did so immediately. After getting out and locking the car, the gentleman came over and told me that he was responsible for safety on the block and that if I had any trouble, I could usually find him walking somewhere on the block. Short of that just ask anyone for Earnie.

Buoyed by this sudden feeling of safety and security, I thanked Earnie and walked toward the school. Odd, I thought, that Earnie had referred to the school as "The Fortress." I searched my mind for a working definition of the term. The best that I could summon up was that a fortress was a stronghold built to protect a human populace residing within its walls. Hmmmm!

The main entrance to the school was gained by ascending a marble stairway that rose to a landing marked by four steel-grey colored doors, none of which had outside handles. These doors were installed into archways which were punctuated with oval shaped carved designs directly above the doors most reminiscent of the Moorish influence I'd seen in the Palace of the Alhambra in Grenada, Spain. On the stairs just a few feet ahead of me was a small baldish man whom I took to be a teacher at the school.

Excuse me; I called to him, could you direct me to the principal's office? With a hand motion, he beckoned me to follow his lead. To my surprise he led me to a door marked "Principal's Office." To my further surprise he took out his keys, opened the door, and again beckoned me to follow him inside. Meticulously, he removed a wooden hangar from a closet and hung his coat in the closet, being sure to allow "breathing room" between it and other garments previously hung there. He then sat down at his desk, put on his eyeglasses, and said, "Good morning. I am Mr. Biggio, the Principal. And you are?" "Ken Kassell," I replied. "I've been assigned to the school as a substitute teacher by the Board of Education." Having completed the sentence I then nervously produced the telegram and license credential I'd received from the Board for Mr. Biggio's inspection. After examining these papers he looked up and asked me if I knew math. Realizing that school had been in session for nearly two months, it struck me that there was some kind of immediate need for a math teacher. I did not want to be turned away, and while math was a subject that I did not master very well as a college and high school student, I replied to Mr. Biggio's inquiry that I'd gotten by. Instantly Mr. Biggio depressed his intercom button and informed a certain Mrs. Gerstein that he was sending her a Mr. Kassell for immediate processing as a seventh grade math teacher. He then released the intercom button, rose from his chair, came out from behind his desk, walked me over to a door which opened out to the General Office, shook my hand and bid me well, and then turned to go back into his office.

Then he suddenly turned to face me, placed both hands on my shoulders, and said, "You might want to work out a bit so as to be able to combat the daily rigors of classroom teaching." Having said that, he then turned and retreated into his office, closing the door behind him. I did not have the opportunity to thank him for hiring me or for his concern as related to my physical well-being.

It was now 8:20 a.m. The general office was a hub of activity—teachers were arriving while phone calls were going out and coming in.   Mrs. Gerstein, like a hummingbird, was alternately engaged in greetings and conversations with any number of individuals ranging from teachers, to students, to parents. I stood there taking it all in and said to myself, this is where I want to be. In my stupor, I did not realize that Mrs. Gerstein a short, pudgy woman with two #2 pencils protruding from either side of her tightly wrapped bun was briskly walking toward me. As she approached, I smiled and started to introduce myself. That won't be necessary, Mr. Kassell; please be seated, she said pointing in the direction of a small chair adjacent to a similarly small desk. She held out her hand, and I gleefully extended mine. Rejecting the salutatory offer, she said, "Give me your papers." Reaching into my jacket pocket to fetch them out I thought that in some small way I was nothing more to Mrs. Gerstein than a passing stranger whom she was obligated to spend time with, provided I had the proper documentation.

Upon examining the documents I had given her, she indicated that she would have to go to the copying room and that in the interim I was to relax and have a cup of coffee from the coffee-maker behind her desk. Seated at Mrs. Gerstein's desk and sipping a coffee, I reflected on my interview with Mr. Biggio, which had consumed all of seven or eight minutes. Very efficient I thought. In later years, as I would work my way into administration and supervision, I vowed to make my interviews a more probing experience for a prospective teacher of children in my care. After duly reflecting on the interview with Mr. Biggio, I turned my attention to observing the plethora of activities going on in the General Office. I saw arriving teachers taking their time cards from their slots and "punching" them in. Each "hit" was accompanied by a loud bang. Certainly, I thought, there was something wrong with the machine. I would find out later that was the way the machine had worked since the depression, and it was fine. The teachers next checked their mailboxes and removed their room keys from a metal key closet, which was affixed to the wall near the mailbox slots.

I further noted the fact that these arriving teachers hardly spoke to one another, kind of greeted one another with head nods then left the office as quickly as they had arrived. I reasoned that these were truly serious businesslike professionals leaving the office purposefully to assume their duties. Of course I realized later how mistaken my reasoning was. What I assumed to be professional zeal was symptomatic of a depressed, demoralized, and beaten staff, and this was only the fourth week of school.

As I further observed the goings on in the General Office, I noted an older, distinguished looking gentleman seated at a desk in the center of the office. At his ear was a phone receiver into which I read his lips to be saying, how sick are you? While speaking to whomever, the gentleman was feverishly writing out notes on small pieces of paper, and occasionally calling the name of one of the arriving teachers, who in turn would come through the swinging café door, approach his desk and take a note thanklessly from him. In each instance, the receiving individual would leave with a scowl on his face sometimes balling the piece of paper up and throwing it in the garbage can after reading it. I would learn at a later time that this was the process whereby teachers received coverage or extra teaching duties in lieu of an administrative assignment or a preparation period. A hall patrol assignment, a lunch duty assignment, or some other school needs-based activity was preferred to an extra teaching assignment. In the latter case, the teacher might have used the prep period to mark papers, council students, contact parents, or prepare lesson plans. However, all of these activities were too often foresaken because of excessive absences of colleagues and the school's or district's inability to attract a corps of "day to day" subs to fill in.

The returning form of Mrs. Gerstein now redirected my focus. As she got nearer to where I was seated, she proclaimed "We're all set; come with me." She led me over to where the distinguished looking gentleman was seated. Mr. Tramm, this is Mr. Kassell. Mr. Biggio asked me to process him as the new seventh grade math teacher. The gentleman got up, extended his hand saying, "Bill Tramm, glad to make your acquaintance. I'm the math chairman, and I'll be with you in a few moments. Shortly, but not before Mr. Tramm distributed several more of his notes, we alighted from the General Office, made our way to a stairwell, and began a trek to the fourth floor, where Mr. Tramm's office was located.

As we climbed the stairs I was consumed with an odor only experienced previously by me on two occasions. The first was when I descended into the 42nd street subway from street level and the second upon entering the men's room at halftime of a Jets game at Shea Stadium in mid September when the air was humid and heavy. As we alighted from the stairwell vestibule out onto the fourth floor hallway, my offended and irritated olfactory senses were relieved by the intake of fresher and much colder air. This invigorating environment was derived as a result of the fact that the heating system, as driven by a pre-WWII boiler in the basement, did not service the fourth floor as well as it did the other three floors. The accepted reasoning was that this floor was an add-on in post war years, while the necessary plumbing and heating upgrades were not. The climate control was made more difficult because of the fact that several hallway windowpanes had been broken out. Walking down the hall, we passed clusters of students, who upon seeing Mr. Tramm scurried away, presumably to their classrooms. The corridor itself was poorly lit. In several places the drab greyish painted walls were peeling and flaking badly. Some students had creatively, via the use of spray cans, tried to hide the unsightly wall condition by incorporating it into "spray art." At least I chose to think so. Other staff members referred to the display as graffitti/vandalism.

In later years I would come to the determination that the physical appearance of the school went a long way in promoting either a positive or negative pre-disposition on the part of students as to how they felt about the school. Later in my career I would be confronted with the problem of being in an old and decaying building that was waiting for years for the school construction authority to make repairs. The principal stated repeatedly that she was powerless to effect changes, as these matters were left to the authority of the school custodian and the Office of School Construction. There came a time when that Principal was disabled as a result of being assaulted by a staff member. During my first week as Acting Principal I met with the PTA and several personnel friends of mine in the construction field. We came up with a list of non-structural maladies that could be repaired, patched up, or fixed over the impending weekend. The PTA agreed to supply continuous foodstuffs. My "friends" supplied materials, expertise, and some of the labor. You had to be there on that Monday morning to see the expression on the faces of the teachers and students, when upon entering the school they found that the vestibule halls were well lit, that blinking lights as a result of electrical shorts were fully operational, that peeling walls on the first floor had been scraped,

23

spackled, and repainted, that the time clock in the main office was working, that the doors on pupil toilet stalls were functioning, that torched bulletin boards had been decorated, that broken sinks and water fountains had been repaired, that the hallway clocks did display the right time, that the school PA system did work more clearly than before. The students were particularly pleased by the fact that several holes in the schoolyard had been recemented and that several backboards without rims now had them. Of course, I was immediately brought to task for violating any number of regulations governing such repairs. This action was formerly presented as a grievance by the school cutodian. When confronted with the charges, I pleaded that I was only an Acting Principal and had not been made aware of the guidelines governing such matters and was acting out of a sense of working together with the community and culling resources all for the betterment of the student body. At the grievance hearing, I was warned by the superintendant to discontinue any plans I might have had for further reparations, or face further disciplinary action. At some point in the not too distant future several of my "friends" met with the custodian similar to the meeting I had had with the superintendent. In the years to follow, I always found him to be extremely cooperative with any request that I made.

After walking the entire length of the hallway, we arrived at Mr. Tramm's office located on the corner end of the hall. Walking in, Mr. Tramm invited me to have a seat, while he routinely and methodically hung his coat on a coat rack, put on a button down sweater, lit up his pipe, and sat down in a leather or vinyl captain's chair. As I scanned the office, I noticed book cases of various sizes, file cabinets with different heights and colors, a conference table accompanied by six folding beach chairs, Mr. Tramm's desk, a telephone, a floor devoid of numerous tiles, a ceiling puckered by years of water seepage from the roof above, shadeless windows, and of course, a portable electric heater. Inwardly my enthusiasm was still high, however I could not help but wonder if indeed I had made the right decision.

In his office Mr. Tramm presented me with the NYC Board of Education Teacher's Guide to Seventh Grade Mathematics, a set of keys containing those to the front and rear door and several closets inside the room, and most importantly, a key to the Men's room. The kit was completed with a complimentary box of white chalk, a board eraser, and a half dozen #2 pencils. As I sat in silent astonishment over Mr. Tramm's matter-of-fact professionalism, I heard him say, "Now you're ready to teach." Looking up and over the rim of his bi-focals, Mr. Tramm asked, do you have any questions? I remained silent. Good, Mr. Tramm exclaimed! Let's go..., I interrupted Mr. Tramm at this juncture by blurting out that I did have a question. The thought had plagued my mind as Mr. Tramm and I had made our journey from the first floor to the fourth and down the length of the hallway, to wit: where were the female students? Mr. Tramm responded that this was an all-male institution. Curious, I thought, that Mr. Tramm would supplant the word school with institution. In retrospect, I should have had a host of questions for Mr. Tramm. Then again, perhaps not! They say, "Experience is the best teacher." As it would turn out I would have some learning experiences over the next thirty-two years that could not be described or anticipated in a verbal debriefing or taught in any Ed. 101 methods class. Mr. Tramm, bless his heart, did take some time to explain that my teaching assignment would include duties as an official teacher with all of the glorious clerical assignments that go with that responsibility. Looking back, I would not have had it any other way. I found that while it was rewarding to teach a variety of different classes all with different needs, there was no bonding experience with those classes. With an official class, even a rookie teacher who would have difficulties in the area of classroom control and instructional delivery, there was a bonding that one had with their own class that was undeniable—a mentality that said they needed me as much as I needed them. This was illustrated very early in my career. I had been having discipline problems with one of my corps classes. Fights would break out in my room, chairs would get broken, and in general the room would look like a wreck after this particular class would leave the room.

During lunch one day, the two deans, the Assistant Principal, and several of the more macho type teachers had to rush to the school yard to break up a fight between members of my official class and members of the class with which I was having so much trouble. As the students in my class were questioned as to the reasons for the fight, one after the other said that the only reason was that the other class had messed with their teacher. Now I'm sure they were not fighting out of some deep-seated loyalty or respect for me, as they were fighting to preserve their self-respect. After all it must have been embarrassing that their teacher was getting his ass kicked by these other kids daily. I would have to make some changes. I was not possessed of startling physical attributes, which some of my colleagues used for intimidation purposes. I certainly was not about to physically confront any of my students. I shall have to assess my own strengths and weaknesses. What were they? I was always uninhibited. I could play sports, particularly "B" ball and baseball. As luck would have it, my class was programmed for gym with my nemesis class.

Coincidentally, my prep period coincided with that class. I decided to go to the gym for the real purpose of observing my kids in a physical activity setting. I wanted to study the degree of aggression and competitiveness they exhibited in the gym class. As it turned out, the regular gym teacher was absent, and no one was paying much attention to the elderly female they had sent over to cover the class. I introduced myself to her and asked if she wouldn't mind if I took charge of my class. Gleefully, she replied, "By all means." I gathered my kids at an opposite end of the gym near one of the basketball hoops. I asked them if they knew how to take a jump shot. After some laughter, several walked away. Turning to one of the remaining kids I said, Lester take a "J," I'll guard you. At first, Lester was reluctant. Then with some encouragement from his buddies, he agreed. He took the ball at his hip, went up to shoot, and was shocked to see that I was holding the ball. Lester then decided he would do better if he took the ball out and went one on one with me. Again I frustrated his efforts. By now the majority of my class had rejoined the group. Not wanting to cause Lester any undo embarrassment, I asked them if they would like to practice some skills that they could use in the school Intra Class Grade Basketball Tournament. Lester would serve as my corporal. I decided not to share the art of such skills as short/shirt grabbing or low bridging with them, nor I daresay elbow flinging after rebounding. These kids were only thirteen or fourteen years old.

My nemesis class, however, were for the most part fourteen and fifteen year olds, who had been held over several times in their young careers. They had no patience for book learning and very little respect for teachers. They were only reachable, when respecting someone who could show them something. After seeing me come down to the gym three weeks in a row, several of the kids came over to challenge my class to a three on three game. They intimidated my kids. As the challengers turned to leave, one of them said you could even play with your teacher if you want to. They looked at me and I nodded in approval. After ten minutes one of their kids had to go to the nurse to close a cut received by someone's flying elbow during a rebound scuffle. Another had to return to the locker because his shorts had gotten torn. The remaining player was invited to

27

get some subs but as he had already had two of his shots blocked, didn't think that subs would enhance his opportunity to win, so declined returning to the locker room to change and get ready for his next class. I now had something some teachers never acquire: respect. For all the wrong reasons I thought. But no, I would learn later, the rule of thumb then, as it is now, is "whatever it takes," or as Malcolm would say later, "by any means necessary."

After handing me a roll book, Mr. Tramm next presented me with a duplicate set of four different math texts, explaining that one set was to keep at home to use in preparing lesson plans, and the other set was to keep on my desk during instruction. My teaching kit was now fully outfitted. I was going to teach seventh grade math, I told my mother that evening. Are they crazy? my mother asked. Do they know that you had to have math tutors just to get through Geometry? It's true what they say about the Board of Education. They don't know what they're doing. While for the most part my mother's declaration that September evening in 1965 would prove prophetic. I took my mother's word as a challenge and drove myself to be the best math teacher those kids would ever have.

The next morning when I arrived at the school, I met Mr. Tramm in the General Office at 8 a.m. He indicated that he was assigning a "buddy" teacher to help with my development. Mr. Cartier will be your buddy. This will be the first and last time I'll make mention of Mr. Cartier. He did not come to work that day as he had been arrested the night before on 42nd street for "hawking." I would not be assigned a replacement "buddy." Before he got started with the task of programming the day's coverage assignments, Mr. Tramm asked me if I had any questions with regards to yesterday's orientation session. None readily popped into my mind. This was after all the second day. How could I anticipate the need to ask what to do when you are called a "white motherfucker," or what to do when students start fighting, or refuse to stay seated, or refuse to answer your questions, or engage one another in idle conversation ignoring your requests to pay attention, or in response to any question you might ask, someone calls out "your mother". No, I could not have anticipated a need to ask Mr. Tramm what to do in situations like these. This was part of the "dues paying process," or the challenge one had to pass before any teaching could be done. The quest for respect begins on day two. For some it never ends. Mr. Tramm informed me that he would accompany me to meet my class.

As we entered the room, I saw that there appeared to be about twenty boys present. Some were seated, while others were huddled up in clusters throughout the room engaged in idle conversation about the events of either the weekend football games or the play of the Knicks in their latest loss. All of a sudden several students hurriedly entered the classroom via the rear door. Apparently word of Mr. Tramm's presence in the class had wafted through the hall grapevine and thus motivated the hasty arrival of these latecomers. I deluded myself into thinking that they really wanted to impress their new teacher. Sadly this was not to be the case. Simultaneously, those who were idly standing about immediately took their seats. As I surveyed the room during this interlude, I was struck by its general appearance of disrepair. There was a large piece of chalkboard missing from the center of the board. The clothing closets did not have doors, nor did the teacher's closet. Two of the three window shades were tattered and torn. The side bulletin boards had obviously been torched; there was no teacher's desk. This last observation was gained when I noticed that there was an adult seated to the side at a student desk and was engaged in some clerical task as not to notice our arrival or anything else for that matter.

Upon closer scrutiny, I recognized him as one of the teachers who had earlier received one of Mr. Tramm's notes in the General Office. He was so tuned out that he did not realize that the entire class was seated and had come to order. Mr. Tramm cleared his throat to speak and the gentleman looked up. As he turned his glance from Mr. Tramm to me, a smile appeared on his face; he got up from his seat and left the room quickly and quietly. In the meantime, the class was obviously engaged in the process of showing proper respect to Mr. Tramm and at the same time sizing up the stranger. This process of sizing up would be an ongoing experience for me, one that would last for thirty-two years. That's what kids do when their environment is influenced by change. Their assessment is usually swift and accurate. They literally compile a complete dossier citing strengths, weaknesses, tolerance levels, habits, teaching abilities, knowledge, and the degree by which one has the "courage of one's convictions." Conversely, we know that in too many schools the adults in charge, be they teachers, counselors, or members of the administration, often are unable to "size up" their student body for the better part of the school year.

My point is easily made via the following anecdote: At a point early in my career I was serving as a behavioral counselor (Dean) for the seventh grade. The grade was so large (26 classes) that the Principal created a second position. An Afro-American named Mr. Willy occupied this latter position. We had a lot in common. Both of us were in the same age brackett, played sports, and had the respect of the student body. There was a popular movie at that time in which the main characters were an Afro-American and a white detective. They were referred to as Salt and Pepper in the movie. The student body would attribute these nicknames to Mr. Willy and me as well. We earned our wings one day when it was revealed to us from one of our reliable "goody two-shoes type students," who wanted to curry favor with us no doubt, that one of our seventh graders was cutting school near a laundromat on 140th and

Lennox. Using my '58 Chevy, we stalked along Lennox Avenue at a snail's pace. There he is, Willy exclaimed. I drove onto the sidewalk and with the breaking of the wheels; Willy had leapt from the car and had the truant in hand within a few strides. For their part the local citizenry were unfazed. Taking us for undercover cops, they did not stop or in any way alter their activities. As we got back into the car which was diagonally parked half in the street and the other half on the sidewalk, we were met there by a beat cop. Willy adorned with his London Fog raincoat, which slightly concealed the appointment of a white button down Brooks Brothers shirt, color-coordinated with a double-breasted Navy all Wool Armani suit, motioned for me to get in the chevy. Of course, Willy never used his Mercedes for such activities. The street cop asked if we were on the job. Of course Willy replied unhesitantly, and with conviction. Then you both have a good day responded the beat cop as he walked off. Happily we returned to the school with our truant.

Within a week or two of this incident, as it had become my custom, following my morning coffee and cigarette, to occasion the men's throne room along with my *New York Post*. On this particular day while concentrating on the throne, I overheard the following exchange between two boys who were obviously cutting class in the hall area just outside the men's room. Yo, Russell, what class you cuttin'? I'm not cutting…I just got kicked out of Science by that prick, Beck. What did you do? I told him I wasn't slicing open no frog, and then I threw it out the window. Which dean you gotta see, salt or pepper? Salt was the reply. You're lucky. Just go in there and talk some shit. He likes to hear students admit to their mistakes and then talk to them about alternatives. That's his favorite word…alternative. Don't forget to say how sorry you are. He likes to hear that too. Even offer to pay for the frog you wasted. I waited for them to move on before I left the bathroom. I quickly returned to my office to arrive there before Russell. I took my seat behind my desk and pretended to be immersed in paperwork. When Russell arrived at my doorway I did not take notice of his arrival until he knocked and asked, Mr. Kassell, can I come in? I looked up at him and said, I really don't have time for you right now. What are you here for and don't talk no shit! Russell was speechless. He sat down immediately and began his tale of woe. This was one time that student "sizing up" knowledge would bare false fruit.

Mr. Tramm wrote my name on the board in syllabic form, Kas-sell. He then asked the class to orally repeat the pronunciation of the name three times. They did so loudly and distinctly. Satisfied that there would be no reason to ever hear that someone in the class did not know how to pronounce my name, he then began a monologue about how fortunate they were in getting their own teacher, and how he would expect them to cooperate in all ways with me. He told them that beginning tomorrow they would receive assignments and lessons from me. Subsequently, for some reason all I could think of were the pictures of Christians being thrown to the lions. One could sense the licking of the chops, the piercing eyes, and most significantly, the willingness to wait, knowing that their prey had nowhere to run and nowhere to hide. As Mr. Tramm pontificated, my mind focused on the belief that beginning tomorrow I would have an opportunity to exert a great influence on these boys. I'm gonna teach them! As Mr. Tramm concluded his remarks, he took note of the time and decided to dismiss the class to their period one assignment. At his direction the class stood and lined up single file on the near wall and began the process of exiting the room in single file. In doing so each student passed me as they exited the class. As they walked past me, I found myself looking up to see their faces. Although I didn't realize it then, it was going to be a long time before I would be able to execute such a disciplined dismissal routine.

Chapter IV

The Second Day...

As I approached the school's perimeter, I again went through the process of circling the block in search of a legal parking spot. Finally I settled on one that allowed for three feet of space between my front bumper and a fire hydrant. Not wanting to be late, I decided to trust my luck. Where was Earnie when I needed him? As the events of the day played out, you will see that this was not to be one in which luck would be my ally. I eagerly entered the General Office and endeavored to mimmick the routines I had observed arriving teachers perform yesterday, while I was waiting for Mrs. Gerstein to process my papers. I went to the "punch-in" clock and searched the time card rack for my card. There were none with my name on it. Then my side vision picked up a "come here hand motion" given by Mrs. Gerstein. Responding to her beck and call, I approached her desk and heard her say, "I didn't think you would be back." I'll have one for you later this morning. Mr. Tramm will initial your card verifying that you were here on time. I said thank you and was about to leave when Mrs. Gerstein out of guilt for having hurt my feelings, I suspect, tried to defend her actions by telling me that I was the third teacher in the past week to have taken the grand tour and not to have returned. I replied that this would not be the case with me. This was to be my job, what I wanted to do, and no one would prevent, dissuade, or in any way convince me to leave. Not realizing that my voice had risen, I turned to find Mr. Tramm peering up at me from behind his bi-focals. He had even stopped writing his little notes. As I made my way to the office exit, several teachers hastily stepped aside. Leaving the office, I grabbed the designated room keys from their rack and heard Mrs. Gerstein say, "I'll have your card ready by lunch hour." Entering the stairwell vestibule, Mrs. Gerstein's last words echoed in my ears,...I'll have your card ready for you by lunch hour...if you last that long! No, she didn't say that, I thought, as I began the climb to the fourth floor. Upon entering the room I surveyed my domain. To my surprise and amazement there in the far corner of the room adjacent to the chalkboard and room window was a teacher's desk made of oak and a captain's chair in matching oak. On top of the desk was an envelope with a note from Mr. Tramm which read as follows:

Dear Mr. Kassell,

Good morning. I hope you like the desk and chair. I've asked the custodial staff to try with all haste to find the missing drawers. Good luck on this your first real day!

Sincerely,

Bill Tramm

The previous day and well into the night I spent studying the math curriculum texts and syllabus Mr. Tramm had given me. I even went so far as to prepare several lesson plans to use the next day. Looking back, I dare say that these plans were overly ambitious to say the least; I never used them.

My mother, not wanting to get in my way, or interrupt what she believed to be a genius at work, busied herself with making phone calls to relatives to inform them that I had finished examining various possibilities and had decided that I was going to teach. Later in the evening she brought me some refreshments and asked me what I was doing. When I told her that I was preparing lesson plans to teach with, she said, "I don't understand why they won't let you teach something you know." As she walked away I heard her murmur to herself "no wonder the schools are in such bad shape." That was 1965 and today we hear the same refrain. I ran after my mother and told her that I was less than forthright with the Principal when he asked me if I knew math. I knew that this was the only available position, and I had made up my mind to have it. I further asserted that she would find me up every night studying the curriculum bulletin, marking papers, and in general trying to stay one or two days ahead of my students. I was going to succeed!

If you've noticed a similarity between my mother and Mrs. Gerstein, you are correct. The former didn't think I knew enough to succeed, while the latter thought I didn't have what it takes. At that time I was the only person who believed in me. That would have to do. I never discussed my plans with my father. He held the opinion that college was an unnecessary expense and that I should have joined the armed forces and learned a trade at the government's expense. The problem with that thinking was that the only trade they were teaching then was how to lay land mines in the jungles of Vietnam.

Chapter V

Two Weeks Later

My strategy of staying several days ahead of my students by preparing myself and understanding the goals and objectives of the math syllabus was paying off. By planning, I was able to get help with those areas of the curriculum that I didn't understand and thus be prepared to teach at least minimum essentials related to a particular topic. When on occasion a student would ask a probing question on that same topic, I would usually respond by saying, "That is an excellent question, and we'll pick up tomorrow's lesson with that question." Of course I was buying time, so that I could check with Mr. Tramm on the appropriate response. No harm, no foul! This strategy worked quite well for an extended period of time, until I was visited one day by the Assistant Principal, Mr. Brachman, who bore a striking resemblance to Hermann Goering, and who had the reputation of running through rookie teachers the way a knife does soft butter.

At the time of his visit, I was teaching a lesson on addition and subtraction of fractions with unlike denominators. After illustrating the method prescribed by the curriculum guide and having allotted time for practicum reinforcement activities, followed up with a summary consisting of questions posed to the students whose responses would indicate to me that either they did understand the aim of the lesson or they didn't, one of my students offered that his mother had shown him a different way to do the fractions, and could I teach the class his mother's method. Of course, I said. We'll begin with that technique tomorrow. For now we have to get ready to change classes. Immediately Mr. Brachman stood and said, "Mr. Kassell, there's no time like the present. Explain the method now!" Somewhat shocked and definitely embarrassed, my reply was, "I don't know it, why don't you?" Not waiting for Mr. Brachman's response, I exited the room and made my way to the teacher's lounge, which by contractual agreement was off limits to the administration. After approximately five minutes I heard Mr. Brachman page my name over the school PA system to report to his office. During the course of that meeting Mr. Brachman suggested that I had been insubordinate, guilty of dereliction of duty, and inadequately prepared to teach. I told him that I was not nor ever would be a whipping boy for him or anyone else. I finished by saying that I thought it would be best for both of us if I resigned. How so a stunned Mr. Brachman asked? So that you don't have to add the charge of assault to those you've already mentioned. Upon entering the General Office, fully intending to give my resignation personally to Mr. Biggio, I found him waiting for me. He escorted me into his office to tell me that Mr. Brachman had called him and had informed him of the essence of our conference. He asked me to recount the events in my own terms which led to my decision to resign. After listening to my account of the events, he told me that he had received very high praise from the Math Department Chairman Bill Tramm and that he thought that I had made excellent progress in the brief time I had been there. He went on to say that he would be speaking with Mr. Brachman later in the day and that he wanted me to go home, relax, and be back bright and early the next day to begin with renewed vigor. After all, isn't this what you want to be—a teacher?

Of course, Mr. Biggio was right. It was what I wanted to be. That night I made up my mind that if doing what I wanted to do meant swallowing my pride occasionally, then that's what I would do. I went to work the next day intending to make amends with Mr. Brachman for any disrespect I'd shown him. When I attempted to speak with him he replied that he was very busy, and it wasn't a good time. In the immediate future Brachman avoided me at all costs, but the seeds for a vendetta had been sown. I would have to be alert.

Chapter VI

A Month Later

Sometime in early November I made a decision, which would likely become the hallmark of my educational philosophy, to wit: do what's best for your students, the hell with everything else, and let the chips fall where they may! Having gained my respect via the gym, I was no longer encountering disrespectful comments or episodes of classroom fighting. On the academic front, however, I was not making much progress at all. Yes, I continued to work hard on my lesson planning. Yes, I delivered instruction in the traditional developmental style. Yes, I continued to "brainstorm" with Mr. Tramm. Math to be sure is an exact science. What was the problem?—no pun intended. One either comes up with the correct solution or one doesn't. My kids could not on average come up with correct solutions. They did not know the multiplication tables and did not see a need to go home and memorize them. Nor did they understand very well the other three math operational functions and saw no need to. Each one did understand that I was required to teach whatever was prescribed in the Board of Education curriculum bulletin. They also knew that I was aware that they were completely turned off to the math curriculum as I was presenting it. They just didn't care. The threat or the possible reality of failing grades did not seem to faze them. I knew better, though. I felt that if I could put them into a situation by which they could succeed, they would apply themselves. To that end, therefore, high grades would be competed for. Knowing what to do and doing it are two different concepts.

One day I simply began the day's lesson with this question. If you were my boss, what would you have me teach? Algebra a student called out. Yeah, algebra, they all said in chorus. They knew that other math teachers of seventh grade classes higher up than them were teaching algebra. It was not expected that they could learn algebra and so the attempt was not to be made. Indeed, low expectations promote low levels of achievement. I asked them what they knew about algebra. Invariably the answer was that they either had a friend or sibling who was studying algebra and from their perspective it looked important. I told them that I'd have to think it over that night and promised to give their request a response by the next day.

To be sure, I was faced with several issues in making my decision. The first and foremost being the ever lurking presence of Mr. Brachman looking to pounce upon me for performing any act outside of the realm of my normal teaching duties. The second issue reliant upon my thorough understanding of the first issue was when to find the time to give instruction for a non-prescribed topic. Having looked ahead at the math curriculum, I noted that it called for instruction for two weeks in the area of negative and positive values, followed up with a one-week term review prior to the Christmas recess. I next discussed my student's request with Mr. Tramm. After listening thoroughly, he put down his pipe and said, "You have worked hard with this group for the better part of two months. You've taught them nothing that can be measured, but they like and respect you. No one in the administration much cares what goes on in our bottom exponent classes, so you do what you think is right. I'll support you in any way I can. Besides if you have success, we can collaborate on a grant proposal. By the way, your colleagues have been lodging protests with Mr. Brachman relating to some of your unorthodox methods. I suspect jealousy as their motivation. I'll do as much as I can to keep the dogs at bay." Thanks, I replied, as I exited Mr. Tramm's office.

The next day I explained to the class that the math guide that I had to follow required a two-week unit on negative and positive integers. Moreover, I told them that I would need time to brush up on my algebra. I explained to them that I would be willing to do that at home if I could get a verbal commitment from them that they would do their best to grasp the concepts I would be presenting over the next two weeks. Unanimously they all replied with a resounding affirmation. By the way, Mr. Kassell, what are positive and negative integers, one of my students called out? I laughed then illustrated a -1 and then a +1. That's about as much as I know right now. We'll get into it tomorrow, I can assure you. Before class ended I asked how many knew how to play cards? They all said that they did. What card games did they play, I asked. Without hesitation they all said Poker.

When class resumed the next day, I divided it into four groups of six students, and then I gave each group a deck of playing cards and some paper script money in the amount of three dollars. On more than one occasion I noticed Mr. Tramm observing through the front door window. In each instance he wandered away as suddenly as he had appeared.

As the lesson began, I instructed each group to begin their poker playing. After five minutes, I began to circulate from group to group. I noted the fact that several players were experiencing a decline in their paper chips. In fact one player was at a "0" chip value. I stopped the proceedings at this juncture and called the unfortunate player up to the board. I asked him if he was going to be allowed to continue playing. His response was yes. He went on to say that as wagers were made, he would move the exact amount of the wager from the pot to the side, which would indicate to everyone a "shy" amount. If he won, then he would receive the entire pot and the shy amount would have no bearing. If, however, he lost, then the amount would represent what he owed the winner. I asked the class if we could put his explanation on the board in mathematical terms. I told them to try it in their notebooks first. After a few minutes, one of the students came up to the board and wrote the following: +$3.00-$3.00=0. Not quite I said. What has happened here is that the player lost more than his original amount. Let's assume that he lost $3.50. How could we show that mathematically? After a few moments, another student came forth and illustrated thus: +$3.00-$3.50=-$.50. Hence we began the process of understanding negative and positive integers. As long as I was able to provide them with examples based on issues surrounding money I held their interest. Also it was key that in presenting these issues that they reflect personal experiences in their life. In other words I took what they brought to the table and applied it to the learning experience at hand. I then asked them to translate the math sentence into a verbal one. It then was elicited that plus three dollars minus three dollars and fifty cents was equal to minus fifty cents. Or as one student succinctly put it, "Plus is when you have it and minus is when you don't." Subsequently we applied the same principle to the dilemma of overspending or over-budgeting in such other forums as the supermarket, amusement park, candy store, etc. Ultimately, my class was able to graph their findings on a 180-degree scale expressing 0 as the neutral integer separating negative from positive value as follows:

$$-9\text{-}8\text{-}7\text{-}6\text{-}5\text{-}4\text{-}3\text{-}2\text{-}1 \quad 0 \quad +1+2+3+4+5+6+7+8+9$$

Later in the term I had to plan a unit on fractions and decimals. Such vehicular tools as the daily racing section of the *New York Daily News* proved to be a wonderful resource. Most of the information contained in the form was expressed in terms of fractions and decimals. Again, many of my students had indicated that they had been to the racetrack with their parents or other relatives and wanted to know how to read the racing form so that they could surprise their relatives. The curriculum guide which

Kenneth S. Karcinell

suggested the traditional "pizza pie" method for illustrating fractional values was set aside in favor of the *New York Daily News*. I arranged for my students to receive the paper for two weeks. Of course a bi-product to our math activities was that they began to check out other sections of the paper. This led to developing interests in current events, stock market activities, and the puzzle sections.

Getting back to cases, I had completed the positive/negative integer unit with three days to spare. I began the algebra lesson with a working definition of the term. Over the three-day period we concentrated on simple algebraic equations with one step transposition, i.e. 3x +6=18. We learned that the first task was to separate numbers from letters. We then learned that the next step was to balance the equation. Employing the following rule did this. What we do to one side we must do exactly to the other side. Thus from the original equation we progressed via a 3 step method as shown below:

$$3x + 6 = 18$$
$$3x (+6 - 6) = 18 - 6$$
$$3x = 12$$

Now, it didn't matter to me that some were able to successfully solve for x and others couldn't. I knew that these kids were highly competitive and that if they were interested they would really learn the times tables, so that they could get the proper solution.

To my shock and amazement, Principal Biggio visited me within several days of my having completed the algebra unit. After all, it was almost Christmas recess, and he was making his rounds wishing everyone a happy and healthy holiday season. While visiting he meandered about the room and paused at the bulletin board displays which reflected evidence of pupil work in the algebra unit we had just completed. It was the first time since I had taken the assignment that I had put any decorations up reflecting the pupil's work. Principal Biggio beckoned me over to where he was standing and said that he was very pleased at the progress I was making as a teacher and at the positive reports he was receiving about the low amount of behavioral incidents with my students. He added that these papers, pointing at my display of them with ratings of 85% to 95%, have the wrong answers. If it's right answers you want, please come back in March, I replied. He never did.

My successes were not going unnoticed. Veteran teachers who had my class for the other subject disciplines were not enjoying the same positive results that I was. Of course, for the most part, these same teachers were predisposed to the fact that the kids in my class could only attain so much. Thus the axiom of limited expectations yield limited results reared its ugly head. These same teachers had it within themselves to be creative. They were rarely asked to be so, however. Consequently their instructional style of delivery was the same for all classes regardless of individual academic abilities. Where does the answer to this type of apathy lie? Supervision and training—where does one find the time you ask? Actually, it has always been there and continues to be there. To mention just a few examples: weekly and monthly grade and departmental meetings, monthly faculty conferences, one-to-one teacher supervisory sessions, demonstrations, outside consultants, additional college methods courses, intervisitation schedules, peer intervention programs, "buddying up," and mentoring. Any supervisor who is not doing these things is violating the "prime directive" of their license. Supervision in this case meaning the removing of all obstacles to the presentation of material designed to upgrade instruction.

These same teachers in an effort to smear me were responsible for informing my nemesis, Brachman, that gambling was going on in my class, and I was encouraging it.

Having been forewarned by Mr. Tramm that Brachman had informed him of the complaint lodged by these teachers with him and that he intended to ask for my dismissal because I was corrupting the morals of minors, I prepared my defense accordingly. Brachman himself never observed any of the "gambling lessons." Nor did he examine my lesson plans that clearly indicated my aims and strategies as implemented. He did, however, summon me to his office shortly thereafter. Upon my arrival Mr. Brachman presented me with a letter to sign, the contents of which accused me of promoting an unwholesome learning environment in my classroom, to wit: gambling. Mr. Brachman informed me that the letter was for placement in my file and would be presented to the Principal with his request for my immediate dismissal. I declined the request to sign the letter and simply left his office, not having the opportunity to offer my defense. I'd made up my mind that if Brachman was going to be successful in his desire to have my services terminated at last, then he was going to have to experience a "truck driver's dispute conference." I was going to kick his ass. Fortunately, the issue never approached the level to which I was prepared to ascend. Principal Biggio summoned me to his office at 2:45 p.m. Present there also were Mr. Tramm, Math Department Chairman, Mrs. Gerstein, and Mr. Lopez who represented the teacher's union (UFT).

Mr. Biggio went to great lengths to impress upon me that this was a meeting of a most serious nature. So much so that he wanted to hear all the relevant facts in the presence of the parties that he had invited. He explained that Mrs. Gerstein would take minutes so that there could be no mistake in what was said and what was recorded. He asked me if I didn't mind. Not at all I said. Then Mr. Lopez, whom after three months of working in the school had never before approached me, leaned over and said that I shouldn't answer any questions unless I first checked with him. To which I whispered "fuck off." Turning back to the assemblage I exclaimed "ready."

Mr. Biggio began the proceedings by asking me if I had had any conferences with Mr. Brachman concerning the issues his letter addressed prior to being asked by Mr. Brachman to sign for the letter. No, I replied. Mr. Biggio then asked Mr. Brachman if he had personally observed lessons being taught by Mr. Kassell that prompted his writing of the letter. His reply was negative. Mr. Biggio asked if I had indicated in my lesson plans under the category of methodology any strategies that would suggest the use of playing cards and the horse-racing page of the *New York Daily News*. My reply was yes. He followed this question up with another related question. Did you submit your plans as per school policy to Mr. Brachman for weekly review? Yes, I replied. When you received your plans back from Mr. Brachman, were there any suggestions for improvement or request for conference planning? No, I replied. Have you completed teaching this unit, and if so when? I completed the unit a little over one week ago. Mr. Kassell, do you have any statement you would like to make with regards to the issues raised by Mr. Brachman's letter? Yes, I do. To begin with, Poker playing was a game that all of my students were familiar with because of prior knowledge. I did not spend any instructional time teaching its concepts. In the case of having students read the horse-racing section of the *New York Daily News*, this experience has led to pupil interest in the stock market section, weather section, sports section, and leisure reading of the newspaper on a daily basis. I thought that with all these by-products to the initial learning goal that the outcome was a desirable one, that is to say to motivate pupil interest in reading. Certainly, I will stop at once if directed by the administration to do so. That is all I have to say. Mr. Brachman, do you have a statement that you should like to make at this time? Brachman was beside himself with frustration. His jowls were puffed so that you could clearly see bursted blood vessels marking a path from cheek to cheek, linked by those already on display at the tip of his bulbous nose, the latter clearly a sign of one stein too many. Briefly Brachman promised to monitor my plans and activities more closely. I told him my mother would be pleased. That should do it proclaimed Mr. Biggio. Following the meeting, Mr. Biggio asked me to remain. I'm aware that you are familiar with gambling lingo he said with a sly grin. Therefore, I know that you will fully understand me when I tell you that as of today, you have used up your chips for this year. Have a good day!

Chapter VII

April Through September '66

For the most part, following "the Brachman Scenario," I spent the months of March, April, May, and June listening, studying, and learning my trade. I had formed some bonding relationships with several of the veteran teachers. These teachers had enjoyed successes in the instructional delivery of their content area. From time to time I visited and observed them as they taught their lessons. Mr. Tramm had suggested that I pay particular attention to pacing, transitional or pivotal questioning, and lesson planning.

With summer approaching, I enrolled at Hunter College in the Bronx for six methods credits. As the new term began in the fall, I reasoned that I would have several advantages when compared to my "rocky" beginning of the previous year. To begin with, I knew that I could survive and "play the game" if I had to. The second advantage was that I had an idea as to how to communicate with the kids. A third advantage being that I now had some "rep" and the respect that goes with it. The fact that I knew the subject matter a little better couldn't hurt. Finally, I was not going to be the third teacher in a series of failed substitute instructors.

The fall term saw me assigned as the Official Teacher of class 7-16, housed in an unused science room. The room was outfitted with stone slab tabletops accompanied by tall, unbacked bar stools, sinks and built-in bunson burners at every table. Even though this was the room that I would be teaching math in, I saw the potential for danger. A meeting with Mr. Biggio got me the "as soon as possible" response. A meeting with Mr. O'Keefe, the head custodian, coupled with the presentation of a fifth of Johnny Walker Red assured me that the water faucets and the gas lines feeding into the bunson burners would be cut off by the morning.

One of the classroom management concepts that I had grasped well was that tenet which bespoke of the need to establish at the outset clear and distinct rules and codes of behavior and not to waiver from them. Allow for no indiscretions. Be fair and consistent in applying them. Articulate your standards and expectations and post them. For me there were two rules and regulations emphasized more than all the others: Preparedness and Courtesy. To demonstrate, I showed them my lesson plan book and explained that I was expected and required to prepare their lessons in advance. Therefore, these lessons required that they do their homework, as I would expect thatof them. On one occasion when I was checking homework, I stopped at the desk of a student who hadn't done the assignment. Why not? Because I went to the Mets game last night was the reply. At this point in as much of an indignant tone of voice that I could summon, I said METS GAME! I couldn't go to the METS game. I would have liked to have gone to the Mets game. But I couldn't because I was marking your test papers, so that I could be prepared to review them today. I found that when I was able to illustrate to the students that I wasn't asking them to do anything more than what I was doing (time-wise), they usually responded favorably. A case in point occurred one winter morning when the school received a bomb scare. The procedure was such that classes were to exit the building from whatever subject room they were in. They were not to return to their official classes for coats but to report to the schoolyard where their subject teachers would supervise them. Many of these teachers retreated into the comforts of their nearby parked cars and heaters, thereby burdening teachers like myself who remained in the yard doing our jobs. The kids while complaining of the cold maintained their discipline as they witnessed the fact that the teachers who were supervising them were just as cold.

I stressed good manners and courtesy at every possible opportunity. As these virtues are values and subject to interpretation, the only way to reinforce them was by modeling. I felt that good manners promoted self- respect and respect for others. If you had something to say, then say it loud enough for all to hear, and all were expected to listen. We did some group guidance work in our official class, and as a result we learned about stereotyping, prejudice and bias. We also learned about open-mindedness. Within the scope of good manners, there would be no gum chewing or candy eating. There would be no hat wearing or coat wearing. No foul language or physical confrontations. Of course there were. Invariably when there were such instances, I would drag out the counseling process to its max, so as time went on the frequency of violent occurrences diminished. The verbal confrontations began to get settled as quickly as they had begun.

Within a short period, the atmosphere in the classroom during the official class period had begun to change to that of a high school study hall. Arriving students knew that for the next twenty minutes they could catch up on missed notes or owed assignments, study, prepare for the day ahead, or consult with me on any matter that was of concern to them. On one such consultation one student wanted my advice on coming up with an excuse for not showing up at a gang fight. He didn't want to be mocked, and he didn't want to lose face. Having grown up in a city housing project, I was fully aware of the dynamics of peer pressure and its influence on the decision-making process regarding right and wrong behavioral choices. I told him that he should beg off, on the pretense that he had to go with his mother to the doctor's. On Monday morning the young man left a note on my desk as he departed for 1st period class, which simply said, "Thanks, it worked."

Of continuing annoyance was that each and every morning these twenty-minute sessions were interrupted with a series of inane and garbled announcements via the school PA system. In all my years of service, at all the schools in which I served, I can count on one hand those instances in which the morning announcements were worthwhile. The indecipherable messages were a result of years of maintenance neglect. In turn this neglect arose out of the fact that the Board of Education did not allocate anticipatory repair funds in its capital budget. It did react to repair requests on an emergency basis. If, however, the Board did not prioritize your request as an emergency, that request went unfulfilled.

The first five weeks of the term were progressing fairly well and without incident. I was growing and developing professionally. I was evolving into a teacher and enjoying every minute of it. No, I wasn't there yet, but eventually I would be. In the meantime, a process of acculturation had begun within my psyche of which I was not immediately aware.

At the end of the block on which the school was housed, there was a candy store/luncheonette managed by three middle-aged black women with distinct southern accents. Each morning usually at 9:30 a.m. at the expense of a prep or administrative period, I found myself there ordering breakfast. I found the setting very relaxing. I was able to read *The Post* and catch up on the late night scores. Also, I could simply mark some papers over a second cup of coffee. Initially, I paid little attention to the language styles or the amenities implied by them, as the ladies expressed such terms of endearment as: "What will it be, honey?" or "How are you today, baby?" or "What can I get for you, sugar?" It wasn't just the sumptuous breakfast making me feel good or my teaching successes, but rather I could count on being addressed this way every day that reinforced all of the above. Perhaps there's a message here for all of us.

As I got to know these ladies, Martha, Cecile, and Shirley, I was able to enhance my efforts at reaching out to parents and gaining understandings as to the home environments of many of my students. I was able to get messages to families that I had previously been unable to contact. For reasons from no phone, broken into mailboxes, to a reluctance to meet me in the school, these parents were not a part of the partnership that was vital to the educational development of their children. Eventually, with the ladies' help, I was able to meet these parents in the luncheonette. On occasion when the parent had to be at work very early, I would meet them at the luncheonette at 7 a.m. You cannot imagine how the degrees of cooperation between my parents and me grew. On "Open School Night" all of my parents showed up.

Somewhere along the line my breakfast appetite had developed a taste for grits, fishcakes, and oatmeal. My lunches very often included some form of Black Eyed Peas and Rice or Salmon croquettes. I was feeling quite secure within my working environment. I was at peace with the world and at ease on the job. Speaking of peace and security, I wondered why I hadn't yet encountered Earnie. Here it was the first of October and not a single sighting.

Chapter VIII

The Fire Drill

It was October 3rd 1966. The weather was typical—cool and brisk for that time of the year. There were just two remaining periods left in the day. Period six found me on administrative hall "patrol" duty at the main entrance to the school. I was thinking of rushing home to catch the rest of the World Series game that had begun at 1:30. Of course, of more significance was that I was celebrating my 24th birthday. The fact that I was twenty-four and that Willie Mays, my favorite baseball player, wore the same number had to have some connection. Later I would stop at OTB and play the 2/4 exacta in every race at Yonkers that evening. As I contemplated these plans, the school fire alarm signals began to sound. Not having a class to supervise, I stayed at my post and monitored the exiting of the building of those classes and teachers using that particular exit. The classes left the building in good order, filing past me, escorted by their teachers as they went, and heading off down the block in the direction of the luncheonette. After four or five minutes Mr. Biggio approached me and asked if I had noticed any problems. I told him that I hadn't. Via a walkie-talkie Mr. Biggio communicated back to the main office. Within a few seconds an "all clear" gong was sounded, and Mr. Biggio retreated into the building. I continued to man my post, assisting in the orderly return of the classes into the school. In so doing it occurred to me that whereas at the beginning of the fire drill every class was accompanied by a teacher, upon re-entering it appeared that a teacher accompanied every other class. I turned to scan the block for stragglers; prior to securing the entrance doors I glimpsed the sudden and hurried approach of four male colleagues who were

54

leaving a building directly across the street from the school. Hold the door, they shouted, so I did. As I waited for them to enter the school, I saw Earnie walking up the block in my direction. At that moment the bell rang signaling the beginning of period seven. I had a choice, wait and say hello to Earnie or be on time for my seventh-period class. I chose the latter.

The morning of October 4th found me in the luncheonette having coffee and a buttered roll while scanning the results from Yonkers Raceway the previous night. To my great delight the 2/4 exacta combination came out twice. I would be collecting $275 later in the day.

"What ya smilin about?" the friendly voice of one of the senior teachers who had taken me under his wing called out. Looking up I laughed and invited "Uncle Artie" to join me. After I explained the reason for my joy, I told him what I had observed during the fire drill yesterday. His response was a shocker. His advice was right on. "Boy I been trying to set you straight on a few things for the longest. This is Harlem, NYC, anything goes, and things ain't what they seem. Big Earnie, he ain't no kinda cop. He is the lookout for one of the biggest numbers and whorehouse rackets in New York, and you know what?" No, startled I asked what? "It's right across the street from the school. The only reason Earnie is treating you kindly is because he wants to make sure that no one is botherin' you, so you don't go and call the police. That would be bad for business. Now the other matter of you seeing those four colleagues coming out of that building;...forget it."

Forget it, I did until 1971. That would be the first year of my functioning as Assistant Principal. In this particular instance, I was functioning as the Supervisor in charge of the graduating class. Previously in June, the Administrative Assistant to the Principal had retired, and Mr. Lindle had been moved up from grade 8 Assistant Principal to the vacant Administrative Assistant's position. This left a vacancy in the grade Assistant Principal's corps. The position was advertised and with Mr. Lindle's urging I applied, went through the Interviewing process and was selected by Dr. McNaughton to assume the role.

Being in charge of the graduating class in this school, in addition to academic departments assigned to you, meant in Dr. McNaughton's words that you were totally accountable for the disposition of that grade. In 1971 the graduating class consisted of twenty-two classes or 650 pupils. Yearbook planning and its creation was the A.P.'s responsibility. That meant picture-taking, editing, paste-ups, layout, advertising, and publication. The A.P. was similarly expected to collect senior dues, arrange for a suitable prom site, solicit the services of an appropriate graduation keynote speaker, see to the dignified preparation and printing of graduation tickets and invitations, to set the criteria for awards, then arrange for the collection of community based funds in the form of donations for monetary awards for the students during their graduation ceremonies.

From time to time Mr. Lindle would ask me for status reports and reminded me to see Earnie for the annual "Men's Civic Association Award." I hadn't seen much of Earnie following the advice of "Uncle" Artie back in '67. This was made easier by the fact that in 1969, the school was relocated from its original standing to an address further uptown. In retrospect, however, it would become obvious to me that Earnie and his cohorts, via the continued contributions of the "Men's Civic Association," had maintained their relationship with the school. I saw nothing wrong with that fact.

Through the efforts of my lady friends at the luncheonette, I arranged to meet with Earnie in his office in the lobby of the infamous building across the street from the "old school." As I walked in Earnie got up from his chair and with a broad smile greeted me with, "Long time no see!" How're you doin'?" Earnie I'm here because..."I know why you're here," he cut me off. "It's graduation time. No problem. So, you've moved up. I knew you would. I knew it from the first day I met you. I've missed our little coffee sit-downs we used to have down at the luncheonette. Is there anything you need? Any problem you got?" No, nothing right now, I said. "You call me if there is," he said, handing me an envelope marked graduation donation. I thanked him, and then we parted company with a handshake. I departed the building with an envelope in my breast pocket, which I would find out later contained $500. As I walked in the direction of where my car was parked, I heard Earnie call out "Hold on a minute. You know, son, I've got some spare time right about now, and I think there are a few community agencies that would be pleased to support such a worthwhile cause as your school's graduation ceremonies. Come with me, I'll drive," Earnie said. With that Earnie took off in the opposite direction with me in close pursuit. After a brief walk, he opened the passenger door to a golden colored Cadillac Coupe deVille. As I became enveloped in its plush leather interior, Earnie got behind the driver's side, and started the engine, pushed some buttons to adjust the seats, closed all the windows, and put on the air conditioning. I hadn't been in a car this luxurious since my high school prom when I was a part of a couple quartet that had rented out a limo for the night.

After visiting a body shop, a barbershop, and what had to be a bookie shop, and a few other establishments whose purpose I could only imagine, and after having Earnie introduce me as a friend who was working in The Fortress, I received envelopes from each. I made a big deal in thanking them and subsequently was given the unsolicited nickname of "Brother Kassell." We broke all previously existing records for culling community resources that year. In the following years, when the school became engaged in various fundraising activities, I would be asked to reach out to my community contacts. Of course, out of respect, I would secure the go-ahead from Earnie before any attempts at solicitation.

Chapter IX

Anthony, the Dean's Office, and Open School Night

The school year was going well. Had it not been for a strained relationship with one of my students, I could say that my teacher/pupil rapport was a success. Now and then this particular student would mutter anti-white epithets beneath his breath but not so that I couldn't hear them. His favorite was contained within his response to my morning roll call. Anthony I would call. Here white motherfucker, he'd say! He additionally found it very amusing to ignore most of the established class rules and regulations. I knew something would have to be done soon. Attempts to reach Anthony's family by all conventional methods had failed. My friends at the luncheonette did not know Anthony or the family. Unusual I thought. Either no one knew anything about Anthony, or I was asking the wrong people.

Finally I met with the guidance counselor, who told me that Anthony had just arrived from Buffalo, and his records had not yet been received. There was very little to go on in making a class placement for him, the counselor said. Have you called Buffalo, I asked? Do you think I should really do that, asked the counselor? No, you shouldn't, I responded, as I left her office. I headed over to the General Office, picked up the telephone, and got information for the Buffalo school system. I received a general information number, called it, and explained to the person on the other end that I was Anthony's counselor in New York City and wanted to know if his records indicated any health restrictions on his ability to participate in physical education. Just a moment, came the response. Hold on. After a few moments the individual got back on the phone and said, "I don't think so, unless you count a medication called Ritalin." Thank you, I said, placing the receiver back on the phone. Exiting the General Office, I ran into my grade supervisor, Mr. Barham, who also happened to be in charge of science and hygiene. Do you have a minute? I asked him. Sure! Do you know what the drug Ritalin is used for? Certainly. Among youth it's given as a behavioral modifier. What type of behavior is it intended to modify? Oh, the usual over-aggressive, hostile, and belligerent behaviors we see here every day. The more experienced staff members attribute this behavior to excessive enthusiastic teenage exhuberance. You shouldn't worry about someone on Ritalin; they are placed in our CRMD unit up on the top floor.

Later that day I revisited the guidance counselor and informed her of my findings. She told me that nothing could be done without either having his records or getting his parents in for a conference. Strike one and two, I thought to myself. Strike three was that Anthony's problem that included his negative disposition was still mine and would continue to be indefinitely. Given my truck driving mentality, I decided upon a strategy of confrontation as opposed to appeasement. As far as dealing with Anthony's continued indiscretions, he was going to be made accountable for his actions.

For three consecutive school days Anthony had been absent. Upon his return to class on the fourth day, I asked him for his parent note explaining the cause of his absence. I ain't got no damn note, he said. I replied that I'd see him at lunchtime to discuss this further. Anthony turned from me waving his hand at me and exited the classroom. Immediately I sent a monitor with a note describing what had just transpired to the Dean.

As the morning moved along, it began to snow. I was looking forward to my pancakes and grits down at the luncheonette. On my way downstairs, I decided to stop in at the Dean's office to see if he had made any progress with Anthony. As I entered the Dean's office, the only person present was Anthony. He was standing near the window with his back to me. When I called to him I got no response. I then said, I can't talk to your back, please turn around. Still there was no response. I walked over to where he was standing and saw why Anthony could not turn around. What I saw so repulsed me that I fled to the teacher's room to spill my insides. The reason Anthony could not turn around to face me was due to the fact that his hands had been placed outside the window, and the window had been lowered to pin his hands in place. I could only guess as to how long Anthony had remained in this position. I returned to the Dean's office, lifted the window, and told Anthony to follow me to the nurse's office. After explaining to the nurse my reason for personally bringing Anthony, I left her office and went on my way to the luncheonette for some badly needed coffee. I was no longer interested in pancakes and grits. I'll never ask anyone to solve my problems again, I silently vowed to myself as I sloshed along in the snow. As I entered the luncheonette, there was the Dean paying his bill and on his way out. Seeing me come in, he smiled and said, I've taken care of that referral. Fuck you, I exclaimed, as I sat down at the counter barstool. You'll never get another. I picked him up five minutes ago and took him to the nurse's office. Oh yeah, bellowed the Dean, as he walked over to where I was sitting. He poked his finger as close to my face as he could without touching it and said, "That's why you people can't teach here." I jumped off my seat and pushed his hand away; he grabbed me by my jacket lapels, and I suspect would have thrown or punched me to the floor had it not been for the intervention of Earnie who had arrived as a result of being summoned by the ladies. Knock it off, Earnie barked. The Dean let go of my lapels, turned, and left the premises. I thanked Earnie and apologized to the ladies, as I also left to return to the school. I never again referred Anthony or any student of mine to the Dean over a disciplinary matter. Of course, my relationship with Anthony did not improve either. If anything he completely despised me, holding me responsible for the abuse he suffered at the hands of the Dean. A few days later I found my car with two flattened tires and broken front headlights.

After getting towed to a local repair shop, the owner who I had been introduced to by Earnie during my fund raising efforts assured me that he'd have it ready by noon the next day. He then had one of his men drive me home. I was trying to relax that evening, by watching the METS game and thinking about how I was going to deal with Anthony the next day when the phone rang. Hello...who's this? I asked in a half-hearted tone. It's Jimmy, came the response. Jimmy from the projects. How you doing, Jimmy, I asked somewhat more enthusiastically than when I had picked up the phone. I'm a cop, came Jimmy's answer. I'd like to get together with you and reminiscence. How about tomorrow night, asked Jimmy. Maybe we could go up to the clubhouse at Yonkers, have dinner, and bet a few races like we used to. I'd really like to, but I have Open School Night tomorrow evening. I didn't know you had kids, responsed Jimmy. Oh, no I don't. At least I don't think I do. I'm a teacher, and I have to be at my school tomorrow night from 6 to 8 p.m. to discuss my students' work with their parents. No problem, he responded. Could I sit in the back of your room while you speak with them? That way we could leave at eight, get to the track by 8:30, and still have a couple of hours to bullshit. I don't see why not I said. Meet me at the school entrance at six, ok? Sure, Jimmy said. Just one thing, I need the name and location of the school. Having complied with Jimmy's request, I hung the phone back up. My recollection of Jimmy was such that he was smart, liked a good joke, and didn't take any crap. I was looking forward to seeing him. It shouldn't be a problem. Jimmy could occupy his time sitting in the back of the room, and studying the racing form, which I would pick up for him at the newsstand near the subway.

With the break of the new day, I'd reached a resolve concerning Anthony. There would be no more appeasement. I was going to force Anthony's hand. One of his most annoying habits was that he would arrive to class with his green woolen hat on, removing it only when I asked him and only after several requests on my part. All attempts at reaching Anthony's parents had failed. It was time for "crazy to get crazy." My lady friends had gotten word to me that what little they could find out was that Anthony's people were bad folks.

It was 8:40 and the members of my official class were arriving at their usual staggered pace. I had positioned myself at the front entranceway and gave the impression that I was monitoring hall traffic, when in fact I was waiting for Anthony. Within a few moments I glimpsed his entrance out onto the hall from the stairway vestibule. He was slowly sauntering along the hallway in the direction of the classroom. Funny thing, I thought. Not a single student made any effort to greet him as he passed through the hoards of students arriving at the other classrooms along the hallway. I moved just inside the doorway arch of my classroom and waited for Anthony to arrive. Within moments he approached. As he entered the room, he passed directly in front of where I was standing. As he did so, I lifted his green woolen knit hat from atop his head. "Hey what you doin'?" Anthony cried out. Everyone else ceased their activities and fixed their eyes and ears on the unfolding drama in the front of the room. Walking away from Anthony toward the science sink holding Anthony's hat in my right hand and my cigarette lighter in my left, I asked the class if they had ever seen the "woolen flame experiment." Anthony was frozen in the spot I'd left him at when I removed his hat. But he wasn't silent. "You better give me my hat. You can't have my motherfuckin' hat." In answer to my question about the "flame experiment," no one in the class responded. What color do you think we'll get when we burn this hat? I asked. No response. Let's see, I said, as I triggered my cigarette lighter and set fire to Anthony's hat. "You crazy white motherfucker," screamed Anthony. "My father is gonna kick your white motherfuckin' ass," was the last thing Anthony said as he left the room. This time I would not be referring him to the Dean.

The remainder of the day passed uneventfully. This was not a surprise. Most kids on the day of Open School Night do not want to give more bullets to their teachers already well loaded magazine arsenal of parental discussion topics. Of course there was a certain melancholia that set in, not only with my official class but also with later arriving classes who had already heard via the grapevine of my early morning science experiment with Anthony's hat. Anthony did not return. I believed that he would return that evening with his parents. Vandalizing my car wasn't going to get his hat back.

After all nothing about me had changed. I fully believed that once he came to that realization, he would have to get his parents to come up and see me. The cost of the hat would be offered as reparations and as entrée into a friendly discussion of Anthony's overall conduct in the class. It was with this thought that I went off to dinner at Patsy's on 118th Street with several colleagues.

We returned to the school promptly at 6 p.m. Waiting for me on the front stoop was Jimmy. After a brief greeting, we both went up to my classroom. I gave Jimmy a copy of the racing form. Pointing to a brown bag that he had tucked under his arm, he asked me if it would be all right if he ate his sandwich while he was waiting. Sure, I said. As we got to the classroom, several parents had arrived a few minutes earlier and were patiently waiting to meet with me. I apologized for my tardiness and opened the door to begin the proceedings.

During the first hour, I saw fourteen parents. This was a disappointing turnout, I thought. I was the teacher of five different class sections—on register approximately 150 students. Where were their parents? this type of apathy was all too often the scene at PTA meetings and at CSB meetings. It's true that many parents feel overwhelmed and nervous about meeting with school personnel. Of course, for many years these same school people did very little to reach out to parents and enlist their support. Fortunately, this pattern began to dissipate in the late '70's and gradually took on the appearance in the '80's of a productive partnership. Now, however, in the '90's given the prosecutorial atmosphere perpetrated by the Mayor's office and his open contempt for the system, by extension its children and their parents, we can label the '90's as adversarial. Can you imagine: a system that has as its primary responsibility the sole function of educating our children does not willingly seek to interact with the parents of those children. Nor does it plan for staff development in "the art of parent conferencing." Is it any wonder that parents feel alienated from the process?

At approximately 7:45 while seated at my desk and in conference with a parent, I caught sight of Anthony standing at the doorway to the classroom. Come on, he's in here, I heard Anthony call to someone down the hall. Within a couple of seconds Anthony was joined by a very tall, bald, and bad looking gentleman. Within a few moments I concluded my talk with Mrs. Washington, shook hands with her, got up from my desk, and walked her to the door. As I got closer to the door, I carefully took note of whom I presumed was Anthony's father. His face was clean-shaven with the exception of a hint of a goatee. From his neck were hung several gold chains and a gold medallion displaying Africa. His forearms were as big as my thighs. Anthony's father was Sonny Liston, I thought. Of course I had no way of knowing if the gentleman was indeed Anthony's father. Having said goodbye to Mrs. Washington, I summoned up my courage, turned to Anthony and his father, and said, "Good evening, I'm glad to meet you at last. Won't you please come in? I'd like to show you Anthony's work." I ain't interested in no fucking work, I heard the man say. I got something to show you, he said, as he opened his three-quarter length black leather coat enough to reveal the gleaming steel of a concealed machete in his waistband. "Where's the motherfucking hat?" Right here, I said, pointing at the pile of ashes in the sink. What did it cost, two or three dollars? "You gonna pay, alright." I heard the gentleman say. I saw him make a motion with his hand in the direction of his waistband.

At that moment I heard Jimmy's voice from the back of the room. "Hold it right there," Jimmy said, rising from his seat with his gun in his hand and pointed in the direction of Anthony's father. "There ain't no reason for all that," came the gentleman's reply. "I'm just showing the teacher my blade. It's from Africa, and I thought he'd like to see it, considering that he's a history teacher an all. We finished. Me and my boy are gonna leave now...if that's alright with you all." Jimmy looked at me and I kinda nodded my approval. As they got outside I heard Anthony's father say, "Boy, don't you fuck with that man. He keeps protection. Got to be a crazy white motherfucker...I'm tellin' you, don't fuck with him."

Jimmy never did identify himself as a cop. From this incident was born the myth of my being connected. I never denied it. Nor did I ever suggest that I was. If people wanted to let their imaginations run wild, then why spoil the day, especially if it meant a better day for me.

I didn't have any further problems with Anthony for the rest of the term. Sadly, however, he was non-responsive, also. Two months later his records arrived at last. They revealed that Anthony was indeed learning impaired and should be placed in a special education setting.

Chapter X

Career Guidance:
Kids and Teachers That No One Wanted

The year was '68, and Mr. Biggio had begun to show signs of losing his grip the previous spring. As we closed operations in June, the betting was even money that he was on the verge of a nervous breakdown and most probably would not be back. There was any number of contributing factors. The staff had become polarized over the various political issues of the times. Several near riots amongst the staff had to be quelled. Teachers who espoused to the Black Power Movement were openly hostile and belligerent to white teachers, unless those whites were openly sympathetic to their cause and methods. As if all of these issues were not distracting enough, there was the threat of an impending strike in the fall if teacher contract negotiations over the summer proved futile. Given the above, you could see why I was surprised to be summoned by Mr. Biggio's office when we all reported to work the week before Labor Day. Given Mr. Biggio's disdain for long and drawn out interviews, the conference went something like this: "How was your summer, Mr. Kassell?" Fine, and yours? I asked. Very relaxing was Mr. Biggio's reply. Mr. Kassell I've decided to make you the "lead" teacher in our Career Guidance program. Not having any knowledge of this program, I was unsure how to respond. This program is under the supervision of Dr. Kahn and is housed on the top floor. I didn't know much about Dr. Kahn. He was somewhat nondescript, kept to himself, appeared to be near retirement, and was the Assistant Principal in charge of Special Education and special programs. Mr. Biggio continued; by the way, I've taken the liberty to arrange a meeting for you with Dr. Kahn in fifteen minutes. Good luck, Mr. Kassell. I'm counting on you."

As I left Mr. Biggio's office, I found comfort in the thought of no more math! As I made my way up to Dr. Kahn's office, I was hard-pressed to have any recollections of the man. I never saw him on a day-to-day basis. Of course he was present at the monthly obligatory faculty conferences, but he was never asked to speak to any of the agenda items nor did he ever volunteer a particular point of view. As I approached his office, I found the doorway open and caught a glimpse of Dr. Kahn deeply engrossed with the *New York Times*. I rapped my knuckles on the door and immediately Dr. Kahn put his paper down and bid me to come in. He promptly folded the newspaper and as he did so I could tell that he had been busy reading the Stock Market section. I'm sorry to interrupt, but Mr. Biggio told me that he had arranged a meeting for me with you at this time. Never mind all that, Dr. Kahn replied. Welcome. So you are Mr. Kassell? I've heard so much about you. Tell me Mr. Kassell, during your undergraduate years did you take any psych, guidance, or sociology classes? I had; I told him and didn't find them too interesting. Have you ever worked as a counselor or in any related field? No sir. Before I entered teaching I was a truck driver. I also waited tables in the Catskills and worked as a "Soda Jerk" in a neighborhood candy store. Right, was Dr. Kahn's doubtful reply. He went on to say that he had twelve pupil record folders that he'd like me to peruse. He stated that the legal cap for this particular class was eighteen and that it was possible that up to six additional students might be added. I don't attach much significance to what's contained in these folders I heard myself saying and not quite believing that I was saying it in light of my experience with Anthony last year. Nevertheless, I insist that you take time now here in my office to review them. I began the process of reading each pupil profile much the way Lee Marvin did in assembling his "dirty dozen."

For the next hour I read accounts of pupils who had been held over more than once, suspended from school on numerous occasions, and of late had become incarcerated at some of the finer youth detention sites in NYC. The word incorrigible seemed to be the favorite adjective of those who had placed written evaluations in the folders. After I finished I passed the folders back to Dr. Kahn. You've got the wrong man I said, getting up and moving in the direction of Dr. Kahn's office door. Just a minute young man, I haven't painted the whole picture, yet. Sit down please. This program is a career-educational-guidance triad. The program will be housed in the double sized "old" bandroom on the floor beneath us. The students will be bussed in each morning from various locales within the borough. Some will come from halfway houses, others from full-time detention centers, and others from court appointed foster homes. Their hours for attending school are mandated, as from 8:30 a.m.-12:30 p.m. They will be picked up by the busses and taken to places of employment that you have garnered for them. They will then put in a workday from 1 p.m.-5 p.m. Each morning the Board of Education will provide you with donuts, milk, coffee, cocoa, orange juice, cold cereal, and on occasion fresh fruit. It is expected that you and your team of teachers will have breakfast and lunch with your students. Your afternoons will be devoted to follow up in such areas as parent contact, agency articulation, and employer conferences. You and your team will meet regularly to set out lesson planning strategies, review case studies, and in general conduct such other business as deemed vital and necessary to the overall success of the program. You and your team shall be responsible for the instructional delivery of mathematics, social studies, reading, four periods of physical education, and one period of hygiene per week.

I was impressed with Dr. Kahn's masterful and assertive articulation of the program. Any questions so far, asked Dr. Kahn. Yes. Would you go over the part that had to do with me getting them jobs? Certainly. You shall not only secure meaningful parttime jobs for each student in the program, but you will also maintain careful records of their employment, documenting your field visits, employer interviews, and ascertaining their ratings of our students in the following areas: absences, lateness, attitudes (negative or positive), willingness to take direction, and job performance growth. Of course, you will have some leeway in trying to improve upon any unsatisfactory reports. The students will know that if they continually present problems in class or on the job, that they may be removed from the program, providing of course that you can document the fact that you've done everything within your power to rectify the situation. There is one problem wihin the realm of curriculum implementation. The mainstream physical education teachers objected to being assigned to teach this class. They lodged a grievance and won at step two. On the other hand, the state doesn't recognize the grievance won by the gym teachers as a sufficient reason to remove physical education and hygiene from the program. In a letter to me they wrote that upon their inspection of the program, there must be full compliance with all the program guidelines and mandates. What about the other teachers on the team? Who are they? I asked, with some enthusiasm? Pulling out a single sheet from his program folder, Dr. Kahn read the names of Bert Flemming, Arnold Mercado, and Mike O'Kernan. You must be kidding I blurted. These three are almost as incorrigible as some of the pupils I just read about.

How they avoided incarceration is anybody's guess. I've heard tell that you are somewhat incorrigible as well, Mr. Kassell, yet very resourceful. I suspect you'll need the latter talent more than ever. I'll be curious to see how you resolve the physical education problem. I haven't accepted the position yet, I reminded Dr. Kahn. He responded saying that Mr. Biggio is very concerned and committed to the success of this program. The fact that he has handpicked you to make it work is to be regarded as a compliment. I don't think he would look upon the fact that you are reluctant to take this assignment as a good career move on your part. He is waiting for my call now. What shall I tell him, Mr. Kassell? As I pondered Dr. Kahn's last statement, I laughed to myself. I wasn't incorrigible; I was a Prima Donna. I was doing things my way before Frank Sinatra immortalized the words. I'll give it a shot on one condition. Which is...? asked Dr. Kahn. Self-autonomy. No second-guessing by the administration. If I decided to put a student or teacher out of the program then that decision stands. There is to be no interference from any part of the mainstream operation of the school. If any of my people are absent, we shall solve that problem internally. I will comply with the various regulations you've stipulated. Finally I want five days for planning before the first day of classes. Immediately Dr. Kahn was on the phone relaying my demands to Mr. Biggio. Within seconds Dr. Kahn placed the phone back in its cradle and said that Mr. Biggio had directed him to inform me that each of my requests would be honored.

The three teachers who were to be assigned had gained reputations as flakes and misfits. Perhaps they were not cut out to be teachers, or perhaps they had been improperly assigned or hadn't found their niche. Who knows? I decided to put off my meeting with them until the end of the week. I did, however, take a gander at their teacher's files that Dr. Kahn made available to me on the QT.

Bert Flemming was a seventh grade teacher whose official class was located on the first floor. One day while in the midst of a social studies lesson, the fire drill gongs sounded. In the investigation that would follow,

Flemming's unorthodox manner by which he led his class from the building to the street was necessary he would maintain because if the drill were real, he, his children, and countless others would be at risk given the school plan for exiting the building. He went on to say that his window was only 6' off the ground—an easy jump for seventh graders. When the gongs sounded, Flemming placed his teacher's chair (a sturdy oak captain's style piece of furniture) as a step up just in front of the classroom window. Each student in turn used the chair to make their way onto the window ledge and then jump to the sidewalk 6' below the sill. No one got hurt, and everyone including himself was safely out of harm's way within minutes of the fire drill gongs.

The PTA received numerous complaints and pressured Mr. Biggio to get rid of the lunatic. Flemming was relieved of his class assignment and was used by Mr. Tramm on a day-to-day basis to cover the programs of absent teachers. Now he would have the opportunity to return to a regular teaching assignment. Recognizing his good fortune, he gladly accepted the assignment.

Arnold Mercado had served as a School Attendance Officer. The operative word here as you will see is "Officer." Arnold had also been to a hearing, and as a result had been deemed unfit to continue to serve as School Attendance Officer. Consequently he, too, was serving as a day-to-day substitute and was not very happy about it. Simultaneously he was suing the NYC Board of Education for illegally removing him from his assignment as Attendance Officer.

In his job description Arnold was expected to "track down" truants and get them to school. Very often he was expected to bring these same students to Family Court. In either case he carried out his duties in a hostile climate. Students and their parents were not always eager to be found nor were they eager to make court appearances. Arnold's investigations were often thwarted by misleading

Kenneth S. Karcinell

tips, non-cooperative community members, and in some cases, attempts at intimidation via mailed or phoned in threats to his office.

As part of his professional job certification requirement, Arnold was in the midst of obtaining a Master's Degree in criminology. One particular Saturday morning Arnold had gone off to his local library to do some research. In the course of his research Arnold learned that New York State equated the role of a School Attendance Officer with that of a Peace Officer. Upon further research he found that this state law dated back to the mid 1800's and stipulated that the equipment those officers in both categories would possess would be a "dependable" firearm, a "Billy Club" and a whistle. Armed with this information, he applied for and was granted a permit for a pistol. He then purchased a.25 caliber handgun that he kept concealed in a leather shoulder holster beneath his sportjacket.

Shortly thereafter, Arnold had "tracked down" a student who was being sought by Family Court. The student who had been reported as truant from his last known school had simply gotten himself enrolled in a school in another part of town. Arnold had become quite resourceful. He found that if he waited for the first three weeks of the term to pass, he could by telephone survey, determine the number of students who had become enrolled in other schools as transfers from "out of state." The law said that they must be admitted. Students who were for one reason or another fleeing authorities, knowing that they would certainly be caught if they remained in their assigned schools frequently used this ploy to avoid detection. It was through one of Arnold's telephone surveys that he learned that the student he was seeking had indeed become enrolled in another school as an "out of state transfer."

Unfortunately for Arnold this particular student was in attendance at one of the most unruly high schools in NYC. Upon arriving at the school he visited the General Office to notify the Principal that he would be conducting an involuntary removal of one of his students. Good luck, the Principal said, closing his office door behind him. Leaving the General Office, Arnold located the pupil in a first floor classroom halfway around from the front door and security guard post. While in the process of escorting the student from the school, Arnold found his way becoming impeded by hoards of friends and associates of the student who had begun to derisively chant "no way, Jose." According to Arnold's deposition, he felt that his safety was clearly in doubt. Therefore, he produced his handgun and saw the hoards part as miraculously as The Red Sea had done for Moses. At his hearing the Board of Education ruled that their employees were obligated to function within those guidelines established by the NYC Board of Education and not those guidelines found elsewhere. Mr. Mercado was to be summarily removed from his post as School Attendance Officer. My kind of guy, I thought, as I closed his folder.

Mike O'Kernan was truly a rare bird. He was a man of scruples and uncompromising standards. He stood approximately 6'4" and by his mere physical presence combined with his aggressive teaching style he usually did not encounter discipline problems in his class. However, there was always room for the exception or, at the very least, the unexpected. Such would be the case regarding Karen, the daughter and only child of the school PTA president.

According to the description of events contained in O'Kernan's file, the incident that "broke the camel's back" as far as he was concerned went this way: One day while in the midst of one of his language arts lessons, Karen who was a known antagonist and provocateur of other children and who often got away unpunished because of her mother's role as PTA President, got into a shouting match with another female student in the class. Before O'Kernan could stop it the two girls were exchanging blows. The

Kenneth S. Karcinell

worst thing a teacher can become involved in is trying to
break up a girl's fight. Unlike boys they do not conform to
code. They will scratch, claw, or bite to get an advantage.
They will not back off simply because a teacher is on the
scene. They seemingly go into a trance not unlike the
"Vulcan Blood Lust" experienced by Spock on Star Trek.
Undaunted Mike O'Kernan approached the two combatants
and in a loud and assertive voice he instructed the girls to
"back off" or else. One girl (not Karen) attempted to do so.
Seeing a break in the action, O'Kernan stepped between the
girls. His attention was drawn to the girl who had ceased
from the pugilistic activities. She was bleeding from various
scratches on her face that would need medical attention. As
O'Kernan attempted to lead her away, Karen came up
behind him and tried to kick her adversary, only to clip
O'Kernan in the calf. Instinctively he turned and threw
Karen over a desk and onto the floor (a medical checkup
would reveal no serious injury, unless you counted pride).
Karen got up and ran from the classroom. As it turned out,
she continued running until she exited the school in search
of her mother. Within ten minutes Mrs. Lauren's voice
bellowed throughout the school. Where is the
motherfucker? Where is he? Please, someone take me to
him. Hearing her shrieks, Mr. Biggio came out into the
office to investigate. At this point there are several versions
as to what happened next. Here is the one I like: After much
salving and cajoling, Mr. Biggio had succeeded in calming
Mrs. Lauren down. He had gotten her to believe that
O'Kernan was an exceptional teacher who had like any
human being lost control temporarily. He assured Mrs.
Lauren that Mr. O'Kernan would eagerly apologize to her
given the opportunity to do so. He asked her if she had
sufficiently calmed down so that he could send for Mr.
O'Kernan to make his apologies. After nodding her head in
the affirmative, Mr. Biggio instructed his secretary Mrs.
Gerstein to have Mr. O'Kernan report to his office. When

O'Kernan arrived, he was ushered directly into Mr. Biggio's office. To this day I cannot understand how Biggio didn't see the need to take time to debrief O'Kernan as to the commitment he had privately made on his behalf to Mrs. Lauren. In any event, as soon as O'Kernan arrived he was invited to sit down opposite Mrs. Lauren and her daughter Karen and directly opposite from Mr. Biggio who was seated at his Principal's desk.   Mr. Biggio mistakenly believed that he had things under control. Mr. O'Kernan, Mrs. Lauren, and Karen have reviewed the incident that occurred in your classroom a little while ago, he said. We all agree it was regretful.   Mrs. Lauren acknowledges that her daughter's conduct was improper. She wants you to know, however, that she is the child's mother and will discipline her child when necessary. She does not want you or anyone else putting their hands on her child. Is that clear? O'Kernan, according to Mrs. Gerstein's notes on the proceedings, simply nodded affirmatively. Is there anything you would like to say? Yes, O'Kernan said. Mrs. Lauren has been sent for a number of times since school started. Until today I had not met her. That's neither here nor there right now bellowed Biggio. He added, looking back on the whole affair, is there anything you would do differently given a similar set of circumstances tomorrow? Yes, Mr. O'Kernan said again.   Knock Karen down first. I should have done it sooner. Bing, bam, and boom is the way to go. As O'Kernan left the room Mrs. Lauren's invectives could be heard at an even higher pitch than when she had first arrived to the school. As you would expect, O'Kernan was removed from his teaching duties and placed in charge of the bookroom and schoolwide supply distribution pending further hearings. He too was delighted at Mr. Biggio's offer of Career Guidance instruction. It took him two seconds to say yes to the offer.

So, this was my assignment—incorrigible students and deranged teachers. Placing the teacher's file folders on Dr.

Kahn's desk, I thanked him. As I got up to leave, I asked Dr. Kahn if he could arrange for me to pick up the room keys for the "Old Band Room," as well as the NYC Board of Education curriculum for Career Guidance. I'd like to stop by in the morning and pick them up. I don't see that as a problem, responded Dr. Kahn. On second thought, I said, I'll need four sets of keys and four curriculum guides. Again, Dr. Kahn's no problem response followed me out into the hallway.

Later that day I discussed my assignment with several colleagues with whom I had struck up a friendship during the past year and whose opinions I valued. Their responses varied from Why? to "I know it makes no sense to tell you that you can't do something; that type of talk seems to ignite your competitive fires." You're so right, expressed another colleague. Wasn't it a year ago that Mrs. Gerstein did not prepare a time card for you because she thought that you would come to the realization that you couldn't teach? We all know how that turned out. Go get 'em; my friends encouraged me. As we parted company, I thanked my two colleagues for their words of encouragement and promised to keep them posted.

The next morning I reported to Dr. Kahn's office at 8:30 promptly. As I entered his office, Dr. Kahn greeted me warmly. Good morning Mr. Kassell. I've arranged for the items you requested yesterday. They are all in that box near the file cabinet. I've also taken the liberty to pick up a couple of containers of coffee and muffins from the luncheonette down the block. I hope you like bran. You shouldn't have, I replied. You see, I wasn't planning on staying long, as I have a lot to do today. Surely a few minutes for breakfast won't hinder those plans, came Dr. Kahn's response. His commanding tone suggested to me that he had orchestrated the coffee clique for a purpose. Accordingly, I sat down and asked, which is mine, pointing at the two coffee containers? If you take sugar and cream it's the one on the left. The other is black without sugar. Take whichever you like, it doesn't matter to me. Joining me, he asked if I would mind telling him how I intended to spend the next five days? I don't mind, I heard myself say to a somewhat startled Dr. Kahn. I want to seize upon this opportunity to prove to you that I am not difficult to supervise. I'll take two days to visit and interview the students, their site counselors, and social workers at the various locations in which they are housed. I'll also want to talk with their parents. But you've already read their files, protested Dr. Kahn. Yes I have; however, there may have been changes since they were updated. The kids may have improved in certain areas. They may have retrogressed as well. Why waste time with their parents; you can see them on Open School Night, Dr. Kahn suggested. I said that I don't think it's very helpful to articulate with parents in November those things that are going to impact upon their children in September. Don't you agree, Dr. Kahn, that parents have the right to know immediately as to what the Board of Education is planning to do with their child? I suppose, came Dr. Kahn's less than enthusiastic reply. I'll need a day to see Earnie; I went on. Who is Earnie, asked Dr. Kahn? You don't want to know, I said. I'll meet with the teachers on Thursday and Friday, for a full debriefing and planning session. I've really got to get going. Thanks so much for the breakfast, the keys, and books. Picking up the carton I turned back toward Dr. Kahn and said, you know there is a favor I'd like to ask. Name it, replied Dr. Kahn. Could you get word to Mssrs. Flemming, Mercado, and O'Kernan to meet me at "the old band room" this morning at ten? Consider it done, I heard Dr. Kahn say as I exited his office. Walking down the hall my thought was that the first meeting had to be with Earnie. Everything would depend upon it. Earnie would have to help me with the two biggest problems I was faced with thus far: finding jobs and a physical education instruction site.

It was 9:15 when I walked into the luncheonette. Good morning, sugar, came Martha's greeting. "How're you doin' today?" she asked cheerily. "How was your summer? You look good." Fine was my collective response to Martha's battery of questions. Well, what can I fix you this morning? Just a coffee, Martha. I'm very pressed for time. Also, I need a favor. What is it baby? she said. I need to see Earnie desperately by noon today. Who's messing with you? came Martha's anguished inquiry. No, it's nothing like that I assured her. I just need his advice on a couple of school matters. You mean help not advice, came Martha's reply. Nodding in the affirmative I asked anxiously, do you think you can get him here by noon on such short notice? You be here, don't be late, was Martha's admonition. Thanks, Martha, I owe you. Not a thing, I heard her say as I left the luncheonette.

It was 10:05 when I approached the "old band room." True to his word Dr. Kahn had arranged for Mssrs. Flemming, Mercado, and O'Kernan to meet me there. Good morning, gentlemen, I said extending my hand to each. I'm Ken Kassell. We know, Flemming responded. Mr. Biggio told us that you had requested our assignment to your program. Right, I said with a slight smile. Let's see what's behind door #1, I said, while placing my key into the door cylinder. As the door opened, I took a stride in, flicked on the light switch, and stood frozen in a state of shock over what I saw. Come on in, I urged each of the other team members. They too had to be in a state of shock at what they saw. For a brief moment we all simply stood there scanning the room in utter disbelief. Similar, I suppose, to the reaction of an aficionado when confronted by Michaelangelo's "David" for the first time. Speechless! As promised the room was the full size of two regular classrooms. As was not promised let alone mentioned, the room apparently had been used for warehousing old and broken furniture and piles of torn books. Litter was

80

everywhere, some used condoms, and in the corner a very old and dead rat. Almost immediately I sensed Flemming turning to leave. Where are you going I said, with an edge to my voice that communicated my displeasure with his decision to leave. I'm going to see Biggio, Flemming responded. I won't work in these conditions. Listen to me carefully, Mr. Fleming, Mr. Mercado, and you, Mr. O'Kernan. Contrary to what Mr. Biggio may have told you, I did not ask for this assignment nor did I ask that any of you be assigned to it. The difference between us, however, is that this is not going to be my last chance. It will be for you if we don't reach an understanding today as to how this is going to work. To begin with, in that box you will find a set of room keys for each of you along with the NYC Board of Education syllabus for Career Guidance Curriculum. Everything that we do here will be borne out of careful committee discussion and my final approval. It's my way or the highway. Do I make myself clear, gentlemen? Fleming, you will not be visiting Mr. Biggio or anyone else in the administration. None of you will give any details or statements to anyone inquiring about our business from here on out. Is that clear? Any and all such inquiries are to be directed to my attention. I have several appointments over the next three days. I'll meet you here on Thursday at 8:30 promptly. Try to organize this place by then. Also, prepare a list of supply needs, texts, maps and anything else you can think of. I won't ask if there are any questions for now, because it doesn't matter. This is your last shot, gentlemen. Make it count. Leaving the room and walking down the hall, I thought, did I win them or lose them?

I walked into the luncheonette at 11:45. I scanned the room quickly and to my great relief there was Earnie seated at the rear booth with the *New York Daily News* opened wide in front of him. Did the Mets win or lose last night? Putting down the paper, he got up with a smile on his face and said hey kid how you doin'? Sit down. I understand you

81

got a problem. Martha came over with a cup of coffee for me and smiled while offering to refill Earnie's cup for which he nodded his approval. It took me about a half- hour to explain my assignment and the nature of the program to Earnie, including the teacher histories and the pupil backgrounds. Tough kids and some tough teachers, Earnie observed. I hadn't thought of it quite that way, but I could see the merit in his evaluation. You still haven't told me what you need from me, Earnie said. Parttime jobs for each kid and a place to do physical education four hours a week. What type of jobs? Hard but meaningful work. Non-abusive bosses. What guarantees can I give that the kids won't steal or be a problem, Earnie said. None, was my quick reply. Upon hearing of such a complaint, I would immediately remove them from the job and program. Each kid would know this going in, I said. Earnie paused, scratching his beard, and then said the following: I'll need two days to get the job thing together. Are you familiar, he asked, with the JFK center over on 135th street? No, I was again quick to respond. It's an After School and evening community center. Anyway, I'll see you back here on Wednesday at noon. Thanks, Earnie. No problem, kid. I liked you from day one. Any teacher who wants to help our kids gets my help. Always remember that, kid—you got Earnie.

My meeting with Earnie ended a little past 2 p.m., and there wasn't much left to do with day one other than plan out my activities for days two and three. I set up a schedule that allowed me to visit half of the students on Tuesday morning and the other half in the afternoon. I would use Wednesday morning to see as many of their parents as possible so that I could keep my lunchtime engagement with Earnie. I made no schedule to confer with the social workers and site counselors. There would be no revelations there. It made no sense to listen to the pontifications of these individuals. They were not Ph.D's, and had no answers. These kids were for any number of reasons turned off to education, turned off to authority, turned off to going along with the program, and turned off to each other and even to themselves. What would it take? I pondered the question. How will I find a common unifying factor that will give them a purpose for their being?

As planned I was able to meet briefly with each of the twelve students on Tuesday. They all professed to be eager to return to school. They expressed concerns about the job opportunities and the Career Education program. They did, however, recognize the fact that that part of the program was a must and could not be avoided. In each interview I made it very clear that any displays of negative behavior either in the classroom or on the job could lead to being discharged from the program.

For the most part after reading their profiles, meeting some of their site supervisors and most of their parents, I could safely say that these children were non-violent. They were misfits. Their offenses ranged from being dull-witted, but not stupid, to severe truancy, to being runaways or victims of a system that did not provide for children slipping through the seams of a non-flexible educational environment. They were alternately withdrawn, indifferent, non-competitive, and goalless. To compound matters, some of them had been abused at the hands of their parents or guardians so much so that there were court orders prohibiting or seriously restricting parent involvement. In such cases when parent involvement would have ordinarily been thought of as a necessary ingredient to the educational planning component for a child, the educator was to call in various child advocacy personnel. I'll have more to say about these individuals, later.

On Wednesday, as planned, Earnie and I sat down for lunch. Martha promised a sumptuous meal of black-eyed peas and rice with fish cakes. After feasting on Martha's Bill of Faire and engaging one another in such small talk discussion topics as the Mets' chance for winning this year

83

and the promises made by John Lindsay in his bid for the mayoralty, we got down to business.

Then Earnie said, by the way kid, I asked a pal of mine to meet us. You'll enjoy him, and I think he can help. I know that he wants to help. I'll let him explain when he gets here. Reaching into his shirt pocket, Earnie produced a folded piece of notepaper and handed it to me. You can see, he went on, that there are twenty businesses and their phone numbers. Why so many Ernie? I said. I only needed twelve. Earnie responded, do you really think that each kid is going to be successful at the job you assign him or her to? You're right, I exclaimed. I would have never thought of that. I know, came Ernie's reply, with a slight hint of a snicker. Then I took a moment to survey the list. There was variety—dishwashing, newspaper delivery, grocery store stock clerk, bookstore clerk, car wash attendant, and meat market assistant were just some of the jobs detailed on Ernie's list. While mostly menial, they were seemingly acceptable within the parameters I'd given to Ernie on Monday. Fred, come on over, Ernie called to a gentleman just entering the luncheonette. A tall, dark skinned man wearing a NYC Parks Department uniform joined us. Sit down, Ernie instructed. Kid, this is Fred Coleman. He's the director of the JFK Community Center I mentioned to you the other day. Other than kid, how would you like me to call you, Fred said, extending his hand, Ken...Ken Kassell, I said, eagerly shaking his hand. Then it'll be Ken, Fred said. Ernie has told me a lot about you and what you wanna do for these kids. Here's what you need to know. Officially, the center doesn't open until 3:30 every afternoon. Fred must have seen my frown, but that won't be a problem, he quickly added. It won't, I gleefully asked. No. You see I arrive daily at 9 a.m. I have any number of chores to take care of each day that requires my presence early on. None of that need concern you Ken. Unfortunately, my staff does not report until 3 p.m. That shouldn't pose a problem I responded excitedly. You see I'll have three of my own staff plus me. I hope they have some special skills. What do you mean, Fred? Didn't Ernie tell you what we had goin' on down at the center? No,...no he didn't. Ernie had a smile on his face that told me how pleasantly surprised I was about to become. We have a full-size gym, an above ground level running track, and an Olympic size swimming pool, four basketball courts, volleyball nets, a locker room area, towels, and shower stalls. You have to be from Heaven, I said. How could I ever thank you? Make it work, was Fred's answer. I've really got to be goin', Fred said, getting up to leave, Fred reached into his shirt pocket and produced a business card. Giving it to me he said "here's my card, Ken. Call me when you're ready to set up the program." I said, Wednesdays and Fridays from 10-12 starting next week. That'll be fine. Call me anyway, Fred said. Remember, you can't use the pool without a certified lifeguard. We all shook hands then left the luncheonette together. We were three happy men. You're the best Ernie. I know, kid, I know, he said walking away in the direction of his gold Cadillac.

I went directly home. My mind was racing with ideas and plans that I had to get down on paper for fear of forgetting them if I allowed for too much time to pass. I was, as some say pumped. I could hardly wait to get to school Thursday morning. Walking up the stairs as fast as I could, I had carefully planned what I was going to say and how I was going to say it. I had prepared a rexo stencil containing the morning meeting agenda. It would be established today that all of our meetings would be documented, although not always in advance. I knew that this program was going to be closely monitored. I also knew that the "bigwigs" were well protected in terms of deniability in case things got out of "whack," but stood ready to accept the accolades when they went well. I didn't begrudge them their status; I simply recognized it as the nature of the beast. I always maintained that if you understood what made the system work, then you could work the system.

As I neared the room, I saw that the door was wide open. Walking in, I knew the answer to the question I had asked myself on Monday. All of the delapidated furniture was gone. All of the old texts and materials were similarly disposed of. It was obvious to me that the room had been fully "policed." Absent was the deceased rat and used condoms. Making their first appearances were four teacher desks and oak captain's chairs. There were four oak bookcases and four portable chalkboards. The room itself had been subdivided into four distinct learning centers via the use of the chalkboards as room dividers. In the middle of the room there was placed a large conference table with four oak chairs. The coup de grace had to be a stainless-steel sideboard which held a very large coffee urn, several stacks of paper coffee containers, a small basket of stirrers and sugar packets, an assortment of miniature breakfast cereals, a box of cocoa packets, at least a dozen assorted rolls and an equal amount of donuts, six miniature milk cartons and as many miniature orange juice cartons. I was astounded. It started Tuesday morning offered O'Kernan. The Board of Education delivered it as part of the school's daily food delivery. They even supplied the stainless-steel sideboard to be in full compliance with the Board of Health regulations. O'Kernan casually observed that the milk and juice allocations would have to be increased when all of the students were in place. He offered to personally follow up on that account. I thanked him. Then he asked, Mr. Kassell do you have twenty-five dollars? You see we all chipped in that amount so as to enlist the cooperation of the custodial staff. They have since assured us that whatever our future needs might be, they will find a way to make it happen. That's great Mr. O'Kernan. Here's my $25. Then Mr. Flemming said, I've prepared the supply and textbook needs list if you care to go over it. In a little while, I said. Gentlemen, I cannot thank you enough. You've shown the kind of initiative that is going to be vital to our success. In the end you'll see that we will be successful. Let's have breakfast. I'd won.

We all took our food over to the conference table. Casually I asked, do all of you want to stay in teaching? As one, they answered yes. That's fine. Then don't think of this as your last opportunity, but as your first. Now I want to lay out some additional ground rules to those I previously alluded to on Monday. Don't look at your agenda; they are not listed in any of the "Items of Concern." First, there is no room for bullshit. I won't ever bullshit you and I expect the same courtesy. Second, we solve our own problems. Third, as I turned to make eye contact with O'Kernan, I said, no brutality. Looking at Mercado, I responded that there is no use of any accessory other than perscribed by the NYC Board of Education. Looking at Flemming, I said, "and lastly, since there are no elevators we shall enter and leave this building via the stairwells and doors made available to everyone."

Let's turn to our agenda. You will see that I've indicated in our organization the following assignments: Social Studies...Flemming, Math...Mercado. How did you make that determination, Mr. Kassell? asked Mercado. Before we go any further gentlemen, when we are out of earshot of our students, amongst ourselves, let's use first names. Agreed? Everyone nodded yes. Arnold, I know that you worked in the Bureau of Attendance. Therefore, I reasoned that you are very good in addition and subtraction. Multiplication and division can't be that much of a stretch. Can we move on? Everyone chuckled, including Mercado. Language Arts,...O'Kernan. The second "item for concern" was listed as Daily routine. Each and every morning barring such unforeseen incidents as inclement weather, traffic accident, or mechanical failure, our students will arrive by bus at 8:30. It will become habitual that as they arrive they will take their breakfast from the buffet and join us at the conference table. We will engage them and ourselves in discussing such things as favorite movies, radio stations, music, sports teams, TV shows, foods, and any other easy to talk about subjects. It's during these sessions that the students are apt to be more talkative and revealing as to their true nature. After breakfast they will be not only more alert but also hopefully become more at ease with us.

Next item...dress code. Shirts and ties, gentlemen. This is not going to be Woodstock. We are not missionaries. We are teachers. Does anyone have a problem? Good. Let's move along. Programming is our next area of concern. Unwittingly gentlemen, the Board of Education and Mr. Biggio, in particular, have given us the opportunity to pursue a concept of teaching that is in its early stages and has only been seen in specially selected areas of the country, specifically, "Team Teaching" in a self-contained environment. To that end you have crafted the room magnificently. By the way, Arnold, do you think you can see our new friends, and ask them if they can empty the huge rear instrument closet? We will use this room as our office and emergency conference center. I will get Dr. Kahn's permission to have a phone installed. Who is Dr. Kahn, asked Burt Flemming? Laughing, I said that he was the school supervisor in charge of the program.

And, Arnold, before I forget, we'll need a minimum of twelve and a maximum of eighteen pupil desks and chairs. Speaking of pupils, when are they coming, asked Arnold? Monday morning, I said. Now to this item: How will the program function? The class will be subdivided into three distinct groups. Each of you will serve as an official teacher for that group. I'm doing this because I believe it is necessary that kids have the opportunity to bond with "their own teacher." The classes will be differentiated simply as The Knicks, The Mets, and The Jets. Numbers like group 1,

2, or 3 often suggest an order of importance or intelligence, which could lead to stigmatization and fights. The same can be said with the use of letters. The instructional day will run as follows: 9:30-10:15, 10:16-11:00, and then 11:01-11:45. During that time schedule the students will rotate from each of you completing a three- period cycle until lunch. Lunch is from 11:50-12:30. At that time we will accompany the group to the pupil cafeteria for lunch, and eat with them. After a while we will desist from this practice hopefully because they will have bonded among themselves and will have been accepted into the main stream of the cafeteria student body. Not to mention the fact that they would probably rather have their privacy so that they could talk about us. Everyone laughed. The buses will pick them up at 12:30 and deliver them to their job sites. Job sites, blurted Flemming inquisitively. Yes. This program is called Career Guidance. To that end a major component is job training. You have noted by now that I have no specific teaching assignment. My preferred academic interests are history, geography, social studies, and with some hesitancy, math. I will be the first substitute. By the way I want each of us to have one another's phone numbers. Unless you are in a coma or in some other way non-functional, absence is not an option.

Additionally, I shall be responsible for all of the program liaison work. There will be a plethora of forms to keep up with and all kinds of field monitoring, ranging from spot checks with the pupil's employers to on the job conferences with parents. Any other questions? Good. Let's look at our last agenda item—Specialty Skills. Briefly, in turn, tell me about your hobbies and any talents you have. You know, like playing an instrument, stamp collecting, sports, swimming—get the idea. Flemming was first, stating that he enjoyed visiting historic areas and would like to be able to take the kids on educational field trips. That might be problematic given the fact that we only have them until

11:45. We'll keep it in mind however. I don't want to thwart any of your hopes or goals. After all, how high is heaven or whats a heaven for? Arnold was next. I don't know if you'll think this is special, but I like to spend time at the ocean, he said. I even work there in the summer as a lifeguard. At the end of the day I amuse myself collecting seashells. Bingo, I thought. Do you have a lifeguard certificate? Absolutely came Arnold's reply. I shoot hoops and read romance novels, chirped O'Kernan.

What's with all the specialty stuff, asked Flemming. Good question, I replied. You must understand, gentlemen, this is a state-mandated program. As such, they have imposed certain non-flexible guidelines. These guidelines define such things as instructional time limits, hence the forty-five minute sequences. The guidelines also specify types of instruction. In the Career Guidance Program the state specifies ninety weekly minutes of Physical Education and ninety monthly minutes of Hygiene instruction. When Mr. Biggio informed the UFT chairman that this program was going to be in place this year and that the gym teachers would be expected to provide the gym and hygiene instruction as specified, they balked and filed a grievance which hinged on the fact that they were lacking in prerequisite special educational coursework. Can you imagine a gym teacher using the term prerequisite? What's the world coming to? At any event, Biggio caved. He did not want to lose an unwinnable grievance. As a result of a meeting I had with several concerned community leaders, we will have our physical education instruction on Wednesdays and Fridays off campus over at the JFK Community Center on 135th Street from 10-11:30.

The director, Mr. Fred Coleman, is very anxious to see our kids have fun and get turned back on to education. I am going to try and make arrangements with the Outreach Program at Harlem Hospital to see if we can get an intern or nurse to voluntarily come over to the center on a once-a-month basis and provide instruction in such areas as anti-smoking, anti-drug use, sexual experimentation, and other topics as may be appropriate. For all I know there may be a state curriculum guideline for Hygiene instruction. There is, interrupted Mike. Let's try to get our hands on one. What else does the center have? asked Arnold enthusiastically. Basketball courts, an upper-level indoor track, a locker room area, and an Olympic sized pool. Arnold, clearly you will supervise and provide instruction in this area. Mike, yeah I know basketball. Bert? I'll try the upper-level track. I used to jog quite a bit. Good. I'll supervise the lockers. By the way, Fred, as he likes to be called, told me that each of you can have a locker there all term and are welcome to use the pool whenever you feel like it. I'd like to spend the rest of the time going through the twelve pupil record folders and deciding upon the groupings.

In the ensuing weeks and months the program flourished. The atmosphere was one of relaxed determination. Certainly there was any number of adjustments. The most rewarding observation that I made was the bonding that took place between the teachers and the students. We all did everything together. The twice-a-week sessions at the JFK Center served to relieve stress for both pupils and educators. We ran, shot hoops, and swam together. This atmosphere of mutual concerns and interests promoted the vitally needed verbal exchange between teacher and student. We were, I daresay, the original "Club Med" of education. Actually it wasn't until the 1970's that educators recognized the validity of having professional retreats as a means of fostering a bonding relationship between teachers and administrators. We already employed all of those techniques. Eating together, playing together, and talking or dialoging together were the three most distinct aspects of our program.

With the passage of time the Board of Education sent us three additional students, thus capping our register at fifteen. Each teacher had a class section of five. It didn't matter. When the new students saw how their peers were so positively involved, they "bought in" quickly. We enjoyed our success. However, we never stopped analyzing our efforts. We spent countless hours in our afternoon sessions trying to identify those things that were working well and those that weren't. We frequently reassessed our goals and our strategies. From time to time we dismissed some of our strategies as being inappropriate. Of course, our goals of making every student a productive learner and to that extent an asset to society remained in place. As we moved into the spring term, we had not been visited once by any member of the administration or the Board of Education. This suited us fine. We were the proverbial "play within a play."

In one of our winter planning meetings, it was proposed that unless there was a parent interview scheduled prior to 9 a.m. that we could alter our arrival time by twenty minutes once a week. In that way each of us would have the opportunity to arrive once a week at 8:50. I thought this proposal over for several days before giving it a green light. My reasoning was that, put quite simply, why not? We had a very viable program. Teachers were teaching, and kids were learning. Everything that had been done to make the program a success was born from our ingenuity; the use of the JFK Center, our reconstruction of the "old band room," our ongoing curriculum development, our "out of pocket" field expenses, and our positive school: community relationships entitled us to some degree of prerogative.

There was one technical problem inherent in our "tardy" arrival schedule: the time cards. Prior to the teaching profession being officially declared as one by the Supreme Court of the US, we like so many factory workers were expected to "punch" a time card upon our arrival and upon our end of day departure. The time card was placed into a "clock" machine, which would literally "punch" the exact time of your arrival. If you did this a number of times in rapid succession, the markings bled over one another, therefore showing an illegible time marking, but answering the question as to whether or not you were in, if someone wanted to know.

Our program and lives were moving along at a gratifying clip. We were well into the spring term. For many of us there were signs, however, of negative things in the air. Mr. Biggio, it was rumored, had lost his grip. He was desperate to show whenever possible that he was in control when in fact he wasn't. Word had gotten to me to stay clear of him and to avoid any confrontations. I thought to myself, isn't that what I had done from September to April. I took the advice with a "grain of salt" and went about my business. The very next day, it was my turn to arrive at 8:50. That morning brought all of the showers for the month of April. As I arrived, I stood at the time-clock obliterating my arrival time as had become custom, when there came Mr. Biggio's voice booming almost as loud as the passing thunder outside. "You're late," Mr. Kassell, he said, standing at the doorway to his office. I'm not, I replied, while removing my card from the "clock machine." What's that? Mr. Biggio said, taking several steps in my direction. I'm not late. I'm absent, I calmly replied, depositing my card on Mrs. Gerstein's desk. Immediately I exited the General Office. A few moments later, I was in my Bel Air, lighting up a marlboro and warming my engine, wondering if first gear would work given the downpour. I was so preoccupied by this thought that I hadn't noticed Mr. Biggio standing just outside the driver's door gesticulating to me to roll down my window. "You can't be absent; you're already here," he began. Where will you go? It's not like you can go back to sleep, he attempted to reason. The poor man was trying to fend off the rain with his morning *New York Times*. It wasn't working. No more questions, I said. For an entire year neither you nor anyone else showed the slightest interest in what we were doing. You know that you can

93

chalk off the time discrepancy as "compensatory." We've done nothing wrong. I'll be in shortly, I said.

Ultimately, twelve of the fifteen kids graduated and went on to High School. Three of them had deep rooted psychological problems and should not have been placed in our program by the Board of Education. What else is new? Arnold Mercado would end up in Florida working as a Prison Guard. Mike O'Kernan relocated to a small upstate town and from all reports was very happy. Bert Flemming did not return in September, and no one seemed to know what had become of him. Mr. Biggio announced his plans for retirement during our June Faculty Conference. Thank God, I thought. The man was primed for a heart attack.

The '68-'69 school year would be a memorable one for New Yorkers. The Knicks, Mets, and Jets would be joined by the NYC Teacher's Union in claiming victory of monumental proportions. Also, the Fortress would have a new Principal. Of course, none of these things were known as we broke for summer vacation, but they would be very prevalent as topics of conversation in the fall.

Chapter XI

September 1968—A New Beginning

When we returned from summer vacation and reported to work for the customary late August Planning meetings, we were introduced to our new Principal, Dr. Lemuel McNaughton. In our "Welcome Back" Faculty conference Dr. McNaughton shared his vision for the school with us. In his remarks he painted a picture of a school that would be intolerant of discipline problems from students, or unprofessional conduct from its instructional staff. He emphasized that teaching was a profession, so there would be a professional code of ethics in place at all times. He told us that he wanted every teacher to strive to be the best that they could be. To that end he said that it was his high expectation that each and every one of us would have by year's end a regular teaching license as opposed to the substitute licenses possessed by the majority of us. He explained that he and his administrative staff would concentrate heavily in the area of staff development and that after making that kind of investment in time and effort, he did not want to have good teachers "bumped" because they possessed only substitute licenses. This, he explained, was the first step in stabilizing a teaching staff. He also stated that it was his belief that teachers who held or aspired for regular certification had a high degree of self- esteem. He asserted that these characteristics would translate into high expectations for student achievment. "If you want to teach, he would say, then this is the place for you."

We were then introduced to Mr. Hal Lindle, who was Dr. McNaughton's handpicked candidate for the vacant Assistant Principal's position in charge of grade eight. Mr. Lindle would join an administrative staff consisting of two other Assistant Principals, an Administrative Assistant, three Department Chairmen, three Guidance Counselors, two Deans (behavioral modification counselors), and of course the Principal. A true "Baker's Dozen," I thought, somewhat cynically. As Dr. McNaughton introduced Mr. Lindle, he briefly stood at his place and facing the staff, simply nodded and sat back down. He was a tall man of African American descent. His curly black hair was combed straight back *à la* the '50's. He had a fishhook scar on his left cheek, which gave his appearance a certain intimidating factor. I estimated his height at 6'2". When he stood up, his clothing apparel and dress style were straight out of Brook's Brothers, replete in a double-breasted blue blazer contrasted with grey pants, a white shirt held together with gold collar clasp and matching gold cufflinks and matching tie clip holding an Italian silk maroon tie in place, Mr. Lindle was a perfect role model for those of us who did our shopping at Alexander's. What subjects would he be in charge of, I wondered. For that matter, what subject would I be teaching this year? In June I had indicated a preference for Social Studies. I wouldn't have long to ponder the question. At the conclusion of the meeting Mr. Tramm informed me that Dr. McNaughton expected me in his office in ten minutes. Do you know why? I asked. No, was all that Mr. Tramm said, as he turned and left.

As I walked into The General Office I saw that Mrs. Gerstein, who had maintained her position as Secretary to the Principal, immediately got up and went into Dr. McNaughton's office to inform him of my arrival. Have him come right in, I heard Dr. McNaughton instruct her. Pre-empting Mrs. Gerstein's invitation I had already arisen and had passed through the swinging café doors en route to Dr. McNaughton's office. Thank you, I said, passing by Mrs. Gerstein's desk. She smiled reassuringly.

Walking into Dr. McNaughton's office I saw at a glance that he was on the telephone. With a wave of his hand he beckoned me in and pointed to a chair, inviting me to sit down. He covered the receiver with his free hand and whispered that he'd be with me in a minute. Looking about the office, the décor had drastically changed since my last visit more than a year ago. Gone were the pictures of Washington, Lincoln, Roosevelt, Kennedy, and LBJ. They had been replaced with pictures of Frederick Douglass, Thurgood Marshall, and Dr. Martin Luther King. On the windowsills were miniature statuesque busts of such luminaries as Douglass, King, Malcolm X, Jesse Owens, and a host of others. The old metal desk had been replaced with a large oak model, complemented by a protective glass covering on its surface. Dr. McNaughton was seated in a leather or naugahide executive style chair, which appeared to have the ability to rotate and recline. In the center of the room was a large oak conference table with eight oak captain's chairs. I emphasize the chairs because of the fact that within the next ten years these items would disappear from schools everywhere, only to reappear tripled in value on the antique circuit. How they got there is anyone's guess. On the wall immediately behind Dr. McNaughton's desk were displayed various laminated degrees and honorariums. The décor was completed with a brass nameplate displayed at the very front of the oversized oak desk. It was obvious to me that Dr. McNaughton had gone to great lengths to create what he deemed the proper appearance for a Principal's Office. In my mind, he had succeeded. I was impressed.

Soon Dr. McNaughton discontinued his phone conversation and came around to where I was seated. Extending his hand, he said, "Mr. Kassell I'm very pleased to meet you. I've heard so many things about you that I had to take time to meet such a talented staff member as yourself." For someone as young as you to have achieved so much acclaim in such a brief career was a rarity. As I read through your personnel file, I saw the very positive letters written by Math Chairman, Tramm. More impressive, however, was the letter from the State Department of

97

Education received over the summer which cited you for having implemented an exemplary Career Guidance Program last semester. As I continued to read through your file, I noted that you were serving under a substitute license. That simply won't do. I cannot afford or should I say the children cannot afford to have you or any other effective teacher "bumped" by the Board of Education. You need to possess a regular teaching certificate. Please stop by Mrs. Gerstein's desk and ask her for an application for the examination for Teacher of Common Branches, and file for it tomorrow. Hesitantly, I asked, "What is Common Branches?" It is a regular license that enables its possessor to teach any grade from K-6. That same individual may teach in a Junior High School or Middle School up to grade eight by being granted a waiver by the Board of Education upon the Principal's request. This license, Dr. McNaughton went on to explain, makes an individual more versatile and more marketable. No doubt you've heard me say at this morning's faculty conference that I believe that high self-expectations translate into high pupil achievement expectations. Do you agree? Absolutely, I replied unhesitantly. Fine. Now, as to the question of this year's assignment, what subject area do you prefer? I began my career as a math teacher, I said, but I never was very comfortable with the material. Yes, Dr. McNaughton said; I've heard tell of some of your adventures in the area from Mr. Tramm. He is very high on you. He describes you as one who only gives 110% and doesn't accept failure.

Further, he states that you are driven by a sense of competitiveness and street smarts rarely seen in someone as young as yourself. You should know that I've heard equally high praise from some community sources. The ladies in the luncheonette and Big Earnie have gone to great lengths to inform me of your high standing in the community. So you can see, Mr. Kassell, that after having discovered such a highly talented individual as yourself on my staff, that I would want to maximize the use of those talents. I also appreciate the fact that you are a bit of a diplomat. Yes, I know that you filled out a "preference sheet" last June indicating your desire to teach Social Studies. The fact that you didn't remind me that you had when I asked what subject you wanted to teach tells me that you have tact, a valuable commodity. I know from speaking with Earnie and learning how you got him to help you secure the JFK facility for the Career Guidance Program last year that you are resourceful. I also heard of your inadvertent habit of letting your time card get stamped in an illegible fashion. You will have to cease from practising that skill anymore. Yes, sir, I said with a smile on my face. Good, now that we understand each other I'd like to get to the matter of your teaching assignment this year.

I need a teacher for our seventh grade Junior Guidance class. While the students in this class have nothing in common with your Career Guidance students, they will require a guidance style approach. Excuse me, sir, I interrupted. I really appreciate all the complimentary things you said to me earlier, but I would really like to teach Social Studies. I know, was Dr. McNaughton's terse reply. There are no vacancies in any of the grades at this time. But if you allow me to finish profiling the Junior Guidance Program, I think you will be pleasantly surprised. To begin with, the Junior Guidance Class is self-contained. The class does move for shop, gym, music, art, remedial math, and lunch. The official teacher, however, is responsible for instruction in Language Arts, Math, Science, and Social Studies. You may design your own teaching schedule and then submit it to the program chairman, who will fit in the other subjects in the periods not used by you. What can you tell me about the kids? I asked in a somewhat resigned tone of voice. They are youngsters who for reasons of low self-esteem and underachievement, have been identified as ineligible for mainstream classes. Truthfully, they have been held over at least once and suspended any number of times. I think that you are just the type of teacher that can help these kids get over the hump. Besides, you'll get a chance to teach social studies. Can I think it over? Yes. As I turned to leave, I heard Dr. McNaughton say, "Are you finished thinking?" Yes, I said, smiling. Good. See Mr. Lindle for your social studies needs and Mr. Tramm for your math and science needs. I'll arrange for your language arts needs and room keys. By the way, your room will be just down the hall from this office. You shall have my support in all of your academic endeavors. Well, you have a lot to do so you'd better get going, Dr. McNaughton said as he returned to his chair. Don't forget to file that Common Branches exam application. I will, I said, exiting his office and heading straight for Mrs. Gerstein's desk.

As I approached Mrs. Gerstein's desk, she held up a manila folder, saying you'll find everything you need in this folder. There is a ten-dollar test filing application fee. They do not take personal checks, so get a money order from the Post Office. In addition I've attached a test scope profile and a schedule of dates on which the test is given. She concluded by urging me to take the exam ASAP. Thanking her, I took the folder and turned to leave. Good luck, I heard Mrs. Gerstein say. Walking away I thought, "Luck has very little to do with it." Certainly over the course of a 180-day school year there are some instances where good luck may have some bearing on things.

My first year experience taught me, however, that if you don't have a plan you will not last very long. Of course, this can pretty much be said about any endeavor. Yet, teaching is different than most. Very often we see perfectly sound plans fail. Teaching is like "pool playing." You must have immediate and long-range strategies. You have to make every shot count. You must continuously position yourself for a good set up shot. Take the offensive, be aggressive, and maintain high expectations for yourself and your students. Never accept failure. I have found that if a teacher can consistently maintain high standards, that teacher is the one who will enlist parent support and cooperation and attain high levels of pupil success.

Contrary to my personal belief that previewing a pupil's records often prejudice a teacher's thinking about a student. Given my experience with Anthony and some of my Career Guidance students, I decided to screen the records of my new Junior Guidance class. After an hour in which I read through all of the eighteen pupil records, I found the following anti-social common denominator: Junior Guidance kids were notorious underachievers. They very often were suspended from school for committing such serious overt acts of misbehavior as: fighting, throwing chairs and desks about the room, threatening, and even assaulting teachers, weapons possession, cutting classes, school vandalism, and theft. In short, they were (as far as the school system was concerned) a lost cause. The solution that the school system found most convenient was to promote these students through and out from the school to another level and another level until they simply disappeared. Of course, they put a very genteel label on this unwritten policy. They called it "social promotion."

This would be my third year of teaching "problem" children. Some of my colleagues suggested that this was a violation of the teacher's contract and that I should lodge a grievance. They said that there was something called "a fair and equitable rotation" of upper echelon class assignments that would entitle me to have several of the higher exponent classes in my program. I thought about their suggestion and then decided to leave things as they were. My reasoning was that the challenge in education was to succeed where no one thought success was possible. As then, this challenge remains.

In 1967 the majority of urban school children all across this country read below grade level. For thirty-two years the system had attacked this problem by changing tests, curriculum, teacher training styles, educational leaders, materials, and pouring financial resources into the void, so much other vital needs became neglected. We would pay for that folly in the area of pupil support services as witnessed by the tragedy of Columbine and Arkansas. The cost for textbooks and materials had increased threefold over a twenty year period, yet the tax levy award for each child had not increased proportionately over that same twenty year period. Vitally needed support guidance services were slashed. In 1965 every teacher in the Junior High School was required to provide one period a week in the instruction of group guidance. There was specifically designed curriculum for this subject. The topics addressed included stereotyping, social amenities, positive and negative school attitudes, and anti-drinking and anti-smoking lessons, just to mention a few. When these curriculum areas were eliminated, along with the cutting back of guidance positions, the system was transitionalized from one of anticipation to one of reaction. With reference to my remarks concerning Columbine and Arkansas, only after such events do we invest resources. Of course, these services must be provided. As an aside I cannot understand, how a school principal could not have noticed the existence of a sub-culture of forty or more misfits within his population.

In the final analysis it is my belief that wherever you find high degrees of pupil success, you will find high degrees of meaningful supervision. Principals who keep in mind that their main purpose for being is to facilitate the upgrading of instruction in their classrooms and superintendants who keep in mind that their primary function is to supply the schools with the kind of leadership that fosters the first mandate and the resources necessary to accomplish this task are the necessary components in my "success" formula. Contrary to popular belief the abolition of tenure is a non-issue in so far as making things better. It takes five years for a school supervisor to achieve tenure. Does anyone believe that this is insufficient time to weed out ineffective school leaders? Ineffective leaders are in place as a result of going unsupervised year in and year out. The responsibility for this rests in the hands of the superintendants. The superintendants, however, at best on average are in place for only two years in most districts. Community School Boards hire and fire these people on whims, personal bias, political correctness, political influence, and in some cases monetary payoffs to corrupt board members.

With all of this in mind, I said to my colleagues that I was quite content with my Junior Guidance class assignment. Maybe some day I'll write a book, I said laughingly as I departed their company and headed off for Mr. Lindle's office to see about social studies materials.

During my career in teaching, especially with regard to teaching underachievers, I was convinced that better than any other stimulus or motivation was the project-based or "hands on" approach. It promotes a sense of self-determination in the learning process and allows for learning to take place at a rate dictated by the student and not the teacher. This belief would become a centerpiece of my educational philosophy.

To illustrate my point, early on in the term the social studies curriculum contained a unit entitled "Local Area Analysis." Each student was expected to create a map of the streets that they used coming to school and going home from school. In creating this map they were to include all facets of their route. They were to label such establishments as grocery store, laundromat, movie theater, candy store, newsstand, police station, hospital, firehouse, burned out buildings, empty lots, drug dens, parks, liquor stores, etc. Their challenge was to create a second map displaying the changes they would make (if they could) to provide their community with a more wholesome array of goods and services businesses. This was the type of project which promoted creative thinking and provocative pupil interactions during discussion time. It also lent itself to committee work, and sharing.

My Junior Guidance kids, however, were not quite ready for committee work. Many of them had been "enemies" for a number of years and were not into sharing at this point of their development. Some refused to take part openly in the class activities. These students and I did reach an accord, however. If I didn't force them to discuss their work in class, they would submit this work to me privately for grading. After a week on this topic, I realized that for the most part they were all attaining similar understandings about their neighborhood. Those understandings were mostly negative, unfortunately. It fell to me, therefore, to decide whether or not to abandon this "project oriented" approach. I decided that it was correct, but that the topic was unfulfilling and did not sufficiently provide for new learning experiences. I gave a lot of thought to the problem. What kind of activity would promote interest and understanding and employ such vitally needed skill enhancements as: writing, grammar, reading, research, imagination, pride, and reward?

About a week later, I found myself looking through the social studies curriculum guide in anticipation of planning for a unit on "The Colonies." There before me was an illustration of New York during the colonial period on a typical day. There were horse-drawn carriages, boats being unloaded, boarding houses, and a host of other activities to be seen. The next day I displayed this picture on the window shade which served as a great projection screen. I was able to accomplish this feat with the use of a machine called an "Opaque Projector." I never had a classroom without this piece of equipment. It would project any printed matter on a screen. It didn't matter whether or not it was black and white or color. The image would appear in whatever medium they were printed in. At any event, as I projected the illustration, I asked them to study the picture for three minutes. I then shut the machine off. I told the class that I wanted them to open their social studies notebooks and to make a list of as many different types of activities that they could recall seeing in the illustration. I gave them ten minutes to prepare their lists. From time to time as I walked about the room monitoring their efforts, I gave verbal hints to further stimulate their thinking. Keep in mind that in those days New York was the capitol of the colonies. It had the largest seaport. Dignitaries and travelers were frequent arrivals. Ask yourself how did they travel around? I prompted. Finally, after being assured that every student had at least five activities on their notepaper, I stopped them. The next step in the process was to elicit these activities and place them on the board. I told them that this would become our master list and that if one of their activities were called by another student, that they were to cross it off their list and raise their hands only if they had an activity that had not been mentioned. Our list referenced Boarding houses, Pubs, Barns, Blacksmiths, Dock Workers, Horse-Drawn Carriages, Horseback Riders, Dung Loaders, Churches, and many other aspects of colonial life.

There were eighteen students in the class. I gave each student one of the above activities to study. I told them that their homework assignment was to come in the next day with one idea for a business that related to that activity. For instance, if we look at the horse drawn carriage we will see that it has wheels, side lamps, and a fancy painted design. Seems to me, I said, that there must have been a place where the wheels were made, where the lamps were made, or where the designs were painted on. By the way, how did they make paint? After a while they got the idea. This was the type of activity that promoted critical thinking, fun, and guaranteed success because there was no incorrect response possible. I would add that I myself had a great deal of fun as well. My long range plan you see was to actually get the names of eighteen businesses that could trace their beginnings to colonial times. I was then going to have each class member write to that company explaining that they were students and were interested to know how their companies got started. As I researched the possibilities, I found information on Fraunces Tavern, Trinity Church, and any number of present day testaments to colonial times. Ultimately, every student was assigned one such company that they would write to. Of course, this could not be done without lessons on writing a business letter. The next step was to simply mail the letters using their name on the return address in c/o my name. Mrs. Gerstein reluctantly supplied the postage and envelopes.

I explained to the class that it was impossible to predict when the companies might write back. When they did, however, the student receiving a response would have two days to prepare an oral five-minute report on the information they had received. This, of course, created a need to prepare public speaking lessons on how to give such a report. Such skills as using index note cards, outlining, speaking loudly and clearly, and sharing were bi-products to the overall learning experience.

Throughout the process the students asked many questions—some very revealing. "Why do we need to put a stamp on the envelopes?" asked one youngster. The one that promoted a light moment, however, was, "What is a Public Relations Officer?" Someone who is paid by the companies to deal with pests like us, I responded. Everyone laughed. Twenty years later I encountered this same student who was in the PR Department of Con Edison.

Within a week responses began to arrive in my mailbox. In turn I would hand them out unopened during "mail call." For the most part this became a daily routine. You should have seen their faces when they received their own personal mail. Some of the companies simply sent brief letters with a curt thank you for showing interest. Others sent folders with brochures and photos.

In addition to all of the periphery learning skills developed through this exercise, such learning concepts in the subject area as a need for labor, modes of transportation, good soil, water supply, raw materials, public demand, among many others were criteria for the existence of a particular business.

To me, however, the greatest outcome could be found in the air of self-confidence that began to emanate from each student. Not to be confused with ego-driven arrogance or conceit, my students began to take on every assignment I gave them with an attitude that said, "no problem," Mr. K. On Open School Night, every one of my students was represented by a parent, a guardian, or another concerned family member. Each told me that they hadn't seen their kids have so much fun in school since kindergarten. Nor could they recall ever seeing them do so much work. One even told me that she had overheard her son tell one of his "troublemaking" friends that he could not go out with him because he had schoolwork to do. You cannot imagine how gratified I felt. Through it all some teachers not only begrudged me my success but also did everything they could to thwart it. One in particular was an elderly black woman who was responsible for teaching my class remedial math. With her hair rolled into a tight bun and her primary teaching tool being two 18' rulers taped together, she represented to me all that was wrong about the profession. I knew from her remarks at faculty or department meetings that she had a negative predisposition towards whites. I also knew that she was old enough to be my grandmother, and accordingly I always conducted myself with the proper respect and restraint when dealing with her. When Mrs. Babcock refused to give my kids the remedial math workbooks, I asked her, why? "You know why," was all she would say before walking away. It got so bad that none of my kids wanted to go to her class. When I informed Mr. Tramm of the problem, he told me little could be done. I don't want them getting in trouble with the Dean (who still had it in for me over his dealings with Anthony). This scenario was a little different. Mrs. Babcock referred them for cutting; and if they were picked up somewhere in the building, there would be little I could do to avoid having them suspended. Perplexed, I sat down in Mr. Tramm's office and thought. Mr. Tramm sat at his desk, lit up his pipe, and seemed to be thinking as well, occasionally scratching his chin. After a few moments, I blurted out, "I got it." Can you arrange my program so that whenever they have remedial math that I have a free period or administrative assignment? That shouldn't be a problem, was Mr. Tramm's response.

While Mr. Tramm worked on the program changes I had requested, I helped myself to eighteen remedial math workbooks from the math supply closet and then returned to my classroom awaiting the students return from woodshop. After they all were seated, I told them that they had to stop cutting Mrs. Babcock's remedial math class—more than half of them were. Where can we go? one student shouted. Yeah, I'm not going there ever, another one said. You will come here, I said. Whenever you have remedial math, I'll be in this room. The first day after I announced this option when it came time to go to remedial math, they all asked to stay. On the second day Mrs. Babcock came to the room to get them. They don't want to go to your class, I informed her; and I am powerless to force them to. Why don't you tell Dr. McNaughton how badly you miss them? By the way, I found eighteen workbooks for them in the math book room. I know that you would have eventually done the same. Again, she turned and walked away. Why would you allow your hate for me to manifest itself in a discriminatory policy towards children of your own race, I asked. Mrs.

Babcock kept walking. Neither Mr. Tramm or Dr. McNaughton ever brought this matter up to me.

In early December, a monitor arrived at my door. He handed me a sealed envelope. "It's from Mr. Lindle" the boy said. Opening the envelope there was a form attached to a carbon paper that in turn was attached to another similar form. Please see me in my office during your fourth period prep today. Please sign for your receipt of this note and give the monitor the original. Sincerely, H. Lindle.

I was curious as to Mr. Lindle's summoning me. Other than having obtained my social studies materials from him in September and sending him my lesson plans each Monday, there had been no communication between us. At the same time, I knew that he was in charge of social studies, and I wanted to be a full-time social studies teacher, so I looked upon this opportunity as one in which I could hopefully create a favorable impression. With this thought in mind I set off for Mr. Lindle's office at the appointed time.

Arriving at precisely 11:15 a.m., the time at which fourth period began, I knocked on Mr. Lindle's closed office door. It's open, came the reply from inside. Turning the knob, I let myself in. Good morning Mr. Lindle. I got your...yes—let's skip that he interrupted. I've gone through your social studies lesson plans for the past two months, and I have only one question. I'll try to answer it, I said. "Which days and periods do you teach Black History?" was the question Mr. Lindle posed with a cutting voice. I'm sorry, I said, I don't think...He continued, it is the policy of the social studies department in this school that every social studies teacher plan for two weekly periods of Black History instruction. Stymied for a response I offered the excuse that I taught Black History when the topic was referenced by the curriculum guide. You have, unwittingly I'm sure, Mr. Lindle said, stated the reason for my aforementioned policy. The NYC Board of Education's curriculum guide pays only the slightest attention to the contributions of minorities in particular those of African American descent. If it weren't for the slavery issue or G.W. Carver's work with the peanut, we wouldn't be there at all. Do you understand Mr. Kassell? Yes, sir, I replied straight away. I'm going to go home this evening and make a list of as many Black contributors to American History that I know. Tell me, Mr. Kassell, after Jackie Robinson, Louis Armstrong, Nat King Cole, and G.W.Carver, who else would appear on your list? Although Mr. Lindle was prejudging my intellect on this issue, and I was somewhat resentful of it, he was right. I would have thrown in Willie Mays, but I thought better of it at the time. Come, come, you'll have to do better if you want to teach social studies here, Mr. Lindle went on.

After school was over that day, I went to Hunter College and enrolled in two courses. "Early African Kingdoms," and "Black Thinkers and Their Influence On American Society." I learned about the Kingdom of Mali. I learned about Emperor Selassie and the Ethiopian belief that mankind owed its beginningsto their country. I learned how Booker T. Washington tricked the white folk into funding the fledgling Tuskegee Institute and of his quarrels with W.E. Dubois. I took a closer look at the positions of Dr. Martin Luther King and Malcolm X. I read up on the accounts of Black Explorers and became intrigued at the stories about The Buffalo Soldiers. I learned about the plights of Paul Robeson, the contributions and inherent greatness of Frederick Douglass, and the writings of James Baldwin. Along the way I picked up on such trivia as the location and history of The Florida Avenue Grill in D.C., Weeksville in Bed-Stuy Brooklyn, and a host of other cultural sites all over America. I visited old homesteads that were preserved as "underground railroad sites" between Virginia and on up to the Canadian border. I'm pleased and proud to tell you that in later years I was known for running the best "Black History Month Presentations," and I was never again challenged on my knowledge of Black History. All of this as a result of a ten minute conference on a cold December morning in a supervisor's office. I always kept that conference in mind. If I could have that kind of constructive influence when I became a supervisor, I'd be delighted. As a footnote, within three years of this conference I did become a supervisor. It was then that I took Mr. Lindle to issue with his mandated programming of a separate instructional format for Black History as apart from American History. It's artificial, I argued. You have to understand, Mr. Kassell, we have just come out of a decade frought with issues centered on civil and human rights. I don't really believe that it's going to amount to a hill of beans. At least not in the private enterprise or the financial markets. We will see changes markedly, I believe, in education. It won't just be Black History, but Puerto Rican History, Mediterranean History, every ethnic minorities' history will need to be included in the curriculum of our educational institutions. Mark my words!

Chapter XII

The Strike

While 1969 saw the physical transition of The Fortress from its original location to one further uptown, the impending Teachers' Strike was going to be much more traumatic than the task of moving the entire school to a new site. The packing away and subsequent unpacking of texts and materials would not be as "ripping" as were the day in and day out abuses suffered by strikers on picket lines throughout the city. And while the new school rocked and rolled everytime a subway train came and left the 145th Street Lenox Avenue Station, it didn't quiver quite as much as the pickets when suspicious cars slowly rolled by. It was not uncommon for people in these cars to throw bags of feces or urine-filled balloons at the strikers.

With urban America strongly opposed to the war in Vietnam and given the slow rate of impact of the civil rights laws passed in 1964, and what was perceived as financial waste vis a vis the space program, and a president whose strength could be traced to middle America, a faction that he proudly referred to as The Silent Majority, we were, in my opinion, as polarized over these issues in the 1960's as in the 1860's, and closer to civil war then could be imagined.

In the decade of the sixties we had witnessed four political assassinations, more than ten years of anit-war demonstrations, accompanied by violent student campus upheavals tragically leading to the deaths at Kent State. Here we were on the brink of a new decade with a promise of healing. All we had to do was survive. We were going to be okay. Yet, things in NYC are never okay. There was a new Mayor. He had said some foolish things about his planned strategies for negotiating impending labor contracts. It was Michael Quill, the head of the Sanitation Workers union, who issued the first warning. In an interview for one of the news programs, he said, "We are going to give Mr. Lindsay a lesson in collective bargaining." True to his word the Sanitation workers went on strike, and the city literally rotted while Mr. Quill was having three hot meals daily in The Tombs (The NYC Jailhouse). The sanitation strike lasted just under a month. Of course, the police, health, and other uniformed city workers and their unions followed suit. The people had had enough. Not quite! The Teacher's Union led by Albert Shanker had yet to be negotiated with. Could labor be the straw that would break the camel's back? Would the city fall or self-destruct over issues such as these? No, ultimately Mayor Lindsay would capitulate with all of labors' demands. Unions would gain benefits that under ordinary times would take three contract negotiations to achieve. Of course, the folly of all this is realized in the near bankruptcy of NYC in 1975. While NYC survived and emerged quite possibly stronger and financially sounder, the Teacher's Strike would claim casualties.

In 1969 the majority ethnicity of the teaching work force was Jewish. Its negotiating body, the UFT, was made up of predominantly Jewish leadership with Albert Shanker as its president. This strike, which lasted more than a month, incurred the wrath of minority parents throughout the city. They saw it as a power grab or money lust. Unlike the other labor strikes, the sufferers in this strike would be the children, who in the end would lose nearly a month of learning. The word "trust" would be stricken from the parent-teacher lexicon for many years to come. While most people who felt this way took no direct action against the strikers, the professional hate mongers did. They rode in cars harassing and demeaning the strikers. Responsible leaders included a well-known newspaper editor of the time, publicly suggested that the Teacher's Strike was a Jewish

Kenneth S. Karcinell

plot to deny minority children of their constitutional right to be educated. Minority teachers regularly crossed the picket lines, often shouting words of derision at their striking colleagues. Interesting thing, though. To this day I've never heard tell of any one of them returning or refusing to accept the benefits gained by that strike.

When we returned to work, we were divided, suspicious, and cliquish. Of course, there were some isolated instances of brawling to further compound matters. Faculty conferences designed to give voice to the "hot" issue were unsuccessful. Sensitivity workshops could not lessen the tension. People were, it seemed, hopelessly divided. What could reunite these people and suppress the prejudices, stereotyping, and bigotry that had arisen out of the smoldering, burning embers of the Teacher's Strike?

The answer would be found in an amazing series of events. In order of succession they were championship seasons for the Jets, Knicks, and Mets. Whites, Blacks and Latinos patted themselves on the back with each team's victory. I was in The Garden when Willis Reed limped onto the court and sank the first two shots of "the game." Everyone went wild. I was at Shea when the Mets clinched. I remember after the game walking down Roosevelt Avenue for about ten blocks. I must have passed through at least three major ethnic neighborhoods. I ate Cuban, Italian, and African American food all night long. Players like Reed, Namath, Seaver, and Clendennon were every New Yorker's own. People came to their senses. I guess it's true what they say about G-d. He takes care of children and fools.

Chapter XIII

Fulfilling Dr. McNaughton's Mandate
Or
How I Got My Regular Teaching License

Following the Teacher's strike, there was a lot of catching up to do. For me, there would be no assignment of any special class, as had been the case the previous two years. I found myself the Official Teacher of class 7-20. To my great pleasure, however, I was no longer a member of the math department. The previous June for the second year in a row, I had put in a request to teach social studies. My request had been granted. I believe that my prior teaching successes and my initiative to enroll in college courses on Black History convinced Mr. Lindle to give me a shot.

Although I didn't possess a social studies license, I did have a regular "Common Branches" license. As this license entitled me to teach at any level from K-8 and as it was assumed that a possessor of such a license could teach all of the major subjects and then some, I was not in violation of any licensing protocol at that time.

I was never one to place a high premium on test results. I looked upon them askance and with disdain. I can recall vividly when earlier the previous year I was at home marking exam papers and getting more and more annoyed with each paper I marked. The reason for this agitation could be found in the fact that each paper was marked as a failing one. Talking to myself, I said I gave them review questions; I gave a pre-test—what more could I do? Just then my mother happened by and seeing my mood asked what was wrong. I don't know. I don't have a single passing grade in these papers. Oh! Is this another group of slow learners they've given you? She said. Yes, I responded.

They have very low reading scores and poor writing skills, but I know that they listen. You are probably right, she said. My mother's hearing had for years been in decline. She had several operations but none really helped as much as she had hoped. There's one thing I've learned, she said. When people lose or do not develop fully certain senses and abilities they unknowingly over-develop others. Why don't you ask them the questions orally? The next day I halfheartedly asked one of the students a question from the exam I had given. Arthur, can you give me 1 reason why the pilgrims wanted to come to the New World? "Religious Freedom," he blurted out. I was stunned. This was the first question on my short answer section. Arthur's paper showed the wrong answer choice. I pulled out the paper of another student. Robert, I called out. Can you tell me how many stars were in the First American Flag and why? "Thirteen, one for each colony," came the reply.

Sadly, we know that it is not always the most knowledgeable person that gets the job or the college acceptance letter but the best test-taker. It was my contempt for the process that ultimately brought the wrath of Dr. McNaughton down on me the previous spring when I took the Common Branches test the first time. The test itself was segmented into three parts given over a three-week period by an examining body called the Board of Examiners. The candidate could not participate in parts two or three if he or she didn't pass parts one and two respectively. The first part was a written essay wherein the candidate had to write extensive essays to two typical teaching scenarios. The second part of this exam was an appraisal of record, if the candidate was already teaching under a substitute license. The third part was an oral interview given to the candidate by two examiners. I had passed parts one and two and felt confident about part three. I had stayed late after school and received tutoring from Mr. Lindle and several of the veteran teachers in his department. The exam was scheduled for

Saturday morning. I fully intended to make an early night on Friday, have a light and easily digestible supper, brush up on a few pointers given to me by Mr. Lindle, and have a nice, hot relaxing bath.

At about 10 p.m. I got a call from one of my "racetrack" buddies who wanted to know if I could go to Aqueduct with him tomorrow. He was very excited and preceded to tell me that he had come by some information with regard to a "can't miss" horse in the second race. What time does that race go off, I asked. One p.m. came the response. I'd love to go, but here's the problem, I said. I have to take a teaching test tomorrow at 11:00 a.m. at Brooklyn Tech HS. It shouldn't be more than thirty minutes long. Why don't you go ahead, and I'll meet you there. No, that's crazy, he exclaimed. Why take two cars and pay all that extra parking? I'll pick you up at ten and take you to the school. While you're taking your test I'll wait in the car, maybe grab some donuts and coffee. OK, I said. Don't be late, I cannot afford to miss this test. He said, don't worry.

I got up promptly at 9 a.m., did the three S's, put on my blue blazer, white shirt, and blue tie and grey pants then went down to wait for Sonny's arrival. At precisely 10:00 I glimpsed his car, a somewhat battered blue 1964 Nash Rambler coming down my block and trailing a cloud of smoke that Sonny attributed to the fact that the car needed a valve job. Getting into the car, I picked up his copy of the *Daily Telegraph* that listed the racing entries and commentaries for the day's races at Aqueduct. Who's the horse, I asked? Red River in the second; we can back wheel him in the doubles, Sonny said. He should go off at fifteen to one. That'll make it a huge double, I said. You'll be able to get your valve job. We laughed. The joke was that Sonny had had this car for three years and it was smoking when he got it. I would seriously doubt that it would ever get a valve job. Very often when Sonny's cars got to a point of not being drivable, they got stolen. Sonny would then use the

Karcinell

Kenneth S. Karcinell

insurance money to get another junkpile. Looking over the racing form, I noted that Sonny's tip hadn't won a race in two years. Knowing that Sonny's information more often than not was good; I became excited at the prospects. Here we are, I heard Sonny say. He slowed to park in a hydrant space right in front of the school. Good luck, kid, I heard him say as I got out and walked towards the school entrance. I chuckled, as Sonny's parking routine reminded me of my first encounter with Earnie.

Checking in at the lobby "test registration" desk I noted the time as 10:45. Right on schedule I thought. At the desk I received a floor pass to the third floor. As I got off the elevator, a student monitor whom I correctly guessed was earning extra credit in community service greeted me. She escorted me to a desk that was manned by a portly gentleman with bi-focals and a copy of *The New York Times*. No doubt, a Dr. Kahn disciple. After giving my name, the gentleman peered down a list of names on a clipboard and placed a check mark next to my name. He then got up and said, "Follow me." He led me down the hall, passing several individuals who were seated in chairs just outside of unlit and vacant classrooms. I correctly assumed that they were waiting to be tested, as I would be in a few seconds. Here we are, the man said. Have a seat; your examiners will be here shortly. Good luck, young man. It was 10:58. Perfect, I thought. Wanting to pass the time constructively, I took out several 3x5 index cards and reviewed some of the notes I'd made the previous evening.

In the meantime, I noticed that several of the candidates had already been admitted into the test rooms. It was 11:10. Looking up and down the hallway there were only myself and another waiting to be examined. All at once the elevator opened and two gentlemen approached me. Are you Mr. Schwartz? No, it must be him pointing in the direction of the other candidate. By now, candidates who had been let in their rooms earlier were exiting those rooms. It was going to be all right, I thought, noting that they were finished in twenty minutes. It was now 11:30. This was good. If my interviewers showed up within the next few minutes, making the double at Aqueduct was very doable.

Dozing in and out of consciousness, I was awakened by two interviewers who appeared as though they were on loan from some neighboring geriatric ward. We're sorry, came the feeble-toned voice of the matriarch. That's fine, I said. I'd like to get started right away. No, we can't give this exam on another day, the gentleman said, as he adjusted his two hearing aids. Now if you'll hold the door, my colleague and I will get ourselves organized and summon you in a few seconds. As I held the door open, the gentleman beckoned for his lady partner to precede his entrance into the room, and she did so with the aid of her walking cane. He followed and simultaneously replaced his eyeglasses with another pair from just inside his coat. As promised within two or three minutes the gentleman came to the door and beckoned me in. Please sit at the Teacher's desk, he said. Returning to the rear of the room to join his partner, he explained that they would each take turns in asking me a series of questions; and it behooved me to answer these questions as fully as possible. The time was now noon. Aqueduct's first race was 12:45. This would be close. Getting finished at 12:15 would allow for a twenty-minute car ride and parking. At best we would have five minutes to spare. I'm ready. At 12:25 the female interviewer said, "Mr. Kassell we are almost through. Would you mind repeating for us your response to my colleague's first question? I heard her say. The window of opportunity was closing. Sure I said, ask him if he remembered it. That will be all, Mr. Kassell.

Sonny and I got to the track just in time to see Red River cross the finish line five lengths in front of his nearest competitor. Two weeks later I received my "Fail" notice. What I didn't know was that Dr. McNaughton had also

119

received a copy of the "Fail" notice. He took it as a personal affront. He called me into his office to console me and uplift my spirits. He assured me that test taking was difficult and that I had passed parts one and two with relative ease. Part three was what we had to focus on in preparation for the next exam. I know you'll pass it next time. I've had Mrs. Gerstein resubmit your name. There's no application filing necessary. Just your submission of the test-taking fee. Also, my sources tell me, they are redesigning the exam. The oral interview portion will be replaced by a "teaching performance" part wherein a candidate will report to some school in the city and teach a lesson in one of the C.B. areas to a hand-picked group selected by the principal of that school. You're a cinch. You know, on second thought, it might prove helpful to know which questions may have stumped you. I've got some connections downtown. I'm gonna find out. Oh, please don't go to any trouble, I said. No, don't be ridiculous. After all that work, studying, staying after school, you have a right to know. Why don't you go about your business; I'll let you know what I find out later, he said. Thank you, I replied, and returned to my classroom.

An hour later while in the midst of teaching a class, a sub knocked on my door and handed me a sealed envelope. It's from Dr. McNaughton, she said. The note read "come to my office now!" Arriving in The General Office, I saw Mrs. Gerstein standing at the doorway to Dr. McNaughton's Office. As I passed in front of her I heard her say, "You've spoiled everyone's day." Dr. McNaughton was standing near his window with his hands clasped behind his back. There were several moments of silence broken by a barely audible statement from Dr. McNaughton. Sir, I didn't make that out. "ASK HIM IF HE REMEMBERS IT," came Dr. McNaughton's booming reply. Is that what you said? Yes, but you don't understand. No, you don't understand, Mr. Kassell. Let me tell you something. No matter how good

120

you are or think you are, the system doesn't care. Your supervisor, Mr. Lindle, is given to quotes. One of his favorites is, "No man is an island," and "Ask not for whom the bell tolls, it tolls for thee." Don't you ever forget it. You will take that test next month; you will comply with every aspect of its requirements, and you will pass it. You will show the test and the testers the proper reverence and respect or you'll be out of here the next day. Understood? Yes, sir, I said, with an unsure stutter. Will there be anything else? Not now, just go, I heard Dr. McNaughton say. Leaving his office, I walked briskly through the General Office. I could not recall ever having been spoken to in that tone of voice before. I would forever be in his debt.

A month later I awoke to a steady rain and set off to take my "teacher performance" exam for the Common Branches License." As I arrived at the assigned school, the rain had intensified. Reporting to the Principal's Office, I was informed that my task was to teach a lesson on the recorder to a group of second graders. Having been an asthmatic child, I was prohibited from taking music lessons on any windblown instrument. Put down an "F", I said. I cannot play an instrument and do not want to waste the children's time or yours. That's too bad came the Principal's reply. Leaving his office I proceeded to the school exit when the Principal came racing down the hall. You know, there were supposed to be two candidates for testing today. I guess the inclement weather has delayed the other candidate. I don't see anything wrong with you taking her subject. Can you teach a lesson on Cleopatra to a sixth grade class? Happily, I said, "You bet I can."

Two weeks later, as I entered my classroom, I found on my desk a congratulatory note from Dr. McNaughton that simply read "well done." LM.

Chapter XIV

Ellen

From a professional viewpoint, 1970 and '71 proved to be uneventful. Considering the fact that we are talking about life and times in the NYC school system, this statement would seem to be an oxymoron. I'm sure that things were going on all around me. During those years, however, I was in the throes of the "Vulcan Blood Fever."

Having settled down to the life of a successful teacher, I endeavored to maintain my success and find time to divert my interests. Those interests of late had become directed at the newly assigned art teacher just down the hall from my room. Given her penchant for miniskirts and the frequent riotous behavior that emanated from her room (as a result of her students not having fully developed their aesthetic values), I found it necessary to unofficially become her "buddy." I can recall that she was very appreciative. As I made more and more visits, the frequency of student disruptions lessened. Ellen was quite pleased at this bi-product to our relationship. She told me that during her interview with Dr. McNaughton, she had stated that she placed a high priority on classroom discipline and that his response was "excellent." It had to be the miniskirt, I thought.

Given my "Damon Runyonesque" lifestyle, I had not given much thought to settling down. Therefore, while I had the occasional girlfriend, I never prioritized a long or permanent relationship with a member of the opposite sex. After all, I came of age in the '60's—love, peace and the Woodstock Nation. Variety was indeed the spice of life! Having a "bachelor's pad" in Lefrak City, a good cash flow, and "action" seven days a week, I didn't think it could get any better. On those occasions when I dated I had a certain "four-step action plan." Typically the date would begin with a dinner at a Polynesian restaurant located in the lobby of my building, followed up with an evening of racing viewed from The Yonkers Raceway Clubhouse, capped off with a late night stop at an FM Radio Station on the Long Island Expressway for dancing and drinks. If things went well, my "pad" was a mere ten-minute drive down the LIE. As you would expect from a teacher, I had a plan!

Bachelors for the most part are creatures of habit, just like everyone else—the word habit being the operative word. Most of their habits may be regarded as anti-marriage weaponry. Mine had become a way of life that hinged on the following schedule:

> Monday Night: Yonkers raceway
> Tuesday Night: Men's Bowling League
> Wednesday Night: Weekly Poker Game
> Thursday Night: Dinner with Mom
> Friday Night: Dating
> Saturday Afternoon: Aqueduct
> Saturday Night: Knicks or Rangers
> Sunday: Giants and Jets and Lesson Plans

Certainly any of the above activities injected into the lifestyle of a married couple on an occasional basis would be regarded as a healthy experience. As I would find out in the not too distant future, these activities have the same effects on marriage as weeds do on a garden.

As I spent more and more time with Ellen, some of my habits had become altered. Evenings at the racetrack had become evenings at Lincoln Center or the theatre. Saturday afternoons would find us "high browing" at the Met or strolling The Brooklyn or Bronx Botanic Garden. For these strolls, Ellen had bought me a lovely set of handkerchiefs and some over-the-counter anit-allergent pills.

Although we always tried to maintain a discreet and professional relationship on the job, my fawning over Ellen and our lingering goodbyes at "the punch-out clock" had not gone unnoticed. It was shortly before Christmas vacation on a dreary Friday afternoon when I had a late lunch. The cafeteria was all but empty. Barring the noise of the dietician's staff cleaning up in the kitchen, I was able to take some small pleasure in the fact that I could enjoy my peanut butter and jelly sandwich and chocolate milk in relative solemnity.

This feeling was short-lived, however, as I heard the familiar voice of Dr. McNaughton, "Mind if I join you?" Please do, I quickly responded. I thought I was the only grown-up to still enjoy a peanut butter sandwich. We both laughed. How's everything this year, he inquired? Good, I said. He continued, how are your classes? Any problems? Classes are fine, I responded. No problems that I'm aware of. Should I be? No, he said. Are you pursuing your Master's? Ah, I thought, just a friendly reminder from our certification-minded leader. Yes, I am. I'm halfway through a program in Administration and Supervision. Excellent, Dr. McNaughton exclaimed enthusiastically. I couldn't believe my ears at his next question. By the way, how's your social life? You know as Principal, it's my job to provide and promote a wholesome work environment for everyone, while modeling a high set of moral values for everyone. Have I in any way offended those values, Dr. McNaughton? No, not at all, he said. What exactly are your intentions regarding Ms. Fisch? Stunned, I searched my mind for an appropriate response. Stammering, I answered honorably. Which means, prodded Dr. McNaughton? I'm gonna marry her, I blurted out. Very good, he exclaimed. Have a nice weekend was Dr. McNaughton's parting salutation. Over the next month I would propose no less than three times. Finally, the third time after a four-month whirlwind romance, Ellen said, yes. Plans for a wedding on Lincoln's birthday at her parents' home were made. Only immediate family and some close friends would attend.

Looking back, it could have been Dr. McNaughton's prodding that led to the next thirty years of married life producing a wonderful daughter, Sarah, and an equally wonderful son, Joey. I prefer to think that the night I took Ellen out on my famous three-pronged date (polynesian dinner, night at the races, and late night drinks and dancing at the all night FM station) was what sealed my fate. From my best account, by the time we had arrived at the FM cocktail lounge, Ellen had consumed four vodka and club sodas. I refrained, using the need to drive sober as an excuse. I had already won several hundred at the track. But I believed that my luck was going to run even stronger as the night wore on. To be sociable, I consumed two gin and tonics at the FM lounge. My best recollection of the evening however, was that after the FM lounge stop, my mind was blank. The next morning I awoke, and found the following note from Ellen scotch taped to my bathroom mirror:

Dear Kenny,

After the waiter helped me get you to your car, I drove you home. The doorman was kind enough to assist me in getting you upstairs. I didn't think you'd mind that I took your car and myself to my parents' house. Call me. Oh, by the way, you owe me $10.00 as I tipped the waiter and the doorman $5.00 each...Ellen

Chapter XV

1972—Welcome to the Wild and Wacky World of Supervision & Administration

As we returned to school, we learned that Mr. Lindle had been moved from his role as Eighth Grade Assistant Principal to that of Administrative Assistant. The chain reaction effect was that there now existed a vacancy in the administrative/supervisory ranks. At his first faculty conference, Dr. McNaughton announced that he fully intended to fill the vacancy ASAP and set a target date for October 1st. In the interim Dr. McNaughton stated that Mr. Lindle would wear both hats. The next morning, above the time clock, there appeared a posting advertisement for the position of Acting Assistant Principal, and its prerequisite requirements: five years prior teaching experience with twelve graduate credits in administration and supervision, and knowledge of Social Studies, Foreign Language, and Industrial Arts curriculum. I had the five years prior teaching experience. I received my Masters' Degree in Administration and Supervision the previous May and my NYS certificate for SAS (School Administrator and Supervisor). I did teach social studies the previous year. As for the foreign language requirement, I had four years of High School Spanish and four years of College Spanish. The Industrial Arts piece could be a problem. Pondering the situation, I reasoned that not too many (if any) applicants would readily meet all of the aforementioned requirements. I further reasoned that there might not be too many who met four out of five the way I did. I'll go for it, I decided. That evening I prepared a letter of application for the advertised position. I made copies of my M.A., and my satisfactory rating as a social studies teacher the previous year. I further attached copies of my high school and college transcripts highlighting the courses taken in Spanish. I placed all of the documentation in an oversized brown string tied envelope. I addressed the envelope to Dr. McNaughton. The next morning I hand delivered the envelope to Mrs. Gerstein. She assured me that she would personally give it to Dr. McNaughton. I thanked her and walked toward the exit doors, hearkened to hear Mrs. Gerstein's call of good luck. Thanks, I said, looking back at her and smiling.

In those days the process for filling an "acting" supervisory vacancy was simple. Candidates from within the school applied much as I described above. Qualifying candidates would then be scheduled for interviews conducted by a committee composed of the Principal and PTA. The interviewing committee would then select their choice and so notify the individual. Thus, on October 3rd my first birthday present was a letter I removed from my mailbox that morning summoning me to a three p.m. meeting in Dr. McNaughton's office. Turning in that direction, I glimpsed Mrs. Gerstein looking at me with a knowing smile. I returned the smile and left the office with a little "giddy-up" to my step.

At precisely three p.m. I reported to the General Office. Mrs. Gerstein dutifully knocked on Dr. McNaughton's door once and let herself in. Mr. Kassell is here I heard her say. Have him come in Dr. McNaughton directed. I was through the swinging doors in a flash and on the word "in" I was brushing past a retreating Mrs. Gerstein, who whispered congratulations as she exited. Upon entering, Principal McNaughton who met me at the doorway greeted me, hand extended. I believe you know Mr. Lindle. I'd like you to meet Mrs. Lauren, our PTA President. Lo and behold I thought. It was "The" Mrs. Lauren. Her reputation as a stern negotiator and child rights advocate having been established in this very office a little over two years ago during Mr. Biggio's watch. Indirectly, she did me a favor at the time;

Mike O'Kernan, the target of her wrath at the time became my team leader in the Career Guidance Program.

In the center of the room there was a small table covered with a white tablecloth on which stood a bottle of Andres Sparkling Cold Duck, several champagne glasses, some assorted cookies, and two lit candles. The only thing missing was a Challah. For all intents and purposes, the scene was most reminiscent of one I had experienced at my cousin's house a few weeks earlier when I attended the ritualistic celebration of the Bris, or circumcision, of his newborn son. I had been asked to take photos at the moment of truth, and passed out at precisely that moment. Quickly my mind refocused just in time to hear Dr. McNaughton's request that everyone join him in raising his or her glasses in toasting my appointment as "Acting Assistant Principal." His toast was echoed by Mr. Lindle's exclamation of here, here!

I don't quite know what to say, I began. I want to thank everyone for their support and their belief in my ability to do the job. I promise to never disappoint any of you. We know that you won't, interrupted Mrs. Lauren. But it's not us you are never to disappoint—it's the children. I went on to say, I have kept Mrs. Lauren's admonition close to my heart all these years. Every decision I ever made was put to the test question: Is it best for the children? If the answer was no, it didn't matter if the decision had to do with some school based program or district directed program, I would not implement it. For the most part I found that if I presented my objections to my supervisors clearly, they went along.

After allowing for a few moments so Mrs. Lauren's words could become deeply rooted in my mindset, Dr. McNaughton stated that I would begin in the position the following Monday. We need time to find a suitable replacement for your teaching assignment. Also, I want you to go through a week of debriefing that will be conducted by Mr. Lindle. Lastly, I want the week so that I can properly announce your appointment to our staff and the district office. I will notify the D.O. this afternoon. As for our staff, I will post a notice of your appointment above the time clock tomorrow morning and make mention of it in my morning announcements. The remaining part of the week will provide sufficient time for any contestation of your appointment or for anyone who might question the process. With those words, I learned my first administrative lesson. It was a repeat of the Boy Scout motto, "Be Prepared."

As Dr. McNaughton concluded his remarks, Mr. Lindle strode past me toward the door. In doing so, he remarked, "the debriefing begins in my office as soon as the festivities here are concluded." I'll be right there, I called after him. Careful not to spill any of its contents, I placed my glass down on the white tablecloth. Turning towards Dr. McNaughton and Mrs. Lauren I said, "if you both will excuse me"...go right ahead urged Dr. McNaughton. Remember, we're expecting great things from you. Yes, sir, I said, exiting the office. As I left I could swear that I caught a glimpse of Dr. McNaughton smiling. It was not a mocking smile but rather one that communicated pride and self-assuredness in knowing that he had made the right decision.

Leaving Dr. McNaughton's office, I rushed across the hall to the Administrative Assistant's Office. Seeing me approach, Mr. Lindle beckoned me in. Have a seat at the conference table, he said. You'll find several personnel file folders on the table. They are professional profiles of the teachers you will be supervising in the Social Studies, Foreign Language, and Industrial Arts departments. They are not files. Only the Principal may keep teacher files. For our purposes they are "resource folders." In any event, please take them home and peruse them carefully. Joining me at the conference table, Mr. Lindle extended his hand and gave me his personal congratulations. I'm not sure if congratulations are really in order. The job of school administrator and supervisor is a thankless one. If I had to do it over, I would have never left the classroom.

Enough of my digression. I don't know much about your philosophy of administration and supervision nor do I care to. We all have varying tolerances, work styles, and biases. In the final analysis, these things don't matter. It's how you do the job that counts. Or more to the point—can you do the job? This job cannot be done without a system. You must be organized and capable of maintaining a schedule. This latter task being easier said than done. The most important quality, however, that one must have is the ability to get students to buy into their program. All of my observations of you in this area, as well as my fact-finding research into your brief career have confirmed that you do have a good way with the students. I have also reached the conclusion that you value the profession. I became convinced of this when you took those college courses in Black History to better educate your students. I know that you are resourceful, as witnessed by your accomplishments in the Career Guidance program. For sure, you will need to maintain that resourcefulness as you plod your way through the muck and mire of the NYC Board of Education with all its restraints and constraints. Mostly conceived I would add by mealy-mouthed individuals whose sole wish is for plausible deniability, so as to be held blameless in all matters bearing negative results. For all these reasons I supported your candidacy for the position I vacated.

As I understand it, you will inherit all of my supervisory and administrative assignments. To that end we will devote tomorrow's meeting to understanding these responsibilities and planning for them. Remember…a place for everything and everything in its place. Questions such as when to collect lesson plans, the differences between informal and formal observations, the matter of preparing a senior activities time line calendar, duty schedules for you're a.m. and p.m. activities, and lunch patrol schedules will be addressed. Get a good night's sleep and have a hearty breakfast. I'll see you tomorrow. This last statement was my cue to leave. Getting up I gripped the folders and said thank you. Part of the job Mr. Lindle replied.

The next day's meeting commenced with Mr. Lindle again reviewing my assignments. You'll be in charge of grade eight, the graduating class. This responsibility includes planning for the graduation exercise at the Riverside Church, the senior prom on that same night, the creation of a senior yearbook, and senior field day. With regard to the senior prom, I advise that you try to make arrangements at either The Renaissance or the Autobon Ballrooms. We usually use one or the other on an alternate year basis. It's the Renaissance's turn this year. You should, however, not assume that they are waiting to hear from you. I would call them in early January if I were you.

I was astounded. The Autobon was of course the site of Malcolm X's assassination. The Renaissance owed its legacy to the '20's. It was rivaled only by the famed Cotton Club in attracting the "hoi polloi" of its day when swing was king, and ermine and lace were in.

For your edification and guidance, Mr. Lindle began I've taken the liberty to pull out my last year's calendar of events. Although the dates won't be the same, I'm hoping that you get a sense of timing. For instance, you would want to start the yearbook planning almost immediately. I'd be remiss if I didn't relate this anecdote to you with regards to the yearbook planning. Do you remember Mr. Taylor? Yes, I do. As I recall, he was the yearbook photographer last year. He worked out of an office up on the third floor overlooking the drive and the river. Your recollection is quite accurate, said Mr. Lindle. Unfortunately, Taylor made the regrettable mistake of publishing the yearbook with a photo of Dr. McNaughton that had not been approved by the good doctor. As you might have guessed, when the yearbook was delivered, Dr. McNaughton was extremely critical of his photo. Do you know where Taylor is this year? No, I said. Come to think of it, I haven't seen much of him lately. You won't, he said, unless you have need to be in the basement. Taylor now works out of what can best be described as a walk-in closet that has been converted into his office. He has no view of the river or anything else. Actually, I'm told that of late he's taken to the practice of wearing extra heavy sweaters and usually has a raspy voice that can be attributed to the postnasal drip he has developed given the permanent dampness of his working environment. Wowwwww! When the time comes, I suggest that you take at least a dozen photos of the man and submit them to him for his direct approval.

Next, barked Mr. Lindle. I know from some conversations that we've had that we differ on certain issues, particularly on the manner by which minority students are taught. I'm sure that however you proceed it will be because you think it best. After having read the folders last night you've no doubt come to the realization that with one exception, the social studies department is a veteran one. Do not employ the policy of "new broom, clean sweep." They will test you soon enough. If I were you, I'd adopt a laid back wait and see approach. I nodded understandingly.

The last matter I want to review with you is the Administrative Memorandum #8. Do you see it? Yes, I have it, I said. Good. This memorandum will be distributed to the staff later on this week. Accordingly, I want to direct your attention to Roman numeral IV, sub item 1.1 entitled "Mr. Kassell's Administrative Duties." You will note that they are carefully outlined as to time and location. I've also attached a copy of the names of those teachers who have been assigned to those areas for patrol duty. It will be up to you to prepare a schematic, illustrating position assignments and their accompanying responsibilities. With regard to your lunch duty, you will be assisted by your grade Dean. I advise that you do not give him a fixed position. You may want to divide the lunchroom in half so as to share the supervisory responsibility. As concerns the teachers, cut them no slack. The first time any one of them arrives late using some such excuse as after class tutoring, breaking up a pupil dispute, calling a parent, or some other excuse for not arriving on time, don't tolerate it. You must stress to these people that no one likes patrol assignments, but it's part of the job, and everyone must comply with administrative assignments.

Tonight your assignment is to prepare a "Communications Bulletin" for each of your administrative duty assignments. Be careful to specifically identify posts, personnel assigned, and post functions. Put the bulletin under your name, approved by me. Here's a model of a previous C.B. Note the style. While I'm at it, I want to point out to you that in this school we use three different types of written communications. One is identified as an "Administrative Bulletin." This document usually comes from the Principal, the Board of Education, or the District Office. In any case, its intent must be implemented without exception or question, and in a timely manner. A "Communications Bulletin" is a document that is usually generated by a member of the in-house administrative team. While it is expected that its contents are to be implemented, it does invite feedback and review. We use a "General Memorandum" as reminders and follow up documents. In all cases they are numbered and maintained in my office in catalogue form. Therefore, if you or any of the other Administrators want to publish such a document, it behooves you to check with my secretary as to the identity of the next number to use in that particular bulletin's series.

After you prepare your schematics, plan to meet with the various individuals involved. At these meetings and all future ones have a pre-prepared dated sign in sheet. Do not use a check-off system. They have no legal basis and do not count as documentation at grievance hearings. Always have a "Meeting Agenda" simply listing the topics in outline form that will be discussed. Finally, for every department, grade, or duty meeting, have a master file for each. Be sure to copy samples of everything to those respective files. I'm going to tell you this only once. You will find yourself constantly being tested. The way to succeed in this job and cover your ass at the same time is to have good organizational skills. In the end, you will find that teachers, parents, and your peers will expect this of you. If you are weak or blasé about this aspect of the job, you won't last very long.

I'd like to call your attention to issues that if not handled properly can incur the wrath of your fellow supervisors. While it's true that you are in charge of Social Studies, Foreign Language, and Industrial Arts, and the eighth grade, you are also in charge of the decorum for the entire second floor. Do you see where I'm going here? I think so, I said. There will be teachers on the floor who are members of departments not assigned to me. Exactly, Mr. Lindle said. The question now becomes this: what are the parameters by which you may supervise them? As floor supervisor, you may hold all staff responsible for supervising safe pupil traffic flow during the class period changes. Throughout the floor there will be available for decorating at least a dozen hall bulletin boards. You may assign responsibility for their decoration to any of the floor teachers. You can do this on a rotating basis or a permanent one. You may not, however, dictate a particular theme to teachers who are not in your department. In such cases while they are to decorate the bulletin board, they may decorate it with materials unique to their subject area. Additionally, while you may visit every teacher's classroom on your floor, if you feel that the room of a teacher not in one of your departments is lacking, you are to share that thought with the designated supervisor of that subject area.

Are you hearing me? Yes, I said.   Loud and clear.
Excellent, said Mr. Lindle.   Tomorrow we'll talk about
Assembly schedules, appropriate dress for pupils and
teachers, programs and special events. Do you have any
questions? No, I remarked. Well, I do. Yes. How come with
all that we have been talking about these last two days and
will talk about over the next few days, you don't take notes?
Photographic memory or at least very close to it, I said.
Looking forward to tomorrow's session. Good night. On
leaving Mr. Lindle's office I thought I detected a slight
smile on the former Master Sergeants face.

The rest of the week was pretty much more of the same.
Mr. Lindle tried to cram as much as he could into our three
sessions. During the day, I found myself doing much of the
same with a new teacher whom Dr. McNaughton had
designated as my replacement. One advantage that he would
have is the fact that my class and my instructional program
was an eighth grade one. I would see to it that each class
understood that while I was not their eighth grade Social
Studies Teacher, I was the eighth grade Assistant Principal.
They would be expected to "go along with the program" or
suffer the consequences, as I so deemed appropriate. As this
teacher was newly assigned and fresh out of "Teacher's
College," my hands were full. He did, however, strike me
as someone who wanted to do well. I'd see to it that he got
his chance.

Monday came quicker than I could have imagined. At
8:30, I found myself in the area of the yard designated as
the eighth grade class entryway.   The Dean, a red-haired
former science teacher, who unlike his predecessors
believed in behavior modification via the counseling route,
joined me there. Much like myself he was proactive when it
came to students' rights. The kids knew this about him and
respected his authority. How are you, Ted? Good, the Dean
said. Yourself? Couldn't be better. The bell's gonna ring in
about five minutes. Usually I go up on the second floor to

monitor hall traffic as the kids are let in. Today is going to be different. Do you have a bullhorn? Yes, I do, he said. Would you please get it? Sure, responded the Dean. Ted was back in two minutes holding a bullhorn. Thanks, I said, taking it from him. Tuning the volume to mid range, I depressed the button and spoke into the mike. Good morning, eighth graders. Some stood still and looked in my direction. I turned the volume control button up to full volume. Good morning, eighth graders. Please stand still exactly where you are, stop the conversations, and listen to the announcement so that you know what to do. Before we go upstairs today, I would like the opportunity to talk with all of you at the same time. Therefore, we're going to go directly to the auditorium for an orientation assembly. Since Mr. Lindle has previously assigned you seats, you will continue to occupy those seats. Dean Brown will escort you there now. I will follow shortly. You are to line up in single file along the side of the building and proceed that way toward the auditorium. Remember you are the senior class, and people will be looking at you. Do all of us proud. Line up. As the grade got into a single file line, I told Ted that I'd be along directly. Is there a problem? he said. No, I just have to announce over the PA for all of the eighth grade official teachers as well as period #1 eighth grade teachers to report to the auditorium.

The "march in process" took about ten minutes. By then all of the teachers had arrived. Some came over to me and offered congratulations. I made a mental note of the ones who didn't. Using the bullhorn as an attention getter I asked every official teacher to take a seat with their class and to actively supervise them. I would also ask that every period #1 teacher take seats with those classes respectively. The effect of this "Bull Horn" announcement was the desired one: the student body immediately ceased their private chitchat and focused on me. I gave the bullhorn to Mr. Brown and using the gift God had given me, I greeted my captive audience. Good morning, boys and girls. There was a scattered and weak return salutation. Digging a little deeper I again bade the group a good morning. The response was 75% favorable. We'll deal with the reluctant 25% a little later, I thought. Good morning, teachers. Their response was similar to the first pupil response. I didn't push. I know that your normal assembly is scheduled for two weeks from today. I felt, however, that it was important for us to meet today so as to have some basic understandings that could not wait that long. Of course, those of you who've been in my social studies class are probably thinking you have a good understanding about me already. The rest of you think you do as well because of what your friends have told you. Some of which I suspect may be true. Some not! You are the senior grade. I consider it a personal honor to be your Assistant Principal. If I ever treat you in any way that suggests otherwise, I need you to tell me so. This statement applies to every single individual in this room.

The remainder of the program pretty much dealt with things that would not be tolerated. I gave Dean Brown the opportunity to speak as well. As you would expect he dwelt on warning students of the consequences about committing such major offenses as fighting, class cutting, teacher disrespect, drug or weapons possession, and smoking in or near the school. I dismissed the auditorium on a class-by-class basis, with teacher escorts. Almost immediately Mr. Broussard, a member of the Social Studies department and the official teacher for class 8-211, approached me. Mr. Kassell, this was very unprofessional of you. The teachers have a right to know when you are planning assemblies. What the teachers have a right to Mr. Broussard is to teach, I said. The students on the other hand have a right to know immediately about changes. Studies have shown that grown-ups such as yourself adapt more readily to change. If not they tend to fall by the wayside. Now you have a good day, I said, turning to walk away. You do the same, I heard Broussard say. Waiting for me in the rear of the auditorium was Dean Brown. Walking up to the second floor together, I said that I'd like to walk once around the floor, monitor the change of period, and then meet with him in my office. He agreed to meet me there in five minutes.

You know, I said, there are a lot of people who do not think much of my selection to the A.P.'s position. I know. Some think I'm too young, and others think I'm the wrong color. I know, Ted said somewhat stoically. Fuck 'em! But why did you have the assembly program this morning without telling anyone? I'm glad you asked, I said. To begin with, whether I'm white, or pink, straight or gay, liked or not, the teaching staff has one function. They must teach. Short of that I will charge them with dereliction of duty.

Students, however, in addition to being charged with the task of learning, must buy into the authoritative program of those directly in charge of them. Therefore, they must always be made aware of changes immediately. You cannot allow for blocks of time to pass during which you are constantly springing things on them. Certainly, I will try not to ruffle feathers. I will try to maintain a professional air with everyone. You have to know, however, I was raised in a Bronx housing project, attended DeWitt Clinton HS, got my ass kicked and kicked some ass. I drove trucks for two years. I know when someone is fucking with me, and I know what to do about it. I said these things to Dean Brown, because I knew that through him I could send a message that could not appear on any written meeting agenda. I want to talk about our relationship, if you don't mind. I see you, to quote the parlance of The British Admiralty as my #2. I will keep you well versed in all aspects of my activities. I expect you to be a major player in the administration of the grade. In my absence you will be directly in charge. I will reiterate this philosophy at the grade meetings later this week. With regard to the kids, I think we are two of a kind. From what little I know of you, I believe that you will spend incessant amounts of time to peacefully settle pupil disputes. You would not be able to do this if the kids didn't respect you. I also know that you frequently stay after school and play basketball with them. I'll be joining you for that activity in the very near future. Lastly, I know that in spite of your out of the classroom assignment as Dean, you are a member of the teaching ranks. You have my word that I shall never knowingly do anything to compromise that status. I don't expect you to rat out fellow teachers. I do, however, expect that if I inquire of you the degree by which a teacher is being cooperative in any of our endeavors regarding any corrective action plans for pupil behavior, that you will be forthright with me. Fair enough, Ted replied.

I believe in consistency. I want the kids and the teachers to know exactly what to expect from me. To that end it shall be my practice to begin each and every morning with a walk around, stopping ever so briefly in each eighth grade class. I will survey the rooms' physical appearance—chalkboards, daily schedule, bulletin boards, teacher desk surfaces, and pupil preparedness. From time to time, when you talk with the kids, ask them to produce their program cards. Check out their looseleafs. Also, I want you to consider the creation of a Dean's bulletin board to be located right outside your office door. If you like the idea, we'll have the custodian install one. What would I display on it? he said Oh, "Dean things" I suppose. Do you ever put kids on probation? Yes, frequently. Then you might want to have a probationary status listing. I'm also going to give you the responsibility of scanning the weekly class section sheets. At our monthly assembly, you shall issue a "Dean's Commendation Card" for the class with the highest section sheet scores. Next month, I'll ask you to attend the eighth grade PTA meeting. At that time you can ask the PTA if they would support our section sheet behavioral

Kenneth S. Karcinell

modification incentive program with some special treats for the three highest classes at the end of each marking period. Such things as pizza parties, roller-skating trips, Yankees or Mets outings, or theatre tickets could be activities that would be fitting for them to sponsor. Do you agree? For the first time during our conference I saw a light in Ted Brown's eyes. That's a great idea, he exclaimed.

In the secondary school, the Dean is the cop. After a while he does not see himself as an educator. He forgets from whence he came. He loses touch with the academic concerns of the school. For that reason, when I was a Dean and more so when I became an Assistant Principal, I spent every opportunity I could to get in front of a class. Not to show off but simply to maintain my tradecraft. I shared this thought with Ted before we broke from our meeting. About a week later, I found him inside an eighth grade classroom during my period one walk around. Seeing me at the doorway, Ted came over and explained that earlier that morning he was in the Main Office and picked up an incoming call from Mrs. Thompkins who said that she was delayed and would not be in until period two. Since Ted had taught math, he reasoned that it would be in the best interests of the students if he took the coverage. Of course, I gotta believe he was recalling the last part of our articulation conference. Frequently, Ted and I took classes when emergencies presented themselves. No teachers could ever say of either one of us that we set ourselves above them. More importantly, the kids were always amazed that we knew the subject matter and could teach. Over the long haul these behaviors unified all of us.

Thus far I'd pretty much followed Mr. Lindle's advice about not making changes right away. My first meeting with the Social Studies department was scheduled for that Friday. There would be some changes.

Good morning, ladies and gentlemen. Please be sure to sign the attendance sheet in the space next to your name.

We have a lengthy agenda this morning, and I'd like to get right to it. I'll ask that you introduce questions in those areas we are discussing now. Any others not addressed by the agenda may be raised when we reach that portion of the agenda labeled as "Open." Items 1, 2, and 3 went rather smoothly. For the most part they were reiterations of previously established policy set out by Mr. Lindle. Item 4 is Lesson Plans. I see that Mr. Broussard has a question. Yes I do. I understand from your agenda that you will be collecting lesson plans on Tuesday mornings. When will you collect Black History lesson plans? I won't, I said. There will be no further requirement to prepare separate Black History lesson plans. Nor will I continue to promote the practice of setting two periods aside each week for the presentation of these studies. With the exception of Mr. Fried who has just joined our department, all of us, and I include myself in this statement, have been teaching Black History as a separate curriculum for at least two years if not more. There is no doubt in my mind that we are totally familiar with that curriculum.

I want us, however, to move our minds into a more multi-cultural awareness. I want us to present the social studies curriculum in as natural and unbiased fashion as we can. We will continue to highlight special holidays and events in our lesson planning, on our bulletin boards, and in our assembly programs. The only place where I will accept a separatist approach to the presentation of minority studies would be as bulletin board displays. Is it to be our understanding, Mr. Kassell that you don't believe in the contributions of Blacks to our history raged Mr. Broussard? No, I exclaimed. I don't see how you could draw that conclusion from what I've just said. Allow me to illustrate. If you are about to teach a lesson about slavery on the southern plantations, I would expect that your plans leading up to that issue would begin with the "stealing" of these slaves from various African kingdoms in the 1700's. I would also expect that you would attempt to provide students with the facts regarding the very high cultural and family values that these kingdoms promoted. Then point out that while slavery was a white man's get rich scheme, it could not have been accomplished without the treachery of Black tribal leaders.

You might want to further indicate to students that the idea of slavery owes its roots to biblical times. Moving along, if you are teaching about the American Revolution, then I would expect that you will include in your plans the fact that Crispus Attucks was a black man who was the first American to be killed. He was a free man fighting for the colonists. Explain how the British and Colonists competed for the enlistment of Black soldiers in their armies. Emphasize how George Washington used the pub and boarding house of Samuel Fraunces as his own private espionage conduit employing every member of the Fraunces family as spies. You might want to take your class on a trip there. It is a functioning restaurant in the Wall Street area. You might also want to review how the Revolution was in large part financed by Jews from Newport, Rhode Island.

If you are at that part of the curriculum that deals with westward expansion, then I had better see mention of the contributions of the Chinese "coolies" in your plans. In addition, where would you fit in the Buffalo Soldiers, and how did they get that name? No need to answer the question. Do all of you understand my policy? I don't agree, Mr. Broussard stated. That wasn't the question, I said. I expect any number of instances in which there is not agreement with what I will say in these meetings. The question is, does everyone understand that my philosophy as concerns the presentation of minority studies to our students is such that I wish to emphasize the contributions to our history of all cultures as they occurred, done without personal bias? I can see by your reaction that we are in accord. I can also see by the clock that we have just about used all of our conference time on item #3. I promise to cut down on my lengthy attempts at clarification in the future. We will table items 4 and 5 for our next meeting. Have a good day.

Oh, Mr. Broussard, a word if you don't mind. Broussard put on his most ferocious scowl and walked in my direction as the others slowly filed out. Broussard was I suspect ready for further confrontation. I need two favors, was my opening. I'm listening, he said. I continued, you are the senior member of the social studies department. I respect that you voiced your dissension openly. Of course, I hope that you will similarly express your satisfaction in the weeks and months ahead. I shall value your opinions in whatever light they're spoken. You said you needed two favors. Yes, I said. The first is that I'd like to assign Mr. Fried to you for "buddy" assistance. Done, he responded. The second? I'd like you to chair a social studies curriculum committee. This committee will be made up of two other department members one of which must be Mr. Fried, the other I'll leave to your choosing. This committee will be charged with developing a map studies program for each of the grades. The program should have at its core a philosophy statement, a resource of materials, and a staff development piece.

The second request has to do with my policy statement on the presentation of minority materials in the instructional delivery of social studies. I would like to see a time line developed beginning in the early 1600's until the present. This would cover the NYC seventh and eighth grade social studies curriculum. Unlike that curriculum we will enrich it with the appropriate and natural input of minority contributions as indicated on our time line. Have Fried do the research. It'll be a good learning experience for him. Not as good as those college courses interjected Mr. Broussard. I heard that some white folk have been known to take a course or two on minority studies there. Broussard smiled. I didn't think anyone..., Mr. Lindle was very impressed when you took that initiative. No one here including myself wants you to fail. We especially don't want to fail the children. We have been together a long time and don't take well to changes. Go slowly. We know who you are, and we hear what you're saying. Make sure when it's your turn that you hear what we're saying. You know it's a nice touch. What's that? The map studies project. Lindle wanted desparately to develop a strong map studies and graphics program within the social studies curricula. Yes, I know. He lamented the fact that it was an unrealized goal. I'd like to have this project identified as a "mission" statement with which to begin our next department meeting. We'll kick it around and try to establish a short and long-range plan for implementation. Let's see what the colleagues come up with. That's a good idea, was Broussard's parting remark.

At the ensuing department meeting, I formally introduced the social studies curriculum committee. I then called upon Mr. Broussard to elaborate on its goals and objectives. To my delight, he had taken the initiative to prepare a formal outline of the committee's persuits and its "Map Studies Mission Statement." Smiles appeared on the faces of the members, as Broussard enthusiastically debriefed the group. After some discussion, the consensus of the group was to do something now; something that students and parents could readily embrace as a necessary learning skill. It was decided that every homework assignment, quiz, formal exam, and daily lesson would in some way address specific map study skills. As the meeting reached its conclusion, I announced that I expected to receive a monetary allocation for "instructional supplies" in another week or so. I made a commitment to set aside one-third of that allocation for the purchase of such things as "hands on kits," and curriculum friendly wall map displays. To that end, I'm going to ask that the curriculum committee survey the various map companies and invite them to send sales reps to our next two department meetings to afford us the opportunity of seeing what's out there. Any questions? Good we've had a productive meeting. Now let's put our money where our mouths are. Have a good day! In December I submitted purchase orders to Mr. Lindle's secretary that called for the expenditure of $2500 in various map study instructional materials.

In the meantime, I continued to meet and "train" under Mr. Lindle's watchful eye after school. At the beginning of October, he asked me when I was going to begin the process of conducting formal observations. Of course that question gave rise to the creation of an "observation appointment calendar," and more to the point, did I really understand that this function was the single most important function that any supervisor worth his or her salt had to master. Among the items discussed were these: What gets discussed at a Pre-Observation conference? What does a supervisor observe besides the manner of instructional delivery? What gets discussed at the Post Observation conference? As I began to write my reports and submit them to Mr. Lindle for correction, he was relentless. You cannot state that something is wrong or inappropriate unless you indicate a positive alternative. By the same token, if you are saying that something is good or worked well, then you must say why it was so. Our discussions targeted questioning styles, learning activities, and integrated curriculum as matters of supervisory concern. Why can't the reports be written in "check-off" style, I asked. I deduced the answer from Mr. Lindle's blank stare.

Allowing for the significance of his stare to sink in, Mr. Lindle went on to explain that a supervisor's observation report is the only opportunity for the supervisor to be specific and succinct in both his praises and his criticisms. Nothing in this report may be left to one's imagination. Such statements are regarded as vague and arbitrary.

Everything, including the heading, is intended as documentation. In the heading alone, you provide information that there was a pre- and post-observation conference. You identify the class observed, the period of the day, the subject taught, and you quote the lesson aim as it is displayed on the board. You leave nothing unobserved. This includes the condition and appearance of the room in general: What did the teacher's desk look like/ Was the teacher's lesson plan in evidence? Did the bulletin boards provide for displays of current pupil work? Were the subject area displays relevant? Was the chalkboard well organized? Unless you are a person of some ill repute, your observation report is regarded as sacrosanct. It is generally accepted that when a supervisor uses such terms as: I observed, I saw, I noted, or I could not help but to notice, etc., the corrollary to these phrases would be stated in the negative, i.e., I did not observe, see, or notice. Inserting these phrases as "sentence beginners" will make everything that follows valid. Hence, the opportunity to overturn an observation report at a grievance hearing is lessened. Do you understand? Not waiting for my answer, Mr. Lindle went off on another tangent, this time dealing with the value and use of the informal observation. Here he stressed that every time a supervisor walks in to a classroom, even if he stays for only a few minutes, the visit may be referenced as an observation visit; and when that supervisor returns to his office, he should note the visit and what he saw in his daily logs.

As the sessions wore on, I became more and more dependent upon Bayer as a vital life support system. I continued to write and submit my observation reports to Mr. Lindle, and he continued to slice through them like a butcher trimming fat from a piece of meat. More and more, however, the reports were being returned with less red ink than previous attempts. As the year went by, I had become so influenced by Mr. Lindle that many of the teachers had begun to refer to me as "little Lindle."

As I continued to be mentored by Mr. Lindle, it became quite clear to me that he was very bitter when it came to "the system," or "the establishment" that governed the system. Upon second thought, bitter doesn't really give the kind of depiction that would accurately illustrate Mr. Lindle's feelings about the system. In fact he held it beneath his personal contempt. Oftentimes he would refer to it as nest of "jive-timers and fools." He used this terminology as a generic description for most DO staff, community school board members and central headquarters bureaucrats.

Looking back I'm inclined to think that his assessment was accurate. The source of his bitterness could be found in the fact that for the past three years he was functioning as an "acting" administrator; a situation that was destined to last for another two years. It seems that in 1969 a landmark Supreme Court decision was passed. This decision became known as Chance v. Mercado. In essence, the outcome was that the court declared that the NYC method of testing for Administrative positions within the public school system was discriminatory towards minorities. Therefore, the court ordered that the city cease and desist from offering these exams in 1969. From 1969 until 1973 there were no tests given. For Mr. Lindle, insult was added to injury. Having passed the last exam given in 1969 and having placed very high on the promulgated list, for sure, he would have been regularly appointed that year. The court, however, made its decision retroactive to disallow the promulgation of that exam. The consequence of all of this, as far as Mr. Lindle was concerned, was that he was working as an unpaid supervisor, surrounded by paid supervisors and more often than not having a greater workload than that of his peers.

This would change in 1973.

147

Chapter XVI

Appointment by Community School Board Resolution

While the Supreme Court did not reverse its ruling regarding the decision that it found the supervisory exams discriminatory, they did allow for a reconfiguration of the exam process in NYC. The outcome was something called "The On-the-Job Performance Test." Additionally, the court allowed for the appointment to the position of Assistant Principal by a community school board of any candidate who possessed a state certificate or had previously passed a supervisory licensing exam. The court's decision would prove beneficial to both Mr. Lindle and me. While he met the qualification for appointment vis-à-vis his possession of the NYS certificate in School Administration and Supervision (SAS) and had successfully passed the last supervisory exam given, I had neither qualification. The "On-the-Job Performance Test" would be my shot. In November of '73 two gentlemen visited me from the Board of Examiners. These men spent the entire day with me. They examined every aspect of how I carried out my supervisory and administrative responsibilities. As they left my office at four p.m., one of them remarked how impressed he was with my record keeping and file system. A place for everything and everything in its place, I said, half laughing to myself. All those hours with Mr. Lindle had paid off, I thought.   Just before Christmas, I received notification of having passed the exam. The next morning I was met at the time clock by a smiling and obviously proud Dr. McNaughton, who had received a copy of my "pass/fail" notice. Later that day I visited Mr. Lindle and personally thanked him for all of his mentoring and patience. All part of the job, my Man. One day you'll be the

Chancellor. See me this afternoon; I want a status report on the various graduation activities. No problem; I'll see you at three, I said, and turned around and left his office.

The next three months went by rather uneventfully. The morning of April 6, 1974 was a typical one for that time of year. As I drove to work there was a smattering of showers. The radio stations weather forecaster had promised sun and clear skies for the Mets home opener at Shea Stadium later that day. What was not typical was the note I found attached to my time card. It was from Dr. McNaughton. It read simply, "see me period three." At precisely 10:20 a.m. I reported as directed to Dr. McNaughton's office. I was joined on my way by Mr. Lindle who I would find out later had been similarly summoned. Gentlemen, it is my pleasure to inform each of you that your names are going to be placed on a Community School Board Resolution this evening for appointment as Assistant Principal. I would very much appreciate it if you both attend the meeting tonight. I'll be there, I said, excitedly. Glancing at Mr. Lindle I saw him nod affirmatively. Good. The meeting will be held at Holmes Junior High School. I advise that you get there promptly at 7:30. Very often there aren't enough seats, and you don't want to stand all evening. Until this evening gentlemen...Taking that as our cue to leave, I followed Mr. Lindle across the hall to his office. Before I could say anything, Mr. Lindle went into a tirade that suggested that he was anything but pleased at the events planned for the evening. Isn't that something? After almost six years, I am supposed to take delight in the fact that the Community School Board has finally decided to pay me my due. Do you realize that these corrupt and incompetent motherfuckers have had seven superintendents, four community school board elections, at least three of their members arrested or removed from the board for reasons ranging from graft to drug trafficking, and they have the nerve to request my presence? Mr. Lindle, I yelled. Do you like Italian food? Of course I do, he said. Why do you ask? Why don't you join me for an early dinner after school? I know a great place over on 118th Street and First Avenue. We'll have a nice meal and then we can go to the school board meeting together. Why are you so sure I'll attend? He said. Because it's the right thing to do was my response. I learned that from you these last six months. Besides, I'll treat. I made some money at OTB yesterday, and I'm plush. How about 3:30? Your money, your time, he said. See you then.

While I understood Mr. Lindle's contempt for the planned evening's activity, I found myself looking forward to the school board meeting, as it would be my first such experience. The dinner at Patsy's wasexcellent, as I knew it would be. The dinner discussion topic revolved around the status of the various senior activities I was responsible for. This was a plus, as I would not have to take time that week to bring Mr. Lindle up to snuff on the topic. By the way interjected Mr. Lindle, I'm a little late in saying this, but I want to thank you for following up on the map studies program. I like what you've done. Why, thank you, I said. Thank you very much. Check please!

We arrived on the block in which Holmes JHS was located at approximately 7:15. I was lucky enough to find a parking space two blocks away. As we drew near to the school, I was struck by the massive police presence. There were at least four patrol cars, and I guessed several unmarked cars as well. The police had cordoned off a special walkway that stretched from the main entrance to the school over a distance of approximately 500 feet out to the street. As we approached the walkway one of the officers asked, "Are you fellas attending the school board meeting?" Yes, we are, I replied. For what reason was the officer's next question. Sensing Mr. Lindle's growing impatience with the banter, I informed the officer that we were listed on the agenda, and that he could check that if he liked. That won't be necessary, an approaching Sergeant said. Just hurry along, if you don't mind. I would find out later that the reason for the high profile presence of police was tied to the fact that at recent school board meetings around the city, several board members had been pelted with eggs and other assorted fruits and vegetables as they attempted to enter their community school board meeting sites.

As we entered the school auditorium, I spotted Dr. McNaughton who hand motioned us to come over to where he was seated. I'm glad you got here early. I've saved seats for you. Here are copies of tonight's agenda. Handing the six-page document to us, he directed our attention to page six, resolution #11. Dr. McNaughton stressed the fact that we should not lose these agendas, as they documented the fact that our appointments to the position of Assistant Principal were in full compliance with Board of Education Regulations governing this procedure. He went on to say that he would direct Mrs. Gerstein to place copies of the agenda in our professional files tomorrow. Looking at the six-page agenda, I was struck by the theatrics of the evening thus far. After all, the main event had not yet begun. Off Broadway theatre, in its truest form. When I shared these thoughts with Mr. Lindle, he became quite animated. Yes, you're right. Shakespeare would be proud. You have all the ingredients—fools and jesters for characterization and treachery and larson for plots. We both laughed uncontrollably at the thought.

It's appropriate to provide an historical footnote at this juncture, as we will revisit a community school board meeting again:

In 1969/70 the NYS legislature passed the school decentralization laws. The intent was to vest power and choice with local community residents in determining various curriculum goals and school governance personnel. The results, however, were that the schools got placed into the hands of vipers. The city was divided into thirty-two "community school districts." Each was headed by a district office, staffed by a superintendent, a deputy superintendent, and anywhere from ten to twenty "coordinators." Of course, there was secretarial staff for all of these positions. One would think that with control now decentralized that the next step in the process would be the streamlining of the bureaucracy at 110 Livingston Street. To the contrary, it grew. The creation of a Chancellorship to oversee all district operations brought with it a new and meaner bureaucracy. Our tax dollars were now paying for two bloated bureaucracies. For sure each district eventually fell under the influence of its local politicians. Patronage and cronyism ruled. Favors were handed out left and right. School construction jobs were the jackpot with the sale of school principalships running a close second. If you were a principal who tried to run your school independent of these influences, and you didn't have tenure, you were committing professional suicide. To think that these conditions do not exist today is truly naiive. At the beginning the school board members were openly contemptful of school personnel. In some school districts the boards would deliberately and routinely hold back certificates of tenure to individuals even though they knew that by not taking any action either pro or con in this matter that eligible recipients of tenure achieved it by a process known as "estopple." To think that individuals who in many cases had minimum educational development, in some cases did not speak English, or were on probation from prison could presume to deny tenure or direct curriculum was to me a personal affront. I can recall vividly getting into a heated debate with a superintendent who during an interview wherein I was applying for a principalship asked me how I felt about shared decision- making and community involvement. You can't be serious I responded. At the time a Chancellor who had literally fled from a system that had bid him good riddance, was running things in our school system. His philosophical imprint was something he called "Shared-Decision Making." He presumed that school principals did not regularly consult with their school-based cabinets and PTA leaderships not to mention the UFT District 37 labor council, Custodial Union, and its own CSA in the decision making process. Any supervisor would tell you that this system is and has been in place since day one. That will be all, said the somewhat shaken superintendent. As I left the interviewing conference room, two members of the panel, who were community-based members, joined me. We want you to know that we appreciated your candor. We intend to do whatever we can to support your candidacy. I'll ask you not to do that, I unbelievably replied. I made an enemy in there and that would mitigate against my ability to administer a school the way I would want to.

Within a few minutes of our arrival, the school board members paraded onto the stage, to a chorus of boos and derisive cheers. Undaunted, they took their seats at the dais. Early on I took note of a particularly loud and belligerent individual in the row in front of us. He agitated the proceedings all night long. As I would grow in my professional development and attend more community school board meetings in various parts of town, I found this scenario repeated. Not only were there ungrateful agitators such as the one encountered here, but there were organized factions as well. These individuals when confronted with an issue not to their liking would do anything they could to strike it down. Their actions ranged from filibustering to acts of intimidation directed at those who supported the issue they were opposed to. Again great theatre! Tragic results!

We'll began with our customary benediction followed by "Lift Every Voice and Sing," announced the school board chair. Again I found this practice observed in other boroughs as well. I could understand the singing of an anthem at the beginning of a sporting event. And then I realized the similarity between the stalking that goes on at a community school board meeting and the stalking of game by a hunter during hunting season. Amazing. I supposed that the thinking was that the presence of a minister at these meetings gave one a sense of holy sanctity to all that would unfold in the hours ahead. I realized as the evening wore on that this could not possibly be the case.

Following the anthem and benediction, the school board chairman announced that the secretary would read the minutes from the last meeting. When did the bitch learn how to read, shouted my agitator. The audience became raucous. We'll have order immediately, shouted the chairwoman, banging her gavel as she spoke. If there are any questions or comments from the audience I will recognize them now. Yes, she said, recognizing my agitator. A mistake I thought. Do you have a comment or a motion? Yeah. I got a motion that all you motherfuckers resign. The audience went wild. There was mayhem. People everywhere were up out of their seats, shouting and waving their hands. Quickly a police presence assembled in the front of the auditorium and order was restored. This foreplay would heighten and recede throughout the evening. Finally at about 11:15 the secretary read resolution #11. "Be it resolved that Mssrs. Lindle and Kassell having met the prerequisite requirements for the positions of Assistant Principal be so appointed by this board." Are there any objections? Looking around the room there now remained a handful of faithfuls. For the most part they were reclined back in their chairs with looks of exhaustion on their faces and large sweat stains on their shirts and blouses. They were truly spent, I thought. We're in. I was sure that closure was just around the corner. Suddenly my agitator sprung to life. I object! Anybody in here know these motherfuckers? Where are they? Raising his 6'2" 250 lb. Frame, Mr. Lindle said, "I'm one of the motherfuckers. Half standing I heard myself say I'm the other. The agitator looked at us and laughed. I guess they're ok. I withdraw my objection.

Chapter XVII

The Golden Years ('73, '74, '75)

The architectural trend of the late '60's focused on maximizing space as its primary objective. Real estate in NYC was very costly with most of it earmarked for housing development. Of course, the hundreds of dilapidated buildings scattered throughout the five boroughs but confined mainly to the poorer neighborhoods in those boroughs remained as undeveloped eyesores. The city for political reasons did not pursue as vigorously as they should have their right of eminent domain to develop these properties for public housing. Consequently, when it came time to construct new schools, the architects had to come up with new concepts. One was to "build up or upon" some pre-existing structure. To that end architects were called in and proceeded (with little consultation with school designers) to draw up plans for various school construction projects throughout the city. In building their schools, such strategies as not having boys and girls bathrooms adjacent to one another was paid no mind. Similarly, the strategy of not having the pupil cafeteria adjacent to the staff cafeteria was ignored. In themselves these are hardly crimes but certainly fall under the classification of annoyance. At any event in 1969 construction work began at 145th and Lennox Avenue for what would be the site of the "new" fortress. Let me correct myself. Construction did not begin at 145th Street; it began on top of 145th Street. To be exact, the architectural plans called for the school to be built on top of the 145th Street Lennox Avenue subway station, which coincidentally was the last stop on that line. Not only did trains roll in and out all day long, but also as this station was a holding area, trains frequently idled for elapsed periods depending on arrival and departure schedules. If you taught on the first floor, the most vital teaching tool you needed would have to be a bottle of Bufferin. Of course, when the trains came rolling in and out of the station, the entire building vibrated. Affectionately, we referred to the school as San Francisco East.

In retrospect we were more fortunate than many others. The city used landfill areas and remodernized factories as school construction sites. These are now the topic of intense investigation as possible cancer causing clusters.

The "fortress," however, was going to be different. It was going to be the educational panacea for all to model. The new principal would be among the very last to be assigned via the "list eligible" method. Decentralization had not yet begun to plague the system. Everything in the school was new and state of the art. However things did go wrong! Texts were insufficiently ordered. Consequently several others and I were sent out in our cars to some of the private catholic schools as well as some of the better-endowed school districts both within and without the city. We begged for charity and in most cases received it. The school was to have had central air-cooling. It worked in only certain areas and not all as it was intended. Ultimately, to my knowledge, it never did.

We still see problems like this throughout the school system. Here's why. When the School Construction Authority approves of a project, it subcontracts all of the accompanying jobs to the lowest bidder. Frequently these bidders desperate for work or just getting started in the field submit unrealistically low bids. Naturally the city accepts the bid. Invariably what happens next is that after a while in a cost cutting effort the contractor lays off some of his employees. Worse yet, the contractor has taken on several other low bid jobs but does not have enough work force to do all the jobs. He begins to alternate sites. School principals are powerless to do anything other then make complaints. More often then not these complaints were placed in the "circular file." Eventually, the sub-contractor may be confronted with the threat of fines and penalties. Accordingly, he declares bankruptcy and all work stops until the job is rebid. In the meantime, months and years often go by with schools literally under a constant state of construction.

Getting back to "the Fortress." It was going to be an example of modernity in an educational institutional setting—a building of aesthetic beauty, an educational complex housing an Elementary School and Junior High School in the same structure. In reality it was going to be a cost overrun disaster. How you may ask can a regulatory body such as the SCA allow for such a thing? Let's take a closer look at the organization of this bureaucracy as it presented itself in the '60's, '70's, and early '80's. For the most part the SCA office was located in some obscure office near central headquarters. It was staffed by an administrator, and assistant or second in command, a secretary and two or three field workers. This "dream team" was responsible for overseeing all of the NYC Board of Education construction activities. This monetary "Black Hole" was left to its own devices for over thirty years. Only recently have they been reeled in and made accountable for their actions.

Looking back I was very fortunate. In the new school I benefited from one of the aesthetics. My room looked out to the north taking in a beautiful view of the East River and its accompanying boat commerce as well as an occasional pleasure yacht. Additionally, I could view the Yankee Stadium that positioned itself as a kind of sentinel to all that passed down the river. If this was what was right with the building, it was a small reward when compared to all that was wrong with the site. It would take two years of a "settling-in" process during which such annoyances as broken pieces of chalkboard, various pipe leaks, damaged floor tiles, jammed doors, and blinking lights, would have to be endured by all. Somehow we managed to persevere. We implemented a robust educational program for our instructional staff.

As an Acting Assistant Principal in 1973, I was at once a member of both the General Cabinet to the Principal, and the more exclusive Executive Cabinet to the Principal. In the case of the former, other members of the school community such as the UFT Chairperson, a member of the Guidance department, the two behavioral modification counselors (Deans), each subject chair, an Assistant Principal, a PTA member, Student Government reps from each grade, and last but not least the Custodial Engineer all contributed to the development of school policy. They met once a month with the Principal on a consultatory basis. Each voiced "items of concern." As a result of these sessions, the Principal would formalize an agenda for the Executive Cabinet. As an outcome to these meetings on school policy, practices and procedures would be published or announced in any of the pre-existing standard methods of communication, i.e., a Memorandum, a Communications Bulletin, an Administrative Circular, or as part of the daily P.A. announcements. Of course, not every "item of concern," or point of view became school policy. The Principal had to be a diplomat, however, if he were to accomplish aspects of his own agenda. Therefore, he was always sure to pick out certain "reasonable" suggestions made by the General Cabinet, give them his full backing in the Executive Cabinet, and thusly moving his own agenda along.

It was no secret that the school was in dire financial straits. Such enrichment programs as Map studies, AVI instructional delivery modes, school clubs, trip programs, were just some of the non-basic tools that we wanted so desperately to have but couldn't pay for out of our meager tax levy funding. This funding incidentally was based on pupil attendance and had a dollar figure that hadn't changed in more than a decade. This pattern repeated itself right up to my retirement in 1997. Consequently, when you see muckrakers such as the school news reporter from the daily newspapers and the special Board of Education Investigators' Office, scandalize the issue of false attendance reporting, understand, right or wrong, the system allows for it. Every May and June school reorganization teams make plans for the next school year. From the time that process begins until September when school opens, three and a half months pass. During that time and particularly over the summer, many kids either leave the city or move elsewhere within the city. In any case, the original schools do not find out until at best late October when they receive a written request approved by the local community superintendent for the transference of records. By then, however, the school principals have placed all of their "no shows" in a "paper" class and continued to count their number as a part of the total school register. Monetary allocations as well as positional allocations are determined based on school register figures and their projected figures submitted in June. The projection, incidentally, was a standard ten percent increase. Getting back to the case at hand. Do you think that any school principal that genuinely has the concern of his student body at heart is going to turn around in September and willingly forfeit what he has gained by doing what the system has required of him? Of course, someone investigating this in November or December is going to cry scandal. Get real!

Back to cases. We needed thousands to accomplish our goals of having an enriched and vibrant extracurricula program with which to enrich our basic mode of instructional delivery. Therefore, Dr. McNaughton presented the problem to the October 1974 meeting of the General Cabinet. As a part of the feedback, one of the suggestions was to have the English Department plan a theatrical performance for the spring term. A quick cost analysis revealed that at best after expenses the school might realize a $500 profit. Besides, we don't have a very strong English department—lest we forget the "Old Calcutta" incident. Everyone chuckled.

Allow me to digress. A year earlier, Mrs. Haynes, the teacher matriarch of the school had unwittingly taken her eighth grade literature class on a field trip to see "Old Calcutta." She mistakenly thought that it would enrich her students with knowledge of Indian culture. Her trip application was approved simply because the destination read Broadway Play. No, that won't do, stated Dr. McNaughton, although it is an idea worth revisiting in the future. We need something else, however! Perhaps we have the right idea but the wrong department, offered Mr. Lindle. Explain, replied Dr. McNaughton. We have an excellent band and vocal music department. Go on, Dr. McNaughton said encouragingly. Why not a concert spectacular in mid-May, a program that could be offered over a two-night schedule with an encore presentation on a third night? On average we could seat 350 people at each presentation. If we priced the ticket costs at three dollars, we could gross $3,150.00. Allowing for printing costs (tickets, programs) and cleanup costs, I believe we could expect to clear $2,500. A hush fell over the room. Dr. McNaughton sat back in his chair, rubbed his chin, and then leaned forward and asked, do you all agree? Not so fast, blurted out Mr. Green, Chairman of the Music Department. There are all kinds of logistics. Such issues as the program format, pupil capabilities, rehearsal scheduling, printing, do we want spiritual, classical or pop, do we want chorale singing, a capella, or musical accompaniment? Yes, we want all of the above, exclaimed a now visibly excited Dr. McNaughton. I am directing you, Mr. Green, with the task of developing a "rough draft" of a program format and to present that format at Friday's Executive Cabinet meeting. We're adjourned. Mrs. Gerstein, you can shut off the tape recorder now.

Executive Cabinet Meeting-one week hence: We will dispense with our usual meeting protocol. Mr. Green, the floor is yours. Thank you, he said. Aside from all of the inherent problems in planning such an undertaking, there are several biological ones. We are by last count an all male school. We also house a largely adolescent population. Accordingly, those students identified in November and December as sopranos and altos may very well become tenors or worse, basses in May. As Mr. Green continued to make what at best could be described as a negative presentation, a glance at Dr. McNaughton was all one needed to understand the man's frustration when he interrupted, "After all, Mr. Green, this isn't Lincoln Center, you know." It could be, offered Mr. Quarters, the Assistant Principal in charge of the seventh grade. Again a hush fell over the meeting, and Quarters had everyone's attention. Go on, urged Dr. McNaughton. The Vivian Beaumont is forming up a youth chorale and band ensemble with an eye towards summer concerts. I know this because the project director is an old college chum who also attends my weekly poker game. I've discussed our plans with him, and his reaction was more than I could have dreamed. He sees our project as an excellent opportunity to "test the waters." He also thinks that I would be more than willing to forget the $100 he owes me in exchange for one evening performance date given to us for some time in late May. We could sell out the theatre to the tune of (no pun intended) 1000 seats at five dollars each. What the heck, on second thought, eight dollars a seat.

Right, was the first word that ever so slowly emitted from Dr. McNaughton's lips. More hurriedly, he exclaimed, "committees." Mr. Lindle, I'd like you to work with our print shop department and develop a schematic for program and ticket formatting. In addition to standard tickets. Continuing to think aloud, Dr. McNaughton said "we will require a hundred Golden ticket invitations. I shall expect every executive cabinet member to sell twenty of these at a rate of twenty dollars each. By the way, let's specify" Black Tie" in the invitations. Mr. Kassell, you will work closely with the Dean's department in canvassing the community and local merchants for their support. Think in terms of advertisements for our programs. As I recall, you did enjoy some positive community ties at one time or another. Mr. Green, from a time perspective, how long do you anticipate the program being? Three hours commencing promptly at 7 p.m. and ending at 10:30, he said. Seeing the puzzled expression on most of our faces, Mr. Green went on to explain that given the seating reconfigurations and stage movement and considering the encore re-entrances, the extra half-hour needed to be factored in. Bravo, we all exclaimed!

For the remainder of the year every teacher, every student, and seemingly every parent became involved with the planning and promotion of the spring concert. Local ministers made mention of it during their Sunday Service, local radio broadcasts regularly announced the event as a community happening, one of the uptown department stores donated fifty pairs of black trousers, white shirts, and red neckties to the school. PTA members measured the size of all the student participants and then performed the necessary alterations. As for myself, I once again sought out Earnie. Local merchants supported the "booster campaign" to the tune of $1500.

You had to be there that May evening to see folks arriving in taxis and limos, assembling out on the Lincoln Center "patio," and pridefully making their way for the Vivian Beaumont to see their kids perform. You haven't heard anything until you've heard 200 males divided into alto, bass, tenor and soprano groupings, singing Handel's "Hallelujah Chorus" in the Beaumont. The program ended with the singing of "Lift Every Voice." Everyone stood at their seats, joined hands, and sang.

Ultimately when it was all said and done, we raised in excess of $9500. There was joy and some gloating, as you might expect. This glee would, however, prove to be short-lived. In 1975 a series of new words and terms entered the educational lexicon: excess, financial crisis, bumping, and my favorite, reversion.

Unfazed by the formation of the "dark cloud" hovering above, Dr. McNaughton invited the entire planning team to a Sunday brunch at the then landmark establishment known as Frank's. Replete with tuxedo style seats, tiled floors, and ornate metallic ceiling, it wasa perfect setting.

In his speech before the group, Dr. McNaughton said that he couldn't begin to ever thank each of us sufficiently for what we had accomplished. The $9500 will help us to realize all of our dreams and goals for our school. More than that, however, we have set a standard for all to follow. Truly, where there's a will there's a way. I should not want to dampen our pleasure at this time, but I feel compelled to share with you the following memo which I received from our district office this past Friday afternoon: "Dr. McNaughton...in accordance with the mandates of the Mayor's austerity plan for all city agencies, the NYC Board of Education has directed that each school district closely scrutinize all administrative/supervisory positions with an eye towards cutting back. Accordingly, your school is required at this time to declare one of your Assistant Principalships in 'excess.' The declaration of this status is solely based on seniority. According to our records the person designated for excess in your school is Mr. Kassell. He will be placed in a citywide excess pool where all attempts will be made to have him placed in a vacant Assistant Principal's position in any of the other local school districts within the five boroughs. Of course, this will be done on a seniority basis, and Mr. Kassell may be eligible to "bump" someone with less seniority than himself."

Having been made aware of this proclamation by Dr. McNaughton prior to the brunch, I was not as shocked as my colleagues. At the conclusion of his reading the memo, Dr. McNaughton outlined a strategy of combatting the order. Petitions from community members, letters from community stalwarts, letters of protest from students and parents, and any personal political clout that Dr. McNaughton had would all be brought to bare in an effort to persuade the Superintendent to find another "cut back" option.

In my heart, I knew that this was going to be a classic case of a worthwhile goal and an unfulfilled objective. The Superintendent, you see, despised our school and its leader; he had expressed this feeling many times. Consequently, I was not surprised when on June 15th; the superintendent summoned me to a meeting at his office at noon time. Adorned in a brown African Dashiki held in place by a large gold medallion which dangled from an equally large gold chain, the superintendent extended his hand toward me, and then voiced his opinion that I had fought the good fight and that all appeals had been exhausted. I was to report to the community school board which governed the Bedford Stuyvesant community in Brooklyn effective June 29th. Leaving his proffered hand unattended, I asked "Is there anything else?"

Later that summer while working as a Bellhop at one of the Catskill resorts, I took particular delight when I read the following news bleep in the *New York Post*. The headline was this: Harlem School Board Votes to Oust Superintendent During August Meeting. It seems that during the time when the superintendent customarily gives his "state of the district report," the school board was voting his ouster. Not giving any additional thought to what had been, or what was still to come, I proceeded to set up for the afternoon card games.

Kenneth S. Karcinell

Part II

The Brooklyn Years

Kenneth S. Karcinell

Chapter XVIII

Bed-Stuy, My New Base of Operations

My arrival to the smallest, yet most highly politicized school district in NYC went pretty much unheralded. This feeling was reinforced by the fact that I sat idly in the district office for four days with nary a word asked or spoken, not even so much as a "Who are you?" or "May I help you?" from the receptionist, who each morning greeted me with a curt smile and no words. While I sat, I watched and listened. What I saw and heard over that four-day period would prove invaluable in the weeks, months, and years to follow. The Superintendent, who full well knew of my transfer from Harlem, had made no effort to interview me or designate any member of his staff to do so, an indiscretion that I would not soon forget.

When I learned of my transfer to this school district I did some homework. How could a school district underutilized to the tune of 2000 students under the legal limit be allowed to exist? The answer could be found in the fact that one of the state's most powerful African-American politicians called Bed Stuy his home. The school district was untouchable. Certainly for appearances sake, things looked normal. Consequently, my transfer that was to fill a pre-existing vacancy was allowed. Principalships and Superintendent level positions were quite another matter. God bless decentralization! Words such as nepotism and cronyism don't begin to describe the almost incestual web of interpersonal relationships that existed throughout the district. Of course, the goal of quality education, which was often stated, could never be achieved within such a climate. But no one really cared. Occasionally, when some superintendent would attempt to get rid of dead wood, he or she would be quickly dispatched. The 2000 missing students weren't missing at all. Thanks to their parents ingenuity, they were attending better schools in neighboring districts.

Since everyone in the district save one (yours truly) was indebted to someone for their job or knew someone who knewsomeone, yadda yadda yadda, while I had no such indebtedness would serve to empower me to act independently over the next twenty-three years. It was, indeed, an empowerment I wielded tactfully and to great advantage.

Sitting in the district office as I did for four days, I got to recognize at least half of the school board and several of the local political shakers and bakers as they made frequent visits to the Superintendent's office. The Superintendent, as I would learn later, was a male Caucasian who had served as principal in one of the district's junior high schools. He had gained widespread community support during the UFT strike in 1969 by keeping his school open and having classes as scheduled. His reputation was such that as a principal he was dedicated to the idea of quality education for his student body. He would stop at nothing to secure the best for them. Regrettably, he did not apply this philosophy to his superintendancy. On numerous occasions he had the opportunity to fill vacant principalships with quality leaders. He invariably yielded to political pressures and continued the practice of appointing "favorite sons or daughters," who at best maintained the highest levels of mediocrity and aspired for nothing more. The thing that irked me the most, however, was his answer to a question I once asked him about my own future. This district will never appoint a white to a principalship, at least not while I'm superintendent, he replied. I appreciated his candor. Why, I asked. The times, he continued, aren't right, and I don't know that they ever will be. What about you, I asked. He smiled, turned to leave and then turned to face me and said, "I only look white; I think black."

On the morning of my fifth day, I endeavored to repeat the routines of the previous four. I arrived promptly at 8:30 a.m., smiled politely at the receptionist, opened my coffee container, removed my buttered roll from its wax paper, opened my *New York Post* to the sports section, and began reading. Just after dunking my roll for the first time and prior to biting off the coffee sogged tidbit, my attention was distracted by a voice that said, "Good morning! You must be Ken Kassell." I looked up and beheld a stunning woman. She was dressed in a smart charcoal business suit, accompanied by a proper Victorian styled white blouse replete with laced cufflinks and high ruffled collar. I suspected that her entire ensemble was purchased at Saks. As I would continue to work with her in future years, it was my observation that this style of dress, which on the surface was reflective of a somewhat conservative style, did not truly bespeak the lady's true nature. It was not for nothing that many of the district's supervisors referred to her as "the dragon lady." Seeing that my buttered roll was sagging, she said, why don't you take that first bite. Doing so I heard her say, "I'm Lyn Rios, the Deputy Superintendent. When you finish your breakfast, meet me in my office." She turned to leave, and I heard her say, ten minutes, no later! Not waiting for a reply she headed off down the hall. Looking at the receptionist with a puzzled expression, she mouthed the words, "room 162." A stimulating conversationalist, I thought to myself.

Entering Ms. Rios's office, I was taken by the appearance of an all business like environment. The walls did display several plaques and various recognition awards, accompanied by other photographic displays of Ms. Rios and various politicos. The office itself had a standard conference table and eight swivel chairs. Imitation oak paneling covered the walls, and the floor covering was a non-descript steel grey area rug.

Please be seated, Ms. Rios urged, gesturing to a chair directly opposite from her seat, then she opened her top drawer and removed a large folder. Placing it on her desk, she said this is your professional file. I received it yesterday from the Superintendent's secretary. After reading through it, I could not for the life of me understand why you had been transferred to our district. We have supervisors twice your age with not nearly a fraction of your accomplishments. We thought a mistake had been made, and I was directed to seek additional information; and so I "checked you out." Oh, that explains the four day silent treatment—I apologize for that, it was rude. No matter. Leaning over a bit, and looking directly into Ms. Rios eyes, I said, "Here's all you need to know about me professionally...now or ever: I'm very good at what I do. I advocate for children by word and deed. I do not play politics or go about looking to curry favor. I'll listen but not to fools. I'm in no one's pocket. I place a high premium on loyalty. I speak my mind, and lastly, I always get favorable results." Not missing a beat, Ms. Rios nodded her head in agreement and stated, "That pretty much meshes with my findings. I'm going to place you in John Paul Jones JHS. This school is kind of a district favorite son, as our superintendent was formerly its principal. The present principal is Ms. Patricia Mary who was promoted to the position from her rank as school administrative assistant. She shall expect you promptly at 8:30 a.m. Monday morning." Standing, Ms. Rios extended her hand and bid me to have a nice weekend. You do the same, I said, as I shook her hand, turned and left. Within moments of leaving her office, Ms. Rios phone rang. The male voice belonging to the superintendent simply asked,...so? He's a keeper, came Ms. Rios reply.

Driving home, I assessed the day's events. I decided that Ms. Rios was someone to be respected, and more importantly, she had treated me with respect. The fact that

172

she took the time to check me out, told me something of her resourcefulness. The fact that she didn't bat an eye at my somewhat self-serving philosophical declaration as to who I was, told me that she was equally confident in whom she was. In later years she would become superintendent. She would be assailed by whites as being discriminatory against them. She would be assailed by black males as being a feminist to the extreme. She would be accused of currying the favor of powerful female community leaders to accomplish her goals and objectives. While I'm sure that she was guilty of all of these accusations, because of the way she treated me that first day I never joined any of the aforementioned bandwagons. Her reputation for vindictiveness in dealing with her detractors earned her the nickname "dragon lady."

Over the years I gained her respect as a more than capable administrator and supervisor. My reputation and abilities for promoting success for my students and developing teacher skills to an optimum held me in her high esteem. On several occasions she asked me to conduct staff development workshops for my fellow supervisors. In the final analysis, I always knew where I stood with her. She once told me, "Ken, you need to be a principal, but it won't happen here." It wasn't going to happen anywhere else either, I thought. The '70's were a time wherein every school district was playing the favorite son game. It wasn't what you knew but who you knew that counted. In this district, however, the game was not applicable. The favorite daughter one was played here. Whoever invented the web site Amazon.com must have been a male who spent some time teaching in this district.

How could this go on? you ask. Aren't there laws? Certainly. From time to time Federal surveys designed to identify the ethnic makeup of a school district's teaching and administrative staff would be conducted. Those districts which did not meet the federal reference point for acceptable ethnic diversity in its teaching and supervisory pedagogical staff were put on non-compliance notice and given a specified period to become compliant. If they did not, various federal funds earmarked for that district would be held back. The non-compliant districts responded predictably. First, they asked for time extensions and usually received them. Secondly, in so far as the teaching staff was concerned, they simply called downtown and ordered up the missing ethnic ingredients. With regard to meeting the ethnic diversity requirement in their administrative and supervisory ranks they played the game expertly. As per contractual agreement every vacant administrative and supervisory position must be "advertised" for a specific period—usually a month or two. For each vacancy, a minimum of ten applicants must be garnered from the hundreds that come in. Another month or two. The "lucky" ten are then invited to the district offices for interviews. Another month or two. The pool is then reduced to three "lucky" candidates. That's right, another month or two. The superintendent interviews these "lucky" individuals, declares that none are fit, and orders the process redone. Given this procedure, it is easy to see that the process of filling an administrative/supervisory vacancy could take two or three years to complete. By the way, all that I've described is regarded as reasonable and not in any way a violation; it just defies imagination. Also, it promotes instability and lower staff morale within the districts engaged in such a practice.

Of course, it promotes a "swinging door" environment, through which the more talented people in a district seek upward mobility in other districts. In the end, once again the children suffer. Excellence in education, for sure, is attributable to instructional delivery. Teachers who deliver a high level of instruction must be encouraged to keep it up. Teachers who aren't must be aided and assisted to achieve that level. The school supervisor above all other duties must provide for the development of the teaching novice. Without that kind of talented school supervisor, the battle is lost and the children are the ultimate victims.

The '70's and '80's were to education as the roaring '20's were for the American public—good times! Principalships, Assistant (Vice) Principalships, Superintendent positions, Deputy Superintendents' positions, and most of the district coordinatorships all had a pricetag. Occasionally, some muckraker or whistleblower would expose a particular district for such actions; and everyone else would lay low for a year, and then come back in force often doubling their prices to make up for lost time. During my time in the district, I was approached on two occasions with the suggestion that $7500 could secure my selection for a principalship I was interviewing for. I knew that an acceptance of such an offer would do nothing more than serve as a bookmark for my demise. At that point I asked myself the two questions that someone who aspires to be a principal asks: Could I do it? I knew that I could do the job, as I had on no less than three occasions served as "Acting Principal" with a high rate of success. Accordingly, my response to the bribe offer was a polite "No thanks." I never regretted it. The consequence to my actions was such that from time to time I found myself in a position of having to "prop up" lesser qualified individuals who indeed had paid the price. On the flip side, maintaining my position as Assistant Principal kept me in the midst of student affairs. Nothing could be finer. To influence and be looked upon as an influence by the students under your charge was as good as it gets. To enjoy the confidence of their parents and teachers as you make hundreds of decisions each week on their behalf is the highest endorsement one could seek in a school. Whether I was settling a pupil dispute, conferencing with teachers to improve their craft, demonstrating a teaching technique, or communicating with parents, I was an integral component in the "teaching/learning relationship." As such I was at my best!

Chapter XIX

Making New Friends

Following Ms. Rios 's directive I reported to John Paul Jones JHS promptly at 8:30 a.m. on Monday. As I approached the Principal's Office, I took note of a pencil-thin figure dressed in overalls, head adorned with a kerchief not quite covering two protruding pig tails, and hands busily dusting a shelving area near the opposite end of the office doorway. A portable radio newscast was highlighting security plans for the impending Republican convention in Miami. I knocked on the door and inquired as to the whereabouts of Principal Mary. You're looking at her or at least part of her came a shrill reply. Turning to face me, Ms. Mary welcomed me and invited me to sit down. Shortly she halted her dusting and came around to where I was seated. Ms. Rios called me Friday afternoon and advised me that you had been assigned to fill our assistant principal's vacancy. I know your first name is Ken, how do you pronounce your last name? Two syllables...Ka...ssell as opposed to Castle, I said. Easy enough, she said. Studyng Ms. Mary's appearance, I thought I was looking at Daisy Mae of "Lil' Abner" fame from the funny pages of *The Sunday Daily News*. While slight of stature physically, she was a giant in hospitality and courtesy. Have you had breakfast Ken? No, I haven't. Ms. Rios tells me that you're partial to coffee and buttered roll. I hope you don't mind, I've taken the liberty to send out for those items, as well as an iced tea for myself. No, not at all, I responded. Thank you. She then went on to say that she understood that I had spent the better part of last week being ignored. That won't ever happen here. Tell me what subject areas have you supervised? Social Studies, Foreign Language, and Physical Education. Which grade levels have you supervised?

Seventh, eighth, and ninth, including all aspects of the senior activities program…prom, yearbook, guest speaker— the works, I said. Very well, was her reply. I'm assigning you as the seventh grade supervisor in charge of social studies, foreign language, industrial arts, and home economics.

As Ms. Mary finished her statement, seemingly on cue a gnome- like rotund woman entered the room with beads of sweat pouring down her face. I hope I'm not interrupting, she said, in a surprisingly deep voice, but I have what you ordered, Ms. Mary. Great, replied Patricia Mary. This is Ken Kassell; he is our newly assigned Assistant Principal and among other things will take on the supervision of the home economics department. It's good to meet you, I'm Ms. Priddy, if there is ever anything I can do, please don't hesitate to ask. I'll remember that, I said, and thank you for the breakfast snacks. See you all later, Ms. Priddy declared as she retreated from the office. She is invaluable to me, Ms. Mary remarked. She is the Home Economics Department. During the course of the year we have any number of meetings and special events. Her artistry in seeing to it that everything is just right is the envy of every principal in the district. Throughout the year as we celebrate the various "special events themes," it is her expertise that enhances the caliber of our bulletin boards and assembly presentations. The gopher, I thought to myself. Every school has one. That's great, I exclaimed.

As I sat having breakfast with Ms. Mary, she informed me that the school administration had two other Assistant Principals and an Administrative Assistant. Additionally, she related that there were two Guidance Counselors and two Deans (behavioral modification counselors). She went on to say that she had "checked me out" and learned that I had been forcibly transferred because of my lack of seniority, contrary to my principal's wishes. They sure do a lot of checking, I thought to myself. You will find that I'm very supportive and do expect people to carry out their assignments in a timely fashion. I'm very big on role definition. What about suspensions, I asked. We use the same criteria here as in Harlem, Mr. Kassell. Just keep me posted. And now I'm sure you'll want to see your office and set up your files. If there is anything you might need in the way of supplies such as file folders, construction papers, writing tablets, etc., please ask Ms. Priddy. Let's meet back here at 12:30 and bring agenda copies you intend to have for your first subject and grade meetings. I'll see that they are typed for you. That won't be necessary, I said. I prefer to do all my own typing. I just need to have a manual typewriter in my office. I'll put it on my list for Ms. Priddy, she said assuredly. We have three secretaries in the school, Mr. Kassell. Then I guess mine will always be able to assist the others when their typing gets backed up, I said, as I exited the room leaving no room for further discussion. My real reasons for doing my own typing were twofold. I believed that teacher observation reports should be typed and in the teacher's hands within two to three days of the post-observation conference. I always felt that to delay was unprofessional. School secretaries were often sidetracked by any number of clerical assignments in the main office and would usually put the typing of such reports on the back burner. Secondly, if I wanted to reprimand someone in writing, I didn't want the whole school to know about it. Always remember, if you want to know what's going on in a school, ask the secretarial staff. Having brought a number of office supplies with me, I went to my car and picked up the box I'd packed them in. Returning to the school, I was met by Ms. Priddy who happily exclaimed, your typewriter is in your office. The room number is 220. Here are your keys. Thank you, I said; thank you very much.

Early on during the months of September and October, I concentrated on setting a tone and a philosophy by which I would administer my grade and supervise my departments. I held to the belief that teachers and students had a right to be able to predict my behavior as related to the things that they were doing correctly, and not doing correctly. I went to great lengths to establish clearly definable routines and practices for both constituents. Each morning prior to entering the school, I held mini "standing" assemblies in the yard. During this time, I would refer to such matters as tardiness, class cutting, doing ones homework, and test preparation to mention a few. In inclement weather we used the auditorium for our gathering. With regard to daily A.M. initial routines, after allowing ten minutes for settling down, I then visited each class on my grade. The visits weren't terribly long, and eventually they became non-disturbing parts of everyone's routine. During these informal visits, I made mental note of classroom bulletin boards, and overall room appearance. Did they display current or dated pupil work samples? Was the subject area taught by that teacher properly represented? Did the teacher post the necessary administrative notices in their mandated designated areas, i.e., fire drill chart showing the stairwell egresses and bell schedule? Did the front door depict the teacher's program and class program card? What about the condition of the pupil wardrobe? Were there any mechanical problems in the room? Broken furniture? Did the chalkboard reflect the school heading and lesson aim? What did the floors look like? What did the inside of the pupil desks look like? What were the students doing during their fifteen-minute official class time? While it sounds like a lot, all of the things I've cited and more can be gleaned in a matter of minutes to the trained eye. The follow up where warranted would be "informal" written notes either praising a teacher for attempting to provide a wholesome learning atmosphere or reminding a teacher that a specific area needs improvement. By the way, there's no such thing as an informal note. These notes, while not copied to one's professional file, may serve as a building block for referencing a teacher's non-attentiveness to a request by such a note for a specific corrective action. Of course, such mundane matters as monitoring pupil traffic during change of period, dismissing one's class on time, and not putting students "out" were matters of constant address and redress. The carrying out of just such a routine gave rise to the following incident:

It was three days from Halloween. I had warned my students repeatedly about the severe penalties for bringing in or throwing any contraband items about the school or at anyone in the school. I informed my teachers that I expected maximum supervision of their students at all times, especially in the hallways during class changes. It was Friday, October 31st. Thankfully, there had been no incidents leading up to today. As the bell for period one sounded, I took my place in the hall and noted that doors were opening and teachers were dismissing their classes orderly and maintaining a vigil as the hall traffic moved along. Unlike the teachers, I did not remain stationary but rather moved along the hall with the students checking that bathroom doors were secure and that stairwell landings and vestibules had no backlog or jamup. At once everyone froze. The loud "pop" was heard everywhere. After the pause, a stampede of students could be seen running towards me from the opposite end of the hall. Moving towards them, several students reported that another student named Juan had firecrackers and had lit one at the top of the stairwell at the other end of the hallway and thrown it down in the path of students coming up the stairwell. That was no firecracker, I thought to myself. Sounded like a good old-fashioned cherrybomb. Thankfully, there were no injuries reported.

Approaching the suspect stairwell, I was joined by the Dean. Herman Walters stood about 6'2". He was on the thin side and had served in his present capacity for at least ten years. His knowledge of and familiarity with the pupil population and their families was a great natural resource for the school. Opening the door to the staircase vestibule, we saw Juan standing at the upper level. Juan just stand still; drop whatever you're holding, Dean Walters commanded. We escorted Juan back to Dean Walter's office. A search of his bookbag and outer jacket pockets revealed two matchbooks and three cherry bombs. Mr. Walters, I'm going downstairs to report this to Ms. Mary. She's not here, Walters remarked. I was downstairs a few minutes ago to pick up my mail and noticed her leaving the school to attend some district meeting. It's your call, Mr. K! Quickly I recalled that during my orientation meeting with Ms. Mary when the question of suspensions came up, her reply was that it was the same as I had experienced in Harlem, and that I was to "keep her abreast." OK. Let's make sure that we have a detailed anecdotal account as to what happened. Be specific as to date, time, and place of occurrence. Be sure to describe the fact that the incident took place during the change of periods. Attach any statements you can get from student witnesses. Make sure those statements are signed and dated. They should also reference the student's official class.

Turning to Juan, I said, "Juan do you understand that you've done a terrible thing, that you could have seriously hurt someone, even yourself?" Juan nodded affirmatively. He offered the excuse that his older brother gave the cherry bombs to him. I told him that I would have to have his phone number so that I could inform his mother what he had done and that he was going to be suspended for five school days. But she doesn't speak English, Juan exclaimed. Not your problem, I said. Give me the phone number. Mr. Walters, do you think that you can arrange for Ms. Lopez to be relieved from class at this time? She's absent replied Walters. Very well, the next best is me. On the third ring the phone was answered. Buenos dias, I said. Me llamo es Sr. Kassell, el principal assistante de la escuela, John Paul Jones. Juan's eyes lowered in disappointment while

Walter's eyes reflected surprise and with an affirmative head nod approval. I went on to ask Mrs. Gomez if she could come to the school right away to pick Juan up. She told me that she could not but that she would be waiting for him at the end of the day. She then asked to speak to him. I handed the phone to Juan and within moments tears began to fall. The last thing I heard Juan say was, yes, mamma.

Turning to Dean Walters, I asked, is there a specific suspension form that you use? Yes, he said, I have some, and they're pre-signed by Ms. Mary. Do you have any written in Spanish? On the reverse side. Excellent. I filled in the suspension charges with adjectives taken from a Spanish-English dictionary supplied by Mr. Walters. In English they translated to endangering the safety and welfare of others as well as himself, inciting a riot, and possession of contraband. I made four copies of the suspension notification—one for Principal Mary, one for Dean Walters, one for registered mailing, and one for Juan to hand deliver to his mom later that afternoon. I'm going downstairs now. I have a few minutes before lunch duty, and I want to fill out the necessary school incident report. We don't do those in this school, Walters admonished. I haven't been told that, Mr. Walters, and I didn't hear you.

Incident reports are routinely filled out and filed with the NYC Board of Education's Division of School Safety. In the '80's the Teacher's Union protested vehemently that many incidents, particularly those causing injury to their workforce, were going unreported by school principals. In some cases it was alleged that principals perpetrated acts of intimidation towards teachers who wanted to file such reports. In other scenarios, protesting teachers who did not have seniority or regular appointment status were simply dismissed if they objected. While untenured principals were extremely paranoid about the fact that the filing of incident reports could serve as fodder for tenure denials, the division of school safety acting as a separate agency from the central board maintained that the filing of these reports were the determining factor in the number of school security guards that would be assigned to a particular school.

I refer to this situation because for me it marked the beginning of an almost two decade era of ultra-extreme driven liberal policy making by the NYC Board of Education. Ultimately, it can be said that in the face of a climate of constant attack and harangue the system folded its tent. When a system lacks discipline and respect, you do not have a system. To be sure this system caved in to special interests and in the end sacrificed all of its integrity. In the period 1980 to the present, physical attacks on teachers, administrators, and students from parents or intruders, far surpassed any similar period on record. How were such matters handled? For the most part "mealy mouthed" principal superintendent wannabes did everything they could to "squash" the paper trails.

Offending individuals were "wrist-slapped." To compound matters, if an offending student was a special education student, approval had to be given from "downtown" for that student's suspension or removal. More often than not, these "downtown" individuals would take a cavalier attitude and suggest that a more "tolerable" punishment be substituted for the requested one. The irony was that these same downtown people were quick to "call out" a principal if any aspect of mainstream education was being withheld from their youngsters. So why not mainstream justice?

I arrived at the main office just as Ms. Mary was returning from her district meeting. Ms. Mary, do you have a few moments? From what I just heard you'll need more than a few moments. Come on in. Sitting down behind her desk, she said take me through it from A-Z. After I related the entire affair to her, she indicated that she agreed with my recommendation to invoke a principal's five-day suspension on Juan. She instructed me on the number of suspension letter copies to be made and to my surprise admonished me not to forget to fill out an incident report for her signature. I complied with each of her directives.

At 2:45 while sitting in my office, I was pleased to note that it was fast approaching "Miller Time." Thankful that no other untoward incidents had occurred, I prepared to go home. I tidied my desk and placed several folders in my attache case, intending to get to them over the weekend. At that juncture, my phone rang. Picking up the receiver, I heard Ms. Mary's voice. Mr. Kassell, Superintendent Diamond has asked me to inform you that your presence is expected at his office this afternoon at 3:30 to meet with Juan and his advocate. Remembering a conversation I had had with colleagues who knew something of Diamond's modus operandi, that he is non-supportive of the school assistant principals, and coupling this thought with the still fresh memory of his four-day snubbing of me, I replied to Ms. Mary that I had any number of after school activities and appointments which were already in place and regretted that I would not be able to attend his meeting with Juan and his advocate. In an alarmed tone, I heard Ms. Mary say, "Kassell, stay right where you are. I'll call you back." Within a few moments, Ms. Mary called me back and reported that a "pre-suspension" conference was scheduled for 9:30 Monday morning in her office. She went on to say that the meeting would be attended by Juan, his mother, a child advocate, and Mr. Diamond, who was extremely disappointed at my response. I hope he gets over it, I said. As for the others, it gives me a chance to make new friends. Have a nice weekend, Ms. Mary. You too, Mr. Kassell.

Quickly I secured my office, closing and locking the windows, putting a locking mechanism on the phone, shutting the lights off, and locking the door behind me. I hastened off to Dean Walter's office arriving just as he was shutting down. You have a minute, I asked, somewhat out of breath? Sure, he said. He reopened his door, put the light on, and said, what's up? Sitting down and pausing to light a cigarette, I told him of the impending pre-suspension conference for Monday morning. Don't worry; I have all the documentation. That's great. Do you have the cherry bombs? Yes. Good. Let me have one and an envelope. What are you up to, Mr. K? I'm anticipating, Mr. Walters, just anticipating. Walters watched as I cut out a hole from the bottom of the cherry bomb, allowing for the escape of the stored gunpowder from within. I examined the fuse and satisfied that it was in good working order, I placed the cherry bomb in the envelope and marked it as Juan's contraband. Handing it back to Dean Walters, I instructed that he put it back under lock and key and be sure to bring it with him to the hearing. He nodded affirmatively. We left the building together exchanging wishes for a nice weekend.

On Monday morning, I checked with Ms. Mary to confirm the hearing. It's still on, she said. See you then. I wondered about her support. No matter, I had a plan. At precisely 9:30, Dean Walters and I reported to Ms. Mary's office for the hearing. As we entered I noted two vacant chairs at the far end of the table. Walters saw them as well, and we sat ourselves in them. Ms. Mary chaired the head of the table. Superintendent Diamond sat to Ms. Mary's immediate left. He appeared to be scowling at me. No matter. To his right was seated a very prim and proper looking woman wearing a scotch plaid vest over a white cashmere sweater. I took her to be the Advocate. Opposite were seated Juan and his mom, who was nervously fidgeting with some beads worn around her neck. A sixth person I recognized was Ms. Lopez, the seventh grade Spanish teacher. Oh, and let's not forget the tape recorder that was placed in the center of the table. Ms. Mary stated that for purposes of officially recording everyone's presence, each attendant should state his or her name and roll. Thus, I learned that Ms. "Prim" was in reality a certain

Isabel MacGregor, NYC Child Advocate. Upon completing this ritual, Superintendent Diamond took over. We will proceed in this way: I will read into the record the charged violations. After which Juan's representatives may ask questions of anyone present. That said, he read the charges. The charges were re-read in Spanish by Ms. Lopez. At the conclusion of Ms. Lopezs' reading, Ms. MacGregor stood up and stated that she wished to protest these charges and proceedings. She maintained that the entire episode was a violation of Juan's rights. The bookbag search and outerwear pocket search were illegal; and consequently, any so-called contraband recovered because of that search could not be used as evidence to support the charges. Accordingly, she concluded, I ask Superintendent Diamond to overrule Ms. Mary's suspension and to reinstate Juan immediately. To my great amazement I heard Diamond say, "That's not going to happen." MacGregor's face turned beet red, which in turn gave off a real glow when contrasted against her scotch plaid vest. She couldn't have been more than twenty-two or twenty-three. She'll be glowing all right, I thought to myself. Wait until she sees my presentation. This day would not soon be forgotten by her or for that matter anyone else in the room.

As a result of Superintendent Diamond's rebuke, in a somewhat desperate mode, Ms. MacGregor, while frantically searching through her notes, replied that the suspension had been enacted by the assistant principal, which was a violation of Board of Education guidelines that stipulated only the principal could exact a pupil suspension. Once again I was pleasantly surprised to hear Ms. Mary state that if one read that particular regulation to its end, one would find that it contained a provision for the principal to delegate the use of his or her name as a signatory to the suspension letters but that such letters could not be distributed without the principal's full knowledge, understanding, and approval. I can assure everyone here that

Kenneth S. Karcinell

Mr. Kassell thoroughly debriefed me and as a result, I gave my consent to the request for a "principal's five-day suspension" of your client, Juan. I thought MacGregor would explode. Her face was crimson. Diamond looked with amazement in Ms. Mary's direction. I'd like a five-minute break, MacGregor said. Granted, replied Superintendent Diamond. Act I was over. Act II, as in the case of most theatrical productions, would be a bit spicier.

During the break, I tried to assess everyone's position. Ms. Mary was a trooper. Given the opportunity to be supportive, she was. Diamond was another story entirely. Clearly he was a "sellout." He seemed to be waiting for a moment to seize upon some perceived impropriety on my part to justify a compromise proposal he had in mind. The sicilian expression "una persona il de respecto" (a person not to be respected) was a perfect description of the man. Ms. MacGregor, for all intents and purposes had a certain missionary appeal. And poor Mrs. Gomez had a look on her face that clearly wished for expediency over debate.

As the five-minute break expired, Superintendent Diamond reconvened the meeting. He stated that this was a non-adversarial meeting and that he was certain a compromise agreement could be worked out. To hell it could, I thought. We'll begin the meeting with a statement from Mr. Kassell. Looking at me directly, he said you have the floor. Be brief. For sure, he was extending a courtesy. Equally so, he was communicating that a decision in his mind had already been made regardless of what I had to say. Before I begin...Just a moment, interrupted Ms. MacGregor. During the break, I had a discussion with Juan. Juan admits that he was wrong and understands that his behavior was unacceptable. I for one feel that it is ludicrous for Juan to miss five days of school over a harmless firecracker prank, after all no one was hurt, she concluded. I'm inclined to agree, chirped in Superintendent Diamond.

Do I still have the floor, I asked sarcastically. I said you did, responded Diamond in an annoyed tone. Thank you. I'd like to ask Ms. Lopez if she is satisfied that Mrs. Gomez is in complete understanding of all that has been said thus far. Exactly, blurted Ms. MacGregor. She speaks no English. How do you know that she understood you when you called her on the phone? Because I spoke to her in Spanish, Ms. MacGregor. Do you speak Spanish? MacGregor was non-responsive. Please go on with your presentation, urged Superintendent Diamond. Very well, I said. I'd like everyone to follow me to the scene of the crime. Really, exclaimed Ms. MacGregor. Let's proceed, directed Diamond. With that the entire contingency arose and followed me to the number five stairwell. Standing atop the stairwell and peering down at my captive audience, I said, "It wasn't a harmless firecracker that Juan was throwing, Ms. MacGregor. It was a cherry bomb. Ever see one? She shook her head in the negative. Ever hear one? Again, the head shook in the negative. I didn't think so. Mr. Walters, if you don't mind, would you pass me the evidence?" Certainly. In this bag there are three cherry bombs and two books of matches taken from Juan's bookbag. Proceed, Mr. Kassell, prompted Mr. Diamond. Very well. I hold in my right hand a cherry bomb. Really is there some point to all this, Mr. Kassell, screeched MacGregor? Getting there, I said. As you can see they are about the size of a cherry pepper. It is filled with one oz. of gunpowder, which in turn may be set off by lighting the a three second fuse protruding from the top. Holding the cherry bomb I had previously "fixed," I placed the lit end of my cigarette to the fuse and threw the cherry bomb down the stairs where they were gathered. Everyone but me and Walters ran or ducked for cover. Of course, the fuse fizzled and nothing happened. Shortly, I counciled, You can all come back now. Oh, did I neglect to tell you that for purposes of this experiment I had removed the gunpowder? The reaction that was demonstrated by you, Ms. MacGregor, Ms. Lopez, Mrs. Gomez, Juan, Ms. Mary and you, Superintendent Diamond was nothing compared to the reaction of several hundred students who were literally stampeded down the halls in a complete fear-driven panic. I rest my case."

In a trembling voice, Ms. MacGregor muttered, "You're crazy. You should not be allowed anywhere near children. I'm leaving here now." She got up and seemingly stumbled towards the exit stairwell. Dean Walters was quick to come to her aid and personally escorted her out to her car. Returning to Ms. Mary's office, I saw Superintendent Diamond speak directly into the tape recorder mike. "Under the circumstances, I find that the grounds for Juan Gomez' five-day suspension are valid and the suspension stays." As Ms. Lopez had also fled the scene, I translated Mr. Diamond's decision for Ms. Gomez. She got up, extended her hand toward me, and simply said, gracias.

Over the course of the next several years I was reported twice to the Child Advocacy Agency by parents who were upset by my suspension record. In both instances, the agency informed the parents that the resources of the advocate's office were minimal and that their advocates were handling matters that were more highly prioritized than the complaint that they were lodging. They advised the parents to meet with me and make all attempts to "reason" out their differences.

Superintendant Diamond and I continued sparring and jousting over the next several years. One such joust had to do with a Step I grievance adjudicated by him.

Chapter XX

The Brinkman Grievance

Don Brinkman was a man of little distinction barring his usual slobbery appearance. He was about 6' and weighed close to 300 lbs. From all indications he had no real ties to his fellow teachers. He had been transferred into the school after having some difficulty in his previous assignment. His colleagues in the Physical Education Department thought he was "weird." The chairman of the department had informed me that whenever he tried to advise Brinkman, that he was quickly rebuffed.

As I was in charge of this department, I was expected to observe each member during an instructional lesson. When it came time for Brinkman's observation I made sure to go exactly by the book (teacher's contract). I sent him a written form requesting that he meet with me at a specific time for purposes of "pre-observation" conferencing. The note required that he sign for its receipt and indicate if he would attend such a meeting. By contractual agreement, attendance may not be required at a pre-observation meeting. Nevertheless the teacher was obligated to sign the form as to his/her intention to attend. This document then served to show that the opportunity to attend such a planning meeting had been properly extended. In my twenty-five years as a supervisor, Brinkman was the only teacher who declined the invitation. In my observation report, his declination was documented via the use of the terminology "Pre-Observation conference offered and waived on (date)." Of course, the observation went ahead as scheduled. Following the lesson observation visit, the teacher's contract provided for a supervisor/teacher post-observation conference. Attendance by the teacher is required. Usually, at this conference, one tries to create an air of give and take. When Brinkman sat down, I passed him the rough draft of my observation report, lit up a True Blue, and sat back and studied his contorted facial expressions as he read through it. Ordinarily, I would have begun the conference by simply asking the teacher what he/she had thought about the lesson. From the stand point of growth and development, a supervisor should hold to the belief that teachers are apt to be honest about their instructional delivery, and do want to identify weaknesses and do want to find ways to improve. When Brinkman saw that under the heading "corrective criticism" there were no less than fourteen such criticisms, he became very agitated. "Are you fuckin' crazy? You don't know who you're fuckin' with; I'm from Bayridge." Snatching up my notes, he got up and left my office indicating that he "was taking this to the union." Undeterred, I opened my desk drawer and removed a photocopy of those notes and went over to my Raleigh, and began the process of putting my informal notes into a formal lesson observation report. I wanted Brinkman to have it before 3 p.m. Of course, I ran it past Ms. Mary who was somewhat amused by my recounting of Brinkman's reactions during our post-observation conference. She approved the document for file placement and arranged for Mr. Brinkman and the union delegate to report to her office so as to formerly present Brinkman with the report to assure him that its presentation was complying with all professional standards. Brinkman took the report from Ms. Mary and quietly signed it. Almost immediately, the union rep presented Ms. Mary with a request for a Step I grievance hearing, at which time the union would maintain that the report was inaccurate, arbitrary, and capricious. A day later the hearing was held, and a day after that Ms. Mary's findings were such that there was no substantiation to the union's charges; she therefore denied the grievance. The teacher's union fully expected Mary's response to be a denial. Consequently, they filed for a Step II Grievance

Hearing with the Superintendent's secretary. Mr. Diamond scheduled the hearing for three days hence and had his secretary send me by special messenger a typed memo as to the date, time, and place the hearing would be conducted. Of course, I had to sign for it and indicate my intention to attend the hearing and give it right back to the messenger immediately. I found the exercise amusing.

Seated at the superintendent's conference table was Mr. Diamond at its head. To his immediate left was Ms. Mary and to her left, myself. On the opposite side to Mr. Diamond's right were the school union rep, Mr. Outlaw, the district union liaison, Mr. Mittleman, and Mr. Brinkman. Seated at a smaller table just to Superintendent Diamond's right was a recording secretary who would take the minutes. Superintendent Diamond opened the conference by addressing procedural groundrules. Ladies and gentlemen, we'll proceed thusly: I'll allow three minutes at the outset for everyone to have an opportunity to preview the document in question. Following that activity, the union rep will state his specific grievance, then Mr. Brinkman may have the floor for whatever purpose he may require. Ms. Mary or her designee will then have an opportunity to respond. Are we all clear? Everyone quickly nodded in the affirmative. I must be the designee I thought. Does everyone have a copy of the document? Very well then, let's have the grievance, Mr. Outlaw. Once again the union's contention that the report was inaccurate, arbitrary and capricious was stated as the foundation for the grievance. Was there a Step I hearing, asked Mr. Diamond? Yes, there was. Its outcome, asked Superintendent Diamond? Ms. Mary denied the grievance. What specific areas of this report does the grievant wish to contest, Diamond asked. All of it, replied Outlaw. That's impossible, declared Diamond in a raised and agitated voice. Let's take a five-minute break and try to narrow things down somewhat. Following the break, Diamond asked Outlaw which of the fourteen criticisms did his client wish to grieve. Diamond's strategy became quite clear. He was going to compromise matters by simply directing that the three or four most grievous items be identified and that the report be rewritten with those items stricken. Brinkman wasn't going for it. At this point, I wish to yield to my client Mr. Brinkman, who shall continue with our presentation announced Outlaw. Proceed, said a reluctant Diamond.

Brinkman stood up and began to read a diatribe of verbosity attacking each of the fourteen criticisms. After thirty minutes and just prior to Brinkman reading his attack on item ten, Ms. Mary asked for a five-minute recess. Request denied, snarled Diamond. I have to use the ladies' room. Five minutes, he said. After the break Brinkman resumed his reading. And 20 minutes after that he resumed his seat. You may respond, Mr. Kassell directed Superintendent Diamond. To what? I said. Point of Order, sir, if I may. Proceed. Mr. Brinkman, unlike myself, has not had the courtesy to furnish each of us with a copy of the document he just read. I would need at least a day to properly prepare a rebuttal. Standing and slamming his palm onto the surface of the oak conference table and staring directly into my face with his nostrils fully expanded, Diamond bellowed, "That's not going to happen. For the record I'm ordering you to respond to any damn thing you wish to or nothing at all. If you take option two, then I will have no choice but to find in favor of the grievant." In that case, sir, I advise that you clear your calendar because after Brinkman there will be at least seven others coming your way. I make no compromises when it comes to moving against such incompetents. Upon investigation these individuals were allowed to ply their trade during your watch. So you find, however you will, and I'll just keep sending them your way. Maybe you'll get it right this time. I turned and left. I heard no objection, only silence.

Two days later, I received a note from Superintendent Diamond that simply read:

Dear Mr. Kassell,

Thanks for the wakeup call. Your observation report is to stand as written. Carry on!

Barry Diamond

That same day I received a note from the district union rep, Mr. Mittleman, requesting that I meet with him on very urgent business. I called his office and arranged for a 3 p.m. meeting that same day.

Good afternoon, Mr. Mittleman, I said. And to you, Mr. Kassell, I want to congratulate you. That was quite a performance. Thanks for the compliment. It was not a performance. I am a well-trained supervisor who pretty much knows how far he can go in pushing people's buttons. What do you have on your mind? I asked. By the way, is this meeting on or off the record? Off, if you like. I do, I said. Granted. Mittleman sat back in his naugerhide captain's chair and pondered for a moment obviously contemplating his next statement carefully. He was a flashy suave type. His suit was an obvious Armani. The coloring was sharkskin grey. His long sleeved cufflinked shirt, no doubt a Brooks Brothers purchase, which served to validate the overall appearance of self- importance, which was further validated by the presence of a blue star sapphire fire pinky ring. The role of a district union rep was to simply oversee the district wide union operation and to provide support and assistance to the school- based reps. They usually teach an abbreviated schedule and maintain an

Kenneth S. Karcinell

office in their school. They sustain their existence by "not losing."

Leaning over his desktop, he looked me in the eye and simply said, I had you checked out. You're good. He must have been the third person that had had me checked out. My face must have shown my amusement. What's so funny? he asked. I exclaimed, you people in Brooklyn certainly seem to be preoccupied with the business of checking people out. Did you use the same source as Ms. Rios and Ms. Mary? No, I simply called our Harlem rep. Well, you left out the word "fair," I retorted. Now why am I here, Mr. Mittleman? It's about Brinkman. Two years ago he had a nervous breakdown. At the time, the union assisted him in getting proper health care. I assume you mean a shrink, I said. Exactly. The outcome was that he was diagnosed as suffering from paranoia believing that everyone was out to get him. I must tell you that since the hearing he has been telling anyone who'll listen that he believes that you are out to get him, and he cannot let that happen. Tell him I am, and it will happen. Are you out of your fucking mind? You call me here to see if I have the courage of my own convictions, under the guise that one of your members is a lunatic, and you are concerned with my safety. I regard that as a threat, a veiled one albeit, but nevertheless a threat. You'd better get him a union transfer to another school because as soon as I get back tomorrow, I'm going to critique his lesson plans. What do you think a slew of red markings all over his plan book will do for his psyche? I'm telling you get this sick fuck out of the school. It's on you, Mr. Mittleman. Good-bye!

As soon as I left, Mittleman picked up his phone and dialed a number. You were right. We'll have to move Brinkman, and I got a feeling he's just the tip of the iceberg. Wonderful, replied Superintendent Diamond. I didn't realize what a mess I'd left. Kassell is a godsend.

Unaware as to the conspiracy between Diamond and the teacher's union rep I went about my business routinely. I would continue to seek to weed out the ineffectual and incompetent individuals who were under my direct supervision. To give you an idea of the time and effort involved in ridding a school of just one such individual, I've provided for your edification a series of documents involving a teacher we'll call Mr. Broome. To say that his behavior was erratic would be an understatement.

Chapter XXI

The BroomeFile

October 5, 1976

Mr. Broome:

The purpose of this letter is for you to indicate in writing, by whose authority you held your 7th, 8th, and 9th period classes in the schoolyard?

Sincerely,

Kenneth Kassell
Assistant Principal

Broome's Reply: Earth Science.
The Power invested in me by authority of the Board of Education.

October 14, 1976

Mr. Broome:

In spite of the fact that you have been advised not to take science classes to the schoolyard, it has come to my attention that you escorted class 9-5 period #2 on Monday to the school yard.

Once again I ask that you state your reason for doing this and by whose authority you acted?

Sincerely,

Kenneth Kassell
Assistant Principal

XXX_____

Teacher's Signature Acknowledging Receipt

Date:_____

Reply:

October 17, 1976

Mr. Broome:

This letter is to serve as a reminder that your lesson plans were due to me on 10/14/76. As discussed at our Science Dept. Conference (See agenda dated 9/28/76), lesson planning is essential to sound teaching.

Additionally, I remind you that it is the policy of the Principal and district superintendent that all teachers prepare lesson plans and that they be readily available at all times.

Sincerely,

Kenneth Kassell
Assistant Principal
Science Supervisor

Teacher's Signature Acknowledging Receipt: X_____
Date: 10/19/76

> Mark Made by Teacher

Reply:
Observation

11-3-76

Mr. Broome:

As I entered your classroom, I noted that at the rear of the room, seven students were sitting at a table playing cards. As I took my seat, I further noted that in the front of the room, there was a radio on playing Rock music in full blast. The chalkboard was completely bare and appeared to have been recently washed clean. I further noted that there were three students sitting on desktops and two sitting on the windowsills. As I observed the above situation, I noticed that the teacher was engaged in stapling something on the bulletin board. I asked the student who was sitting next to me what the homework assignment was. She stated that "there was none". After sitting in the room for fifteen minutes, it was my conclusion that the teacher made no attempt to rectify or to formally conduct any semblance of a lesson. In response to a note that I sent you for your lesson plan, you made the following statements in the presence of the class:

"I haven't done a lesson plan for 10 years. You, Mr. Kassell, are invading my privacy. Don't come around my room anymore; you are harassing me. You're trying to get rid of me."

Mr. Broome repeatedly asked me, "What are you doing here?" He also stated that, "Mr. Kassell will leave before I do." Referring to himself, Mr. Broome stated, "I cannot be intimidated, but now you (Mr. Kassell) are."

As I continued to conduct my observation, a young lady who appeared to be an intruder, wearing a white science lab jacket, who you, Mr. Broome, identified as Donna, walked over to where I was sitting and stood over me. When I asked her to please move, she in turn berated me.

As stated in my opening paragraph, it was noted that there was no apparent lesson in progress. There was no aim set forth on the chalkboard; I did not hear any classroom discussion; and there was no homework assignment given.

Your responsibility as per school policy is to have a lesson plan each and every day for the classes you teach. Additionally, as per school policy, superintendent's policy, and the Chancellor's policy, you are required to give homework assignments daily. If you disregard these rules (as you stated that "you hadn't done a lesson plan in ten years") it may be judged that you are insubordinate.

Card playing and rock music were inappropriate activities for this science class. These activities did not serve as motivation for the ensuing instructional activities.

Your response to my visit was unprofessional and unsatisfactory. You attempted to engage me in an argument in front of the class. Your tone and manner of speaking was loud and belligerent.

The fact that you knowingly permitted a youngster in your class who is not a JPJ JHS student threatened the safety and security of the class.

I sincerely hope that you will review this report carefully and react in such a way to improve the learning atmosphere for the classes you teach.

Sincerely,

Lesson Rating: UnsatisfactoryKen Kassell
CC: Ms. Patricia Mary, Principal
    Teacher's Professional File

12/1/76

Incident Report

Re: Mr. Broome, Teacher
Prepared By: Mr. K. Kassell, Assistant Principal

On the above date, at approximately 11:45 a.m., a number of students (ten or more—see attached for student statements) came running down the hall, shouting that Mr. Broome "was breaking and throwing chairs." My reaction was to immediately go down the hall directing pupils who were in the halls and running from Mr. Broome's area to their classroom. As I approached Mr. Broome, who was standing in the hall having a heated discussion with a female student, I urged him to calm down. I tried to pat him on the shoulder in a reassuring manner, and at that point Mr. Broome threw up his hands, loudly told me to calm down the students, and then slammed his classroom door in my face.

Upon further investigation a student witness reported that the precipitating incident was an altercation between two boys, and that Mr. Broome's efforts to diffuse the altercation consisted of throwing punches and pushing students in all directions.

Sincerely,

Kenneth Kassell
Assistant Principal

202

February 16, 1977

Mr. Broome:

Today, I was attracted to your room by loud radio music. I indicated to you that we had visitors in the school and that the radio needed to be turned off. As I turned to leave the class I noticed in the rear of the room what was clearly a card game going on. When I mentioned to you that there was a card game going on in the rear of the room you stated loudly and belligerently, "Where is there a card game? If you see it, deal with it." Upon hearing your tone, I merely instructed the boys to cease. They did stop, and as classroom intruders, they left the room.

To permit children to play cards in your classroom (unrelated to the lesson) is immoral. To permit children to gather in your room when they have other classes to attend encourages their corruption and undermines the teaching of your colleagues and is counterproductive to the wishes and goals of their hardworking parents. To continue to allow the radio to play during instructional time at as high a decibel level as you did may in the long-run cause auditory damage to your pupils. Assuredly, its loudness makes it difficult to learn in neighboring classrooms.

Kenneth S. Karcinell

Throughout the two years I've been here, your indiscretions have been of such an overt form (never before seen by myself) and well documented (see notes and letters from the principal, superintendent, and parents) that I am amazed at how you continue with impunity. Nevertheless, albeit, when I remind you or any teacher of unacceptable conditions, I shall expect <u>you</u> to deal with it.

Sincerely,

Kenneth Kassell
Assistant Principal

Cc: File
Supt. Logs~~Teach~~er's Signature
~~X~~4.16.77 .

Teacher's Signature Acknowledging Receipt and Placement in File/Date

3/5/77

Dear Supt. Diamond:

I am continually miffed and amazed at the day-to-day activities of Mr. Broome at JPJJHS. His irrational conduct has become folklore. His provocative behavior towards supervision will one day become an embarrassment to us all. The harm that he is rendering "OUR" children is irreparable, but the blame for his presence is another question entirely, which one day shall indeed, in my opinion, be a question that will not be easily answered.

Day in and day out this man operates under the influence of something other than orange juice. His radical behavior and open hostility towards

204

supervision promotes similar behavior on the part of some of his students toward authority. They quickly learn that if their teacher can go "unchecked," then so can they. The fact that all students seem to know that they can gather at will in his room makes the supervision of the floor impossible. The domino effect is that other teachers no longer seem to respond to supervision as they once did; some who do want to teach are so distracted by Mr. Broome's almost daily outbursts often complain, and ask "can't anything be done?" How shall I answer them?

Sincerely,

Kenneth Kassell
Assistant Principal

4/1/77

Dear Mr. Broome:

You are summoned to attend a disciplinary conference in the Office of the Superintendent on Monday, May 7, 1977 at 3:30 p.m.

This will be a conference for the record. In accordance with the UFT contract, you are entitled to be accompanied by a representative who is employed by the New York City school system or a Union representative who is not a lawyer.

The conference has been called because you allegedly left the building with one of your classes on April 26, 1977 without permission. Additionally, you are charged with playing loud raucous rock music during a period of instruction, after being told by your supervisor to cease and desist from this practise on more than one occasion. Please be advised that your Principal, Ms. Mary and your Assistant Principal Mr. Kassell have been invited to attend this conference as well.

Yours truly,

Barry Diamond
Community Superintendent

Follow up notation:
4/1/77—As of 4:30 p.m. Mr. Broome has not arrived nor the principal either.
KK

4/10/77

Dear Mr. Broome:

You are summoned to appear in the Office of the Community Superintendent on Wednesday, May 16, 1977 at 3:30 p.m. This will be a conference for the record. You are entitled to be accompanied by a representative who is employed by the city school system or an employee of the Union who is not a lawyer.

The conference has been called in response to a report submitted by your principal, Mrs. Patricia Mary that stated that you played loud raucous music during classroom instructional periods and left the building without permission. This conduct occurred on at least two occasions within the last six months. This represents unprofessional and unbecoming behavior. By copies of this letter, I am requesting that Mr. Kenneth Kassell, Assistant Principal, and Mrs. Patricia Mary, Principal, attend the conference.

Very truly yours,

Barry Diamond
Community Superintendant

Follow up Notation:

As of 4 p.m. Mr. Broome did not show up! Absent as well was Mrs. Mary. Mr. Diamond again allowed me to go home and stated that Mr. Broome's failure to be present was grounds for insubordination charges and removal pending the outcome of those charges.

In the last analysis, the thing to remember here is that the teacher in question was not terminated from the system, he was simply removed from the workplace and placed elsewhere; in this case, at the district office pending the promulgation by the superintendent of formal charges. The process would take six months. Ultimately, the teacher's union was able to stall the scheduling of formal hearings until the fall term. All told, the process had been stretched out by two additional months. At the beginning of the fall term, the union requested that its client receive a full medical evaluation from the Board of Education Medical Unit. One has only to visit this unit to see that they themselves are in need of some type of evaluation. Be that as it may, this type of evaluation would consume the remainder of the fall term. My point is not that the particular teacher should be "taken out" of the system but that the process to reach a final determination as to whether he should be removed from the system or whether he should be afforded professional help required almost a year to reach.

If you project this scenario as one that to some degree exists in each of the thirty-two school districts, not to mention the division of High Schools, you can see there may be several hundred individuals of similar plight, costing the city millions.

Chapter XXII

School Board Meeting, Or "Off, Off Broadway"

I came to the belief long ago that when the school in which I was working was to host a school board meeting, that I was professionally obligated to attend and to assist in making those preparations which would bode well for a successful meeting. Therefore, when Ms. Mary asked me if I would be able to attend the school board meeting hosted by our school, I replied, of course. Good, she said, it's tonight. No problem, I assured her. As usual I left the school at 3:15, took my customary forty-five minute ride home, showered, shaved, and took an hour power nap. After a light tuna salad dinner, I was back on the road and on my way to the school where I arrived at 7 p.m., fully one-half hour before the scheduled start of the meeting.

As I entered the school, I was attracted to the auditorium by the muffled tone of several voices. Upon entering the auditorium, my eyes captured the following scene: There was Ms. Priddy and two members of the PTA involved in making such preparations as befitted the occasion. In the rear of the auditorium were placed two 10' long tables. One table contained a coffee urn for thirty-five cups. Alongside it stood a hot water urn and a basket of various tea selections. Of course, there were the usual complement of paper cups, plates and napkins—not the no-name cheap store brand variety. These were the ones that had tasteful floral designs and double ply material. A tray of plastic forks and spoons finished the appointments. On the other table, one could find two large watermelon fruit boats, each containing a very ample assortment of pineapple, cantaloupe, honeydew, and watermelon slices. There also were available a wide selection of homemade baked

209

cookies. Among the choices were: chocolate chip, almond, oatmeal raisin, and butterscotch. Anticipating the presence of youngsters, there were several large bottles of flavored soft drink and two large baskets filled with potato chips and pretzels.

Of further note, each of the tables was covered by an attractive vinyl covering that lent itself to easy washing. Looking about the auditorium, it had been decorated with colorful streamers and various placards welcoming the audience and the school board to John Paul Jones JHS. On the stage again there were the two 10' tables placed side to side in a lengthwise fashion. The tables were cloth-covered and the front areas were skirted by taped-together construction paper. There were seats for eleven individuals—nine board members, a recording secretary, and the superintendent. A microphone was located in the center of the table, as was a pitcher of ice water along with a column of plastic drinking cups. As Ms. Priddy and her assistants scurried about tending to the arrangements, I was reminded of the scene from *Alice in Wonderland* where she encounters the Mad Hatter.

Ladies, can I be of any assistance? Would you go to the office, bring the 200 agenda copies here, and then test out the mike? asked Ms. Priddy. My pleasure, I said, walking off in the direction of the office. Upon my return, Ms. Priddy placed the agenda copies on one of the tables in the rear of the auditorium. Some parents had already arrived and the meeting would be starting shortly. I next tested the mike and determined that it was in good working order. I moved to a rear row and took a seat to observe the proceedings. As the community school board negotiated their way down the center aisle and onto the stage, Ms. Mary and her elves joined me. Ms. Mary suggested that I dim the lights in the audience area to cut down on glare that would reflect back up to the stage. I complied with her wish and retook my seat. It was exactly 7:30. The auditorium was filled to capacity. The security personnel stood at either side of the stage area. The school board led by Superintendent Diamond had made their way onto the stage and had taken their seats. Showtime!

As the audience became quiet, the chairwoman asked that all join in the singing of the anthems, "The Star Spangled Banner," and "Lift Every Voice and Sing." Upon their completion she gave thanks to God. Officially, the meeting commenced with a reading of the minutes from the previous meeting and a motion to accept the minutes as read. Things were moving along at a fairly slow and dull pace. This is usually the case in most Act I scenarios. Things would drastically change in the ensuing moments. Trying to avoid the utter boredom of the moment, I took note of the school board's make-up. To begin with only seven were present. According to their letterhead, there were six women and three men. Thumbing down the list I found what I was looking for: the everpresent "minister."— a man about 6'4" and 250 lbs. I noticed him in reverend garb as the procession was led to the stage at the beginning of the meeting. He fulfilled his role perfectly—tall, dignified, and in possession of a bible tucked under his left armpit. Among the women several who rivaled his girth but not his height. Scanning the agenda I didn't see any item that could be described as provocative. For the most part, each item involved a budgetary concern that needed to be voted on. Usually there has been agreement to these items during the board's executive sessions. By regulation these items have to be presented in an open forum for additional clarification to the public before an official vote can be taken. However, there was one item of particular concern to Ms. Mary. Earlier in the day, I was present in her office when she had summoned the PTA president to remind her that she had better contact our Board member liaison to remind her that she wasn't having any evening center at "her house." This item would prove to be the "show stopper."

The chair called upon the Recording Secretary to read item five into the record. As had been the case with the previous four items, the matter was then opened up for discussion and inquiry from the audience. Ms. Vetrell, our school's PTA president, was the first to speak. We at the John Paul Jones School feel that our facility is inadequately equipped to host an evening center program. What did the bitch say? asked one of the female board members. Shut the goddamn mike off, bellowed the chairwoman, and someone tell that witch to shut her mouth. The audience was immediately alerted to the change of tone and sat upright in their seats anticipating an upbeat tempo in the moments ahead. The mikes as evidenced by the statement, "who you callin' bitch, bitch?" emanating from the inquiring board member, had not been shut off. No matter, the chairwoman had raised her behemoth girth from her seat and was ever so slowly making her way toward her board colleague who had herself risen to meet the challenge. The audience remained silent and glued to the happenings on stage. The security guards made no move to intercede. They were trained in crowd control tactics as applied to negative audience participation and were not to interfere with the proceedings of the board. I said witch...bitch. On the word "bitch," the offended member grabbed a handfull of the chairwoman's hair, and the chairwoman in turn clasped her teeth around her opponent's ear. Ladies, ladies, I beg of you to cease immediately. Rev. White had himself risen from his seat and approached the combatants with Bible in hand. Neither paid him any mind. Gazing upward and proclaiming, "His will be done," the Rev. grabbed the nearest woman, which happened to be the chairwoman, by her arm and spun her free from her entanglement with her fellow board member, and in the same motion smacked her upside the back of her head with his good book sending her sprawling to the stage floor. On cue, the curtains closed and the audience cheered uncontrollably.

Needless to say, item five was defeated!

Chapter XXIII

Transfer Time...

In August of 1981, upon my return from summer vacation, I was summoned to Superintendent Diamond's office. As I had been a good boy the previous semester, I could not guess at what the matter was.

Reporting as directed, Mr. Diamond's secretary announced my arrival. Have him come right in; I heard Diamond's recognizable voice order. I let myself into Mr. Diamond's office. Ken, it's good to see you, began Superintendent Diamond. Have a seat; I have a serious matter to discuss with you. Ken? Hmmn! Why did my neck hairs stand on edge, I wondered to myself. Almost immediately my mind flashed a "Warning...Beware sign." Throughout your brief tenure here in the district you have garnered the respect of many, myself included. True we've had our moments, but I always respected you as a worthy adversary. More important than all of that, however, is what you stand for that has caused me to call upon you today. Here it comes, I thought.

We have a relatively new JHS in the district that to say the least, at the present time is floundering. I was very aware of the school. It was two years old and with each passing day an embarrassment. The building had been designed by Diamond. The Principal and Assistants had been handpicked by Diamond, as had most of the support staff. While the Principal was generally regarded as a "nice man" and a gentleman, his great fault was that he was not a listener, and he did not allow others to share in the decision-making processes. Of course looking back, there weren't too many on that staff with whom I would have shared the decision-making process with either.

214

Diamond continued, I have decided to "sure up" the administrative staff with proven, experienced JHS people. I think that given your skills, penchant for detail, knowledge of the teacher's contract, and ability to relate to the student body, that you are an ideal person to put into that environment. What do you say? Do I really have a say? No, no you don't. Is the Principal aware of your plan? I said. Diamond replied that he enthusiastically endorses it. When? I queried. Allowing for you to gather your things from John Paul Jones, you are expected by noon tomorrow. In response, I had one last question. Am I the only one? No, do you know Ms. Hatcher? Only from supervisory meetings held in the district office. She'll be joining you as well. She brings a wealth of experience and like you is well versed in her knowledge of the job with a proven record of success. You and she should get along very well. I'm a soldier, I said. If getting along were my priority, I wouldn't have gotten this far.

If there isn't anything else...in fact there is, Diamond said. The other shoe was about to drop, I thought. Some matters warrant your special talents. I've indicated to Principal Andrews that it was my expectation that you would look into these matters on a prioritized basis and take such corrective action, as you deem necessary. Diamond had gotten my attention with this bit of intrigue. I'm listening, I said in anticipation. To begin with you'll assume the usual department and grade responsibilities. Your administrative assignments however are a direct mandate from me. What do you know about the school? This was a loaded question, the answer to which I was about to get full debriefing on. Therefore, the few things that I did know were not worth mentioning. Nothing, nothing at all, I replied. The school was opened two years ago; I designed it and supervised its construction, Diamond said. I hand picked the instructional staff, the administrative support team, and the Principal. Considering his track record at John

Paul Jones, I could not determine if Diamond was proud of the fact or if he was divulging his secrets as another embarrassment. I decided not to interrupt him. Within a year there was an electrical fire, which is the reason that the school PA system and its elevator is more often than not inoperable. The central air conditioning system is workable in about fifty percent of the building. More than $50,000 in texts, "small equipment" (typewriters, cameras, VCR's, and TV's) learning kits, and general supplies has never been received.

To all of these problems I want answers and solutions. Diamond sat back in his chair, seemingly inviting me to respond. If the school was only two years old, then why aren't the contractors being held to the task of proper repair? The electrical contractors were "fly by nighters" and cannot be found. The air conditioner installers have declared bankruptcy. The police have had their ears to the ground within the community and have not located a single TV, VCR or camera. They're looking in the wrong place, I calmly said. This startled Diamond. You know where these things are, he blurted. Not specifically, I replied. In general terms, however, they are wherever the books are. Ask yourself, if you were a truck driver delivering these items all over the city and you wanted to market some "excess" goods, where would you look to do business? Who would gladly pay cut-rate prices for such items? Who Diamond shouted? The private schools. You can forget about recovering them. But I'm very curious as to how it was done. I'll keep you informed.

After reporting to the school, I had a meeting with Principal Andrews. Outwardly, he was a tall, thin, stately looking man of African-American descent. He warmly welcomed me, inviting me into his office. Putting his suit jacket on, he joined me at the conference table. I was made aware by the superintendent that you and Ms. Hatcher were being transferred into the school to join the administrative support team here. I want you to know how welcome you are. I intend to say the same to Ms. Hatcher. You shall supervise grade eight, the social studies, and math departments along with physical education. The eighth grade is our senior class. Not a problem, I replied. Good, here are your school keys. There's one for your office, a master key for all classrooms, a key to the men's room, and an elevator key. Do not lose the elevator key. It is irreplaceable; don't lose it. I was told the elevator didn't work. Only twenty-five percent of the time, Andrews said with a smile. I know that problem is one of your special mandates to follow up on, as is the ongoing electrical problem and missing inventory.

So far so good! When I began to ask such technical questions as: May I have a list of the teachers and their license status? Which method of writing observation reports do you prefer? or Is there a uniform day for the submission of weekly lesson plans? Principal Andrew's response was whatever works for you. Now I knew there were problems. Indeed, when I got to meet my department members and broached these questions with them, their response was that no one previously had made an issue of these matters. Unsaid was, why are you? Apparently, I had been "checked out" again, with the conventional wisdom being that I not be provoked. There is some value in having one's reputation precede one, I thought. I carefully explained to each department under my supervision what their rights and privileges were in accordance with their license status. On a formalized agenda, I outlined data concerning observations, formal and informal, and lesson plan writing, and collection routines.

From the questions asked, it was clear to me that these matters had not been a priority until I'd made them such. I surveyed the teachers as to how long they had been at the school, and how many times had they been observed or had a discussion with a supervisor as to their teaching craft. Out

217

of fourteen teachers, two said they had been observed the previous year but had never received a written report attesting to the fact. All of that changes today. By week's end you will receive special lesson plan forms. You are to prepare your plans in duplicate and submit them to me each Monday morning by 9 a.m. I will endeavor to send you any critiques I may have before the day is out. We will meet once a week as provided for in your programs during the period designated for "departmental meeting." Oh, one more thing. Next week's meeting agenda will evolve out of the things I observe this week. Therefore, be sure to bring paper and pencil. Please be sure to set up a folder for the maintenance of these agenda so that you will have them at your fingertips for periodic review. If you are ever absent from a meeting, you may expect to find your agenda in your mailbox or may certainly obtain one from me personally. That'll do it for today. Spend your time productively; there's not enough of it.

As they filed out, I realized that the school had few systems of accountability. In what was supposed to be an institution of learning, we had instead an institution of disillusionment. What must the student body be like or for that matter the parent body? What about the school itself— its inner workings, its resources, and its personality?

My next meeting was with the school custodian. I sent him a formal written request for a meeting at a suitable time. Apparently, being somewhat enraged at the audacity of an Assistant Principal to take up his valuable time, he personally appeared at my doorway bright and early the next morning, holding my memo in his hand. I'm honored, Mr. Ritchie. Please come in. Doing so, he closed the door behind him. Where do you get the "balls" to summon me in writing? You should consider yourself privileged, I said, in that your signature was not required. I heard about you, Kassell. Oh no, I thought. I checked you out. You got some reputation. If you had me checked out as you say and if your sources are as good as you want me to think that they are, then you know the true nature of my assignment. As of this moment and not a moment more, you have a career choice to make, Mr. Ritchie—a simple answer to a simple question. In either case, I am prepared to act forthwith. Do you wish to be a part of the problem or a part of the solution? Sitting back, Ritchie took a moment and then extending his hand, he said, maybe we got off to a bad start. I'll try to be as helpful as I can. Shaking his hand, I thanked him, and asked why doesn't the PA system work? Without it, we can't have an "intruder alert" code or an emergency announcement option. He replied, the company that did the job went south, and no one knows where. The School Construction Authority won't let us sub-contract the job to anyone else. Really, we need a re-wiring job. What about the AC system? I asked. Like the elevator, its failure is tied into the fact that the school's wiring system cannot support the full AC system. I see. Well, I've taken up a lot of your time Mr. Ritchie. Aren't you leaving something out queried Ritchie. In response I said, I don't think so. Don't you want to know about the missing books and stuff? Oh, I know you don't have any information on that subject. That's right! Ritchie exclaimed. How did you know that? Because if you did, then you would have had to be in on it, I said. Have a good day, Mr. Ritchie, and please leave the door open.

Sitting back in my chair, I contemplated my "truck driving days." There were two essential documents used in tracking delivered merchandise. The buyer upon delivery would check the items received against the original purchase order. Too late for that, I thought. The second document known as a "Bill of Lading" was a driver's receipt indicating that at the point of delivery the buyer or his or her designee had signed for the delivered items. The signed document then served as verification that the delivery was made. The truck driver kept the original, and the customer was provided a carbon. I would have to search the main office files for those Bill Of Lading carbons. The usual scam run by deliverers who were crooks went like this. In the first instance, the deliverer had to have a previously determined market for the items he was going to steal. He then had to know which of his delivery sites had a shoddy intake procedure. Having done this, he would arrive at the site, proclaim to the secretary in the main office that he was running late and needed to drop off fifty boxes and get going. The secretary would in turn simply point to some area in the office or a nearby storage area. After ten or so minutes, the delivery man perspiring profusely would approach the secretary's desk and thrust the "Bill of Lading" in front of her, saying, that's it...sign me up and I'm outta here. During the course of making this statement, at least three or four droplets of sweat would have fallen on the secretary's desk, and being repulsed by the smell of the deliveryman's body stench, she was all too happy to sign the document and get him going. The idea of delaying his departure while she counted the delivered boxes would have been abhorrent to her.

Picking up the phone intercom, I called Mrs. Goldstein, the head secretary. Mrs. Goldstein, could you arrange to have the file folders for all of last year's purchase orders and the file folder for all of the Bills of Lading placed in my mailbox within the next half hour? I could, if I knew what a Bill of Lading was. A Bill of Lading is the document signed when a delivery is made to the school by a trucker. Oh, you mean those little teal colored slips. Exactly, Mrs. Goldstein. Oh, I have them in with the purchase orders. Excellent, I said. Send me the purchase folder ASAP. Before I forget, I will want to meet with you and the entire General Office staff, including any parent volunteers tomorrow morning at 9:15. I'll arrange for the office to be covered at that time. Placing the phone back in its cradle, I began to formulate plans for a secure receiving and distribution-tracking format. It had to be simple, precise, and user friendly. A monitor who gave me a note and folder interrupted my contemplation. The note read: Mr. Kassell...Here is the file you requested. Fast enough? Sincerely,...Anna Goldstein. She had a beautiful signature, I thought. Please tell Mrs. Goldstein that I am very thankful; I instructed the monitor.

As the day wore on, I decided on how I was going to track the receiving and distribution of delivered items to the school. I needed three things. The first was a large three ring looseleaf bookbinder. The second was a sheet of double-spaced three-ring looseleaf paper. The third item, a 12" ruler. All were readily available. I carefully scrutinized the dusty books and binders in the bookcase I inherited when I was assigned my present office. Carefully, I selected a voluminous binder entitled "Chancellor's Regulations"...1975-1980. Trashing all of its contents and applying a damp cloth to its vinyl covering, I was pleased at my ingenuity. Reaching into my bottom desk drawer, I extracted one sheet of double-space ruled loose leaf paper. Taking my 12" ruler from my top desk drawer, I ruled out the following columns: Date Received, Vendor, For Whom, # of Items/Boxes, Corresponding PO#, Receiver's Signature, and Date. After meeting with the secretarial and office staff, I would then have to prepare an administrative bulletin to all staff concerning this new procedure.

After dinner that evening, I took out the Purchase Order File Folder sent to me by Mrs. Goldstein. My first task was to separate the PO's from the Bills of Lading and then to place them in chronological order. All was going well. Miraculously there were equal numbers of PO's and Bills of Lading through August. Something was wrong. I could feel it. Something so obvious that it was right in front of me, if only I could see it. I decided to take a cigarette break and check on the Knicks. Coming back to my desk, it occurred to me that schools traditionally do not accept delivery of goods ordered in the spring semester over the summer. PO's are usually stamped in red, "Hold until end of August." The reason being that there is no way to maintain accountability for received items in July or August. How then was it that I was staring at Bills of Lading during the period July 6th— August 18th with Ms. Goldstein's signature? Mrs. Goldstein didn't work in the summer. Perish the thought that sweet little old lady could be part of such a swindle. Repeatedly I stared at her signature. Still something wasn't right. Hold on, I thought. I turned my attention back to the file folder Mrs. Goldstein had sent me earlier. Where is the note? Finding the note, I studied it and was immediately gratified to see that Mrs. Goldstein was not the scoundrel I had thought. In fact, had she not sent me the note, I would never have realized that while the summer Bills of Lading were signed in a severe left handed slant, Mrs. Goldstein's note was clearly written by her right hand. I would, of course, share my findings and theories with Mr. Andrews before forwarding them along with my "special weekly administrative progress report" to Mr. Diamond. I hardly had time to bask in my success when the phone rang.

Vito, I'm glad you got back to me. I need a favor. You got it, Kenny. I need you to come over to the school I'm working at and check out its electrical systems for me. He replied, I don't do that kind of work, Kenny, but I know someone who does. I'll have him call you; his name is Rocco. Thanks "V." I'll see you Thursday night at the alleys.

The next morning I got to school a little early to access the photocopier, before the area was overrun by frantic teachers anxious to make ditto sheets. I needed fifty copies of my new "Merchandise Intake Routing System" and seventy-five copies of my administrative memorandum articulating its use to the teaching staff. In the midst of running the job, I was joined by Principal Andrews, for whom I had developed a certain respect and admiration for during our brief association. Sipping coffee from a container, he inquired as to what I was up to. After explaining, I shared my findings with him concerning the phony signatures on the Bills of Lading. He was elated. You have no idea what this means to everyone in this school and to me. No, I'm afraid I don't, I said. He insisted that I go and get some coffee while he saw to the completion of the duplicating job. I'll explain when you get back.

Upon my return Mr. Andrews explained that not only had the school been deprived of vitally needed educational materials, it had also seen the reputation of every adult in the school tarnished by whispered accusations that some amongst them were linked to the thefts. Have you formulated a corrective action plan? To begin with, and of course with your permission, I'd like to orient you and the other supervisors, as well as the secretarial staff as to these new procedures we just ran off. Excellent, he said. When? At 9:15 this morning, he replied. I'll arrange it. The secretarial staff has already been placed on notice. Good. I'll intercom the AP's. One more thing, Mr. Andrews, I'm expecting a very important call from someone named Rocco. Oh? He's an electrician. I see, Andrews said smiling. Sounds good to me.

The result of my investigation ended in criminal charges being brought against the corrupt truck driver. He further divulged the fact that he had sold the goods to an all too willing ritzy private school in Manhattan. He gave the name of his contact at the school, who in turn quietly resigned. During our annual candy sale fundraiser, we received a check from the school in an amount approximating the costs of the "summer deliveries." Their books charged the expense to the purchase of 2500 boxes of cordial chocolate cherries. Everyone was happy. Subsequently, we dropped charges against the truck driver, and thus brought closure to the entire affair. My new "Merchandise Intake System" served as a model throughout the district.

Hello...yes, Mrs. Goldstein, I do know someone named Rocco. I'll be right down. Seeing Rocco in the main office, I escorted him over to the staff lounge and encouraged him to have some coffee and donuts. He didn't need much encouraging. I'll be right back, I said, exiting the lounge and making my way over to Andrew's office. Knocking on his door then opening it, I was gratified that he was alone. Mr. Andrews, I have Rocco in the lounge. Sensing that Andrew's hesitancy was an outgrowth of the fact that he had forgotten my mentioning of Rocco to him earlier in the week, I started to debrief him. Almost immediately he recalled the conversation. Tell me, aren't we violating some of the custodial contractual stipulations here? We're violating most of them. I've asked the superintendent to schedule a district-wide custodial meeting for this morning covering an agenda filled with his concerns based on things he had seen while visiting the schools in the district. Naturally, I had to tell him why. Mr. Ritchie will be tied up all morning. OK, where do we start? Right here in your office in the Public Address booth. By the way, Mr. Andrews, do you mind if I work out of your office this morning? Rocco doesn't speak very good English and if something comes up...sure go right ahead, he said. It was 9:30 a.m. At 11 a.m. Rocco approached me and said, "All finished boss. No more problems. I go now!" Both Andrews and I looked up in amazement, gazing at Rocco's exiting rear. Shouldn't we test it? Andrews said. My response was, not now. Don't worry, if Rocco said it's fixed, then it's fixed. Tomorrow morning when Ritchie is back in the building, tell him that you are going to try the PA system out hoping that it will "feel like working." Then when it does, he will be no more the wiser. I felt good about what I'd accomplished. It would be a going away present for Superintendent Diamond, whose contract was not going to be renewed.

Chapter XXIV

Hello...Mr. Weiss!

In appearance Alan Weiss was diminutive in height and slight of girth. He wore octagon-framed eyeglasses, a peace medallion around his neck displacing any need for a necktie, an open-collared denim shirt and khaki pants. To complete the '60's image like a cherry on top of an ice cream sundae, his kinky reddish hair was formed into a slight fro—the problem being that for Weiss the balding process had begun. While he may have been going for a radical '60's expression, I immediately took him for the schmuck that he was. His reputation for being a radical and an antagonist of administrators was legendary. Generally, all efforts were made to appease him. By now you must know that he and I were destined to experience some moments of ill rapport.

On the morning of October 3rd, 1982, I had convened a meeting of the senior grade teachers of which Mr. Weiss was a member. Ladies and gentlemen, our purpose this morning is to plan for senior picture day. You have before you an itinerary as to when you will escort your class to the auditorium and the pupil and staff dress codes. Yes, Mr. Weiss. In his whiny voice, Weiss announced that it was a contractual violation for me to impose a dress code on the teaching staff. I was not surprised at Weiss comment. He had insisted at an earlier meeting that male teachers, in spite of my request to wear a white shirt on assembly days, didn't have to wear one. His male colleagues, however, understood my rationale: that we were role models and we should be prepared to do at all times what we were asking of our students. I attempted to reason with Weiss. These yearbooks and their pictures will be keepsakes for the youngsters. I cannot understand why you, Mr. Weiss, would want to appear in a book kept for posterity looking like the misfit that you look like now. That's an insult, he said. I resent it. I demand that you apologize, Mr. Kassell, or I'm going to the union. Suit yourself, I replied. Weiss got up to leave. A word of caution, Mr. Weiss. What? The meeting is not over. If you leave now, you risk a letter placed in your file citing you for insubordination. Weiss sat down. In the unhappy event that there are any in this room who feel simpatico with Mr. Weiss' position, my memory is long. Have a good day; we are adjourned!

The next morning my Dean, Mr. Timpson, and I supervised the picture-taking operation. Classes were sent for in clusters of threes. There were twelve regular education classes and three special education ones. The reporting classes were programmed in such a way so as to facilitate a time when the official teachers could be with their class. When the classes arrived to the auditorium, parent volunteers ushered them to a specific "readiness area." While they waited there, various ladies in the PTA attended to the females. The male students were attended to by me and any male teachers or parents who happened to be there. The photographer's format was such that each class took their place on the stage and were posed on ascending risers, thus being tiered. The center space in row one was reserved for the teacher. Just before things started, I had a brief meeting with the photographer. I suggested that row one be bordered as close to the edge of the stage as possible. I contended that this would discount any possibility of light reflection from the stage flooring back towards the subjects. That is an excellent idea, responded the photographer. That problem occurs quite often. Leaving the photographer, Timpson asked...what's that all about? We've never had that problem. Detail, Mr. Timpson,...detail, I said.

As I observed the photographer working with the classes, I learned that his "trigger" was the word "ready!" Having uttered that word, there was a two or three second pause, as the cameraman's eye gleaned the appearance of a smile on all his subjects for the last time. At that moment a flash went off, and the picture was taken. I won't have much time; I'll have to do it right.

Weiss' class was in the second cluster. True to his word, Weiss was adorned in his usual protest style. The unpressed khakis were complemented with an illustrated Save the Whales t-shirt. As his class was being prepped, I meandered my way over to the center of the pit area beneath the stage and sat down. The photographer was now seating Weiss and his class. Hearing the word "ready," I reached up and in lightening fashion grabbed Weiss by his belt buckle and yanked him off the stage just as the flash went off. Peering down at Weiss who was lying on the floor, I asked, are you all right? Mr. Timpson, please take Mr. Weiss' class back to their room while Mr. Weiss fills out the required accident report. That won't be necessary, snarled Weiss. I'll see you in the Principal's office with my union rep. Look forward to it. See you then I called to a hastily exiting Weiss.

At 2:30 that afternoon, Mrs. Goldstein called me on the intercom to inform me that Mr. Andrews required my presence in his office immediately. Reporting as directed, I found that Mr. Weiss as promised was present with his union rep. They were seated at the conference table along with Mr. Andrews. I took a seat opposite Weiss and his rep. Mr. Kassell, began Mr. Andrews, Mr. Weiss has lodged a complaint charging you with among other things, assault. Weiss was very agitated and interrupted Andrews, screaming, "This man grabbed me by my privates and tore me from the stage onto the floor."

Two classes were in the auditorium, several teachers, PTA members, and the Dean, Mr. Timpson. This is very serious; Mr. Andrews went on, while seemingly recording all that was being said on a yellow legal pad. How do you respond, Mr. Kassell? I'm in shock, I quickly replied. Is this

227

the gratitude I get for saving Mr. Weiss from possible serious personal injury? Just as he lost his footing at the edge of the stage area, I rapidly came to his assistance just in time to cushion his fall. I was somewhat shaken up myself I might add. Well, we have two conflicting reports, observed Mr. Andrews. Do you, Mr. Weiss, have any written witness reports that would corroborate your assertion? Weiss whined that he hadn't. Do you, Mr. Kassell. Yes, I do, Mr. Andrews. I was anticipating the need for witness reports to be attached to the school accident report. It was no accident, yelled Weiss; it was an incident. Mr. Weiss, some decorum if you don't mind, urged Mr. Andrews. May I see those witness accounts? After taking a few minutes to scan the reports, Mr. Andrews stated the following. I'm afraid, Mr. Weiss, that all of these accounts support Mr. Kassell's version. Therefore, I will allow these witness statements to be attached to the Accident Report. There will be no more talk of an Incident Report. The only question I have is what did the cameraman mean when he ended his statement with the sentence "that unfortunately, Mr Weiss' class photo would not have him in it?" Weiss' lip quivered ever so slightly. He turned toward his union rep, who in turn nodded his head ever so slightly from left to right. Noting this non- verbal communication, Principal Andrews proclaimed the meeting to be over.

While I was sure that Andrews was fully aware as to what had really transpired, he never brought it up to me. I think it was his way of evening our accounts.

Chapter XXV

Mr. Weiss, One More Time

On the morning of May 15th, 1982, I found myself conducting the eighth grade Career Day assembly program. My newly assigned Dean, Ms. Alice Rhett, assisted me in this assignment. Previously, Mr. Timpson had asked for a change of his assignment. In place of his "Dean's duties," he had become the school programmer. I first encountered Ms. Rhett when she served as union council to Mr. Weiss during the hearing wherein he alleged that I had assaulted him. She had a reputation for fairness and discipline. I also found her extremely bright and quite helpful to me in making decisions on the administration of the grade.

The program format was one by which there were two phases. The first being that the twelve dignitaries would give brief three-minute biographical introductions but take no questions. Phase two provided each dignitary with the opportunity to have a "Q and A" session with the kids in their classes. Each visitor would be given a schedule whereby he or she was to rotate visits to each classroom over a ten-minute period. The teachers, Ms. Rhett and I, would serve to keep things moving. What could go wrong?

Arriving to work that morning and feeling confident that all was in place, I had a last concern. Stopping at Mr. Timpson's desk, I instructed him to give Mr. Weiss a room assignment change for the day. I then rushed off to meet with Ms. Rhett and the guidance department for one final debriefing. As a result of my rushing off and the various program changes that Timpson was involved with, I never learned that Weiss had declined the room change assignment on the basis that it was a contract violation.

The assembly program went along perfectly. We were right on schedule. As the assembly period drew to a close signifying the end of phase one, I began the class dismissal routine. While doing so I summoned Ms. Rhett. Alice, if you don't mind, I'd like to take a ten-minute coffee break. Can you send word to Mr. Andrews that we are beginning phase two and then escort the dignitaries to the third floor to get things started? I'll be there shortly. No problem, replied Ms. Rhett.

True to my word, I finished my True Blue and coffee break then proceeded up the stairs to the third floor. Just as I hit the third floor landing, I encountered Mr. Andrews coming down the stairs. Something was terribly wrong. His hair was askew, his shirt was half out of his pants, his tie looked as though it had been pulled as tight as it could, and he was almost running down the stairs. Mr. Andrews, what happened? Not breaking stride, I heard Andrews say as he passed me…"No time, have to call the police."

Continuing my ascent to the third floor, I stepped out of the vestibule and onto the floor. The first person I encountered was Ms. Velez, a school aide, whose main function was to monitor pupils coming and going as they used the lavatories. Ms. Velez was a deeply religious woman. Often, I observed her in moments of "down time" reading a small hand-held Bible. Oh, Mr. Kassell, I'm glad you came;…it was terrible. Slow down, Ms. Velez, take a deep breath. Here, let's go over to your seat. After a few moments, I said, are you ready to tell me what happened? Yes, I'll do my best. Good. What happened? Ms. Velez was still very agitated. She took out her rosary beads and as she began to twirl them through her fingers, she grew calmer and related the following account:

At 10:30 just as scheduled, Ms. Rhett led the dignitaries onto the floor. They all walked off in the direction of the classes. The last person was Mr. Andrews. He was going to follow them, but he heard the noise coming from Mr. Weiss' room, so he went to see what was going on. Wait a second, I interrupted. Are you sure it was Mr. Weiss? As sure as I know that I'm talking to you, Mr. Kassell. Ok. Go on, I'm sorry, please go on; I won't stop you again. Mr. Andrews went into the room. I heard Mr. Weiss yelling at Mr. Andrews. Then Mr. Andrews came out of the classroom, and Mr. Weiss followed him out and jumped on his back. They both fell on the floor and Mr. Weiss kept saying, give it back to me. Mr. Andrews pushed Mr. Weiss away and ran down the stairs. I was in shock. Weiss strikes again. Why didn't Timpson do as I'd asked? Knowing that Mr. Andrews was seemingly unhurt, I instructed Ms. Velez to write down everything that she had just told me. Were there any other witnesses? I asked. No, Mr. Kassell, the hall was empty and Ms. Rhett had taken the visitors around the corner. Is Weiss in his room? Yes. Ok. Nothing has changed. In a few minutes phase two will be over. Ms. Rhett and our student ushers will escort the dignitaries to the library for the PTA luncheon. You did well, Ms. Velez. Everything will be fine.

In his anecdote, Mr. Andrews filled in the missing pieces, that is, to say what went on when he entered Weiss' room:

"As I entered room 333, I noted that all of the desks and chairs had been moved to either side of the classroom. The room itself being a double-sized one had its partition fully opened. At either end of the room, there was hung a mini basketball hoop, approximately 10' high. Two teams consisting of three boys were running up and down the classroom floor throwing what appeared to be a nerf ball at the hoops. The teacher, Mr. Weiss, was seated atop the stacked chairs nearest the window and with a clipboard and pencil appeared to be keeping score. The students, to their credit, upon seeing me in the room ceased the activity and stood still. Not saying a word, I walked to one end of the classroom and removed one of the hoops. Mr. Weiss called out to me. What are you doing, Mr. Andrews? You can't have that; it's mine. I paid him no attention and while walking in the opposite direction, I passed the student who was holding the nerf ball. I held out my open palm, and the young man placed the ball in it. Weiss was by now out of his seat and was stalking my every move. I'm telling you, Mr. Andrews, you can't have those things; they are my personal property. I continued to ignore him. I removed the second hoop and exited the classroom. Weiss followed me out into the hall. I'm warning you, Mr. Andrews. The next thing I knew, he had leapt onto my back. I got away from him and went to call the police."

I made the decision not to confront Weiss. Believing that neither he nor Andrews were in no need of any medical assistance, I adhered to the axiom that says, "the show must go on." Accordingly, I went to the library to await Ms. Rhett and the dignitaries. I decided not to let on to anyone what had transpired. On schedule Ms. Rhett escorted the group of visitors into the school library at precisely 11:30 a.m. How are you? Ms. Rhett asked. You wouldn't believe it, I said. Later. Ladies and gentlemen, I know that Mr. Andrews wanted to greet you personally and may still be able to. However, last minute business has deterred him. Our PTA has prepared a sumptuous luncheon, and I bid you all to "dig in." Knowing that Mr. Andrews enjoyed this kind of pomp and circumstance not to mention the photo op, I sent one of the ushers to Mr. Andrews with a note that read...Mr. Andrews, the dignitaries are having lunch now. I made the opening remarks; they will probably be leaving in twenty minutes or so. We are hoping that you can join us and make the closing remarks. Within a few minutes, the usher came back and while gasping for breath told me that Mr. Andrews was being arrested and so was Mr. Weiss. Getting up from my seat I leaned over to Alice Rhett and simply said take over. Don't forget to thank the visitors and the PTA. She started to mouth the word "what," but I turned and left, hitting the staircase in a run. What I saw next was surreal.

I arrived in the lobby area just in time to see the last of a procession of police heading for the exit. Recognizing the Sergeant who appeared to be in charge, I approached him. Red, what the hell is going on? How you doin' Ken...your principal, Mr. Andrews, called in a complaint against a teacher...let me see...Mr. Weiss for assaulting him. Mr. Weiss filed a cross complaint for assault and theft of private property. We're gonna take them both in and see if we can get this straightened out at the precinct. Red, what exactly did the teacher mean by personal property? Hold on; let me check my notes. Here it is...a Nerf basketball and two hoops. Listen to me, Red. How long have you known me? About five years. You trust me, don't you Red? Yeah, you got a good rep. What's all this leading up to, Ken? The teacher's lying. I don't know, Ken, he seemed pretty convincing, especially about the equipment. Look at both men, Red. If Mr. Andrews, a man over 6' tall, had struck or assaulted that whiny little putz there would be physical evidence. Yet, if you examine Andrews, you'll find scratch marks on the left side of his face and a torn shirt collar. I have conducted my own in-house investigation. I have witness statements all contradictory to the teacher's statement. What about the Nerf ball and hoops, Ken? Another lie, Red. We use that equipment for our handicapped physical exercise program. We have purchase orders for them.

The teacher is a nutcase, Red; I'm sure you got some in the precinct, too. Boy, do we, starting with the Captain. I could tell you some stories, Ken. Another time, Red. While we were talking, Andrews and Weiss had been placed in separate police cruisers. Are you sure about the purchase orders, Ken? Didn't you say I was always straight with you guys? Turning toward the waiting police cars, Red ordered "let the principal go. Keep the teacher". Seeing Andrews getting out of his car, Weiss became quite animated. He appeared to be screaming and trying to exit the car he was in. Tell the teacher if he doesn't restrain himself, we'll do it for him, directed Red. In the meantime, Andrews, head down walked deliberately past me and into his office.

Subsequently, Weiss was released from the station house. He was also removed from the school pending a formal hearing by the superintendent into the entire affair. I was never asked to produce the purchase orders for the Nerf Ball. To this day, Andrews never asked me what I'd said to Red to secure his release. He did thank me when we worked together collating the various witness statements in preparation for the impending hearing. The teacher's union got Weiss and Andrews to drop their respective criminal charges, in favor of the professional machinery built into our system for the handling of such matters. Specifically, Andrews re-wrote all of his charges in a formal letter for Weiss' file. Weiss in turn grieved that the letter was totally inaccurate, arbitrary, and capricious. Of course, the union waived Step One, which ordinarily would have been a hearing conducted by the principal and adjudicated by the principal. The union agreed to the stipulation that Step One would simply show the statement "grievance denied." The grievance would then be re-submitted as a Step Two matter to be heard and adjudicated by the superintendent.

Within a month, Mr. Andrews and Mr. Weiss received notification of the scheduling of a Step Two grievance hearing. Dr. Brown, who had succeeded Mr. Diamond, had built a reputation as a tough but fair man. He was in his late 50's and gave the impression of being straight-laced, not surprising given his West Point background. Andrews made Ms. Velez and me aware of the date and time, so that we would be available to testify.

On the afternoon of June 20th at 3:30 p.m., Dr. Brown convened the Step Two grievance. His personal secretary, Mrs. Roberts, took minutes. Present were Weiss, the district union rep, Mr. Mittleman, the school union delegate, Dean Rhett, Mr. Andrews, and myself. With Dr. Brown seated at one end of the long oak conference table and Weiss at the opposite end and the various players on the flanks, we began. Just as Dr. Brown was about to explain the protocol, Weiss stood up and protested my presence. I object to Mr. Kassell being allowed to sit in during these proceedings. I demand that he be removed. To begin with, Mr. Weiss, said Dr. Brown, this is not an inquisition. No one will be removed. We may excuse some individuals as we proceed or we may not. Your objection is noted; your request is denied. You now have fifteen minutes to present your case. The clock is running, Mr. Weiss. I was impressed. Weiss and Mittleman consulted briefly, and Weiss stood to make his presentation. During the course of his diatribe, Weiss referenced the Nerf Ball several times. Dr. Brown interrupted Weiss with an apology for doing so and asked if Weiss had the Nerf Ball with him, as he was not familiar with one himself. Weiss reached down into a large brown grocery store type paper bag and extracted the Nerf Ball and the hoops. He then rolled the Nerf Ball down the length of the table to the waiting hands of Dr. Brown. Dr. Brown examined the ball, squeezing it in various ways, and tossing it in the air. Satisfied, Dr. Brown started to place it on the floor where he was seated, when Weiss admonished, "That's my property Dr. Brown, you may not have it." Brown quickly bent down to retrieve the ball and said, hold on Weiss, I read the hearing briefs, and rolled the ball back down the length of the table. Just as before, all eyes followed the ball much in the way the crowd did at the US Open. For Weiss it was indeed game, set, and match.

In the final analysis, Weiss was denied his grievance. Brown made him an offer he couldn't refuse: that he be sent to the Board's medical unit for a full evaluation, or take a one year unpaid leave of absence with all matters pertaining to the case sealed, thus insuring his ability to re-enter the system a year later. Weiss accepted the terms of the latter scenario.

A year later I heard that Weiss was a computer programmer for the Central Board of Education at Livingston Street.

Chapter XXVI

Three Amigos

Throughout my twenty-five year stay in Brooklyn, I met some great people. There were two men in particular with whom I was very tight—Oliver Timpson and Leo Lawes. Both were physical education teachers. Both worked second jobs after school for the NYC Parks Department. Like myself, both were married with children, all of whom would attend and graduate college. Like me, both had a passion for The Trotters. Earlier you were introduced briefly to Oliver Timpson who was my Dean at the time of the "Weiss senior picture day fiasco." Oliver was on the stocky side. He stood about 5'10" and weighed in at about 220 lbs. He spoke in a raspy, deep voice that got the attention and respect of the students. He was very well liked and respected by his fellow teachers and had a brilliant mind when it came to school programming and day-to-day coverage procedures. He was truly a hard worker. In addition to his parks department jobs, he hustled wall papering and house painting jobs on weekends and holidays. Leo was a striking contrast to Oliver. Standing at about 6'3" and weighing a streamlined 185 lbs., he was a picture of strength and dignity. He was a real throwback. Every day he would arrive to work in a sport jacket, trousers, a shirt, and a tie. He would change into a physical education teacher's outfit he kept in his locker. He completed the appearance with a whistle he wore around his neck. At day's end, he would change again to his "dress up outfit." I once asked him why he just didn't wear the gym outfit straight from home. He looked at me with some contempt and replied, I'm a teacher. The fact that I teach physical education doesn't mean that I should diminish the profession by dressing unprofessionally. I've told that story repeatedly to young teachers who tend to discount the fact that they are role models and are really working at a job that The Supreme Court has declared to be within the scope of "white collar" professions.

Every morning the gym office hosted coffee and donuts for teachers who were in their coffee club. The office was also available to club members for lunch. Invariably, the topic of conversation was sports oriented with a great deal of interest in the previous night's racing results from Yonkers or Roosevelt. Often the three of us would arrange to meet at whichever track was running to spend the evening. More often than not, however, it was Leo and I who would make such jaunts. Oliver, you see, preferred to cover back at The Parks Dept., while sending money for certain bets, not the whole card.

Be that as it may, Leo and I found ourselves as early arrivals one evening at Roosevelt. The traffic coming out from Brooklyn was very light. Post time was 8 p.m., and here we were with two hours to kill. We had dinner at one of the fast food stands, and then sat down on a bench located in the outer grandstand area. Leo didn't study the program too diligently, leaving that task to me. We must have made some pair—Leo in his herringbone jacket, brown pants and matching herringbone cap and me in my sharkskin grey suit. At least that's what some young impressionable college kid thought. He had been eyeballing us for about ten minutes. What he saw was me occasionally checking my watch, pointing out horses that were warming up particularly well, and instructing Leo to make notes on his program. From a distance we must have looked like the touts that the famous sportswriter Damon Runyon immortalized. Sure enough, the young man approached and excitedly asked, "Are you guys trainers?" No, I quickly replied. I'm an owner, and this is my trainer. Wow, exclaimed the young man. You got anything good. Play the #3 horse in the 5th race, I whispered, and don't tell anyone.

Thanks a lot, he said. I always wanted to meet guys like you. He took off, and Leo and I laughed. As the evening progressed, things were not going well. At the end of the 4th race, Leo and I had fourteen dollars between us. Let's save four dollars for some coffee, suggested Leo. Who do you want to bet the ten on? You pick it, Leo. Leo's pick put a period on our gambling for the evening. We were slowly making our way toward the exit, when we heard the excited calls of our young friend. Guys, guys. We turned and saw him running in our direction. You guys are the greatest, he said while waving two handfulls of bills. Turns out the #3 horse we had given him as a lark actually won at odds of 35 to 1. Wait till I tell my friends. Here I want you guys to have this, he said, handing Leo a fifty-dollar bill. Oh we can't...yes interrupted, Leo. Ok, kid thanks. Later, said the departing young man. Well, Leo, this didn't turn out so bad. I just got one thing to say, said Leo. What's that I asked? I want to be the owner next time, and you'll be my trainer. We left the track laughing hysterically.

Chapter XXVII

New Brooms, Clean Sweep

A bookmark year for the NYC Board of Education was 1982. A maverick candidate for the position of chancellor had emerged on the scene. He had the audacity to promise to obliterate corruption and incompetence wherever he saw it. The board, taking the approach that seeing was believing quickly installed him as The Chancellor. He warmed to his commitment by cleaning out the NYC Board of Education's scandalous supply depot in Long Island City. He next moved in on several of the more scurrilous school boards in the five boroughs. In some cases he found that sitting members were in non-compliance with the residency requirement. In such cases they were summarily removed. In other situations where he found widespread corruption within the boards, he suspended them and replaced them with an appointed "chancellor's trustee." It wasn't long before the establishment had given him the nickname "Il Duce."

Over the summer of 1982, Dr. Brown retired from his superintendency. A chancellor's appointee, none other than my old friend, Lyn Rios, replaced him. It seems that Lyn had gone to work at the Board of Education's central office in 1979. She apparently used that time to forge influential ties with the downtown bigwigs. It was her time. Il Duce's mandate was to clean up the district; that is, follow his lead, do something dramatic and attention getting right away. And so on December 7th, 1982, became a "day of infamy" for Paul Anderson. Paul had fallen out of favor with the parent body of the school. It had gotten so bad that he and the PTA president would not even talk to one another, communicating by written memorandum. The undeniable truth, however, was the ongoing low performance of the school. Being a former colleague of Paul's, Ms. Rios designed a dignified approach to the problem. She made Paul an offer he couldn't refuse. Officially, Paul would take a yearlong sabbatical for restoration of health, effective immediately. In turn she would not bring charges that would smack of incompetence against him. The truth be told, Paul was a suffering asthmatic and had become very stressed from the constant harangue of parental attacks on his leadership. Rios's offer was truly not one he could refuse. At 1 p.m. Paul called all of the Assistant Principals to his office. He simply announced that as of that moment, Ken was the Acting Principal. He stated that for reasons of ill health, he was going on immediate sabbatical. Three other assistant principals beside myself were in the room. Everyone expressed shock and concern. We all extended get-well wishes and then quietly filed out.

The word spread like wildfire. Seizing the moment, Ms. Rios announced at one of her principal's conferences that she was targeting at least one more principal in the district. Rumor had it that it was Ms. Mary.

I met with Ms. Rios after school that day. Ken, this is an opportunity for you to show what you've got. Have you taken the Principal's exams, yet? No, I haven't. But I'm going to. I must tell you that The Chancellor has handpicked a replacement principal for the school. He will be assigned in mid-February. He might start making appearances during the month of January. If so I expect that you will cooperate with him in all ways possible. In the meantime, I want you to know that I shall be available to you at any time for support and guidance during the course of your tenure as Acting Principal.

The rest of December was thankfully uneventful. The Christmas vacation was truly a blessing. With the New Year, I directed that every department, minor subjects as well, submit plans for formal mid-term testing. Exams were to be typed and formatted in the same style as the standardized city exams. The last week of January was to be mid-term testing week. In the meantime, Mr. Dave Coleman started making appearances in the school. Not being a Brooklyn guy, I was unaware that he was some kind of a legend among the locals. He went out of his way, however, to avoid contact with me. He spent most of his time interviewing various elements of the school staff, including custodial and kitchen staff. In late January, Ms. Rios summoned me to her office. It was then that I was formally introduced to Dave Coleman. Indeed, he was formidable. Standing at about 6', he had to be at least 250 lbs. The big fat cigar he moved from side to side in his mouth added to his overall surly appearance. Ken, began Ms. Rios, you've done a great job. In a day or two you'll receive that compliment in writing. Thank you, Ms. Rios. I appreciate that. I want you to know that Mr. Coleman will be assigned as Principal next Monday. How do you see yourself as best being able to support his efforts? In the brief time I've had as principal, I can say with some certainty that there isn't enough time to truly do the things one has to do to fulfill the role. The paperwork can enslave a principal to his office. I believe that it is crucial for a new principal to be in the mainstream as much as possible. The students and teachers have to see him as a high profile personality. Given my familiarity with most of the administrative concerns, I see myself as Mr. Coleman' Administrative Assistant. That's great, Ken. Dave, do you agree? Why not? Curious answer, I thought. Sitting there, I felt a certain tenseness, I couldn't put my finger on it immediately.

Dave Coleman struck me as anything but the kind of Principal that Ms. Rioss would appoint. He was a departure from the wimpish male types that she promoted. Point in fact was that until Dave's arrival, she had appointed only one male, opting for a "sister" at every opportunity to make an administrative appointment. Was it any wonder that in some circles the district was quietly referred to as the "ladies club." Wait a second, he was not one of her appointees, he was put in place as she had been, by Il Duce! She had to accept him!

Being somewhat egotistical myself, our relationship was doomed from the outset. Dave Coleman was not one to take criticism or suggestions well. He also made no secret that he wanted to bring a "friend" in as an assistant principal. In order to do that, he needed to create a vacancy. He thought! Among the assistant principals, I was still the youngest and the one with the least seniority. I was, therefore, not surprised when I learned in June that Mr. Coleman had requested that I be transferred from the school. Ms. Rios informed me that I would be transferred back to John Paul Jones JHS.

To add insult to injury, Coleman asked me not to have any hard feelings. I told him that his strategy to create a vacancy to transfer his friend in was obvious. Then I reminded him that had it not been for Il Duce, he would have never been picked by Ms. Rios, and what made him think that she would pick his friend to fill the vacancy. We'll see, he said. It never happened.

Chapter XXVIII

John Paul Jones Revisited

My arrival for a second tour of duty at JPJ was heralded much more than my first posting to the school. It didn't help matters that Ms. Rios had removed all doubt, letting it out that Patricia Mary was indeed on her hit list. I was walking into a true catfight. It wasn't long before Ms. Mary referred to me alternately, as "The Hatchett Man," or the man that replaces principals. To compound matters, unlike my previous tour of duty, the school no longer had four assistant principals; the administrative support team had been reduced to two.

It didn't take long before the fur began to fly. In the two years since I'd left, there remained a core of incompetent long-term substitute teachers, who although continually subjected to public ridicule by Ms. Mary, still flocked to her side, as she was quick to remind them that if it weren't for her, they'd have no jobs. These same individuals remembered well my last tour of duty and the names of their fellow incompetents whom I had cast out. For sure, I was in hostile territory. Over the next year and a half, given the flood of paper exchanged between Ms. Mary accusing me of all sorts of indiscretions and my replies defending against those accusations, I came to appreciate the excellent training I had had in Harlem.

In early October, one of my social studies teachers called in to report that he needed his first period class covered, as he had battery problems. Don't worry about it; I'll take the class, I assured him. Can you make it by 9:45? You can count on it, Mr. K, replied the grateful teacher. By day's end, I found the following letter in my mailbox:

Mr. Kassell

Who the HELL do you think you are to go in opposition to my philosophy??

PM

Thus, the stage was set. I contemplated the note and its vitriolic tone reaching the following decision. I could not hope to in any way dissuade Ms. Marx, from her belief that I was the "superintendent's man." I would not ask the superintendent for relief by way of transfer. What I was very good at, however, was giving as well (if not better) as what I was receiving. If letter writing was to be her weapon of choice, so be it. I could play the documentation game with the best.

The next volley of fire took place in early December. For over a month, I had complained to Ms. Mary. that the second floor was overutilized. So much so that whenever the change of period occurred, it took me five or more minutes to clear the hall. Her answer was to assign on an "occasional" basis additional personnel from the first floor. Of course, the first floor had people to spare because it was severely underutilized. Ms. Mary. had been trained by Mr. Diamond to keep the traffic flow on the first floor at a minimum. Thus, when visitors entered the school they would be presented with an orderly hall appearance and a quiet floor overall. I never knew when her "assignees" were supposed to be on the 2nd floor, as there was no written schedule provided me. On the morning of December 3rd, 1984 I received the attached inquiry from Ms. Mary. My reply was in her letterbox by 8 a.m. the next day.

12/3/84

Mr. Kassell,

Are you utilizing the services of Mr. Johns & especially Mr. Starks, because I don't think your getting much mileage out of the help I've provided for the floor. I received notes in my letterbox about the change in the tone of the 2nd floor because of Mr. Prattler's presence.

12/4/84

Dear Ms. Mary:

On 12/3/84, I called into school to advise that I would be late. Upon my arrival I was <u>gratified</u> to find Mr. Prattler in my office and supervising the 2nd floor. I've always maintained that the floor could use any help it could get. Actually, Mr. Prattler is to be commended. In conversation with him, he indicated that he took the initiative to assist a colleague and to provide help when it was most needed. I would caution the hallelulahs as to the change in floor tone—this is a generality. In the mornings up to period 4, the floor is usually well managed—on periods 5, 6, 7 & 8; it is somewhat more confusing. Perhaps Mr. Prattler could make some suggestions.

As always, I am impressed with the "grapevine of children and other informants you've gathered." I don't underestimate their loyalty to you nor do I care. The notes you received in your letterbox are from those who would divide and conquer—who were they from?

Ken Kassell

P.S. As for Johns and Stark, I hardly see them, as they are usually taking coverage assignments during the time they are supposed to help out on the floor. I assumed that this was done with your knowledge and approval.

In early January, I informed Ms. Mary. that I had been summoned for jury duty effective immediately. Can't you get it postponed? I see no reason to, I answered. Well, we do have midterms scheduled. I can assure you that all of my responsibilities in that area have been fulfilled. Upon my return on January 29th, I found the following letter from Ms. Mary. dated January 10th in my letterbox. Of course, it warranted an immediate written reply. See letter to Ms. Mary. dated January 29th.

January 10, 1985

Dear Mr. Kassell,

In anticipation of the citywide mid-term exams scheduled for the month of January 1985, you received a memo dated November 12th, 1984 from this Office (see attached).

Unfortunately, you <u>did not</u> comply with the said item. The fact that you were summoned to report for jury duty does not excuse or permit you to be remiss of your responsibility. Nothing has changed—the New York City Board of Education always schedules citywide exams on or about the 2nd or 3rd week in January of each year.

It was unfair of you "to saddle" Mr. Prattler with the chore of completing your Social Studies and Science exams. In as much as you are aware of Mr. Prattler's special administrative assignment and his responsibility to prepare exams in ALL subject areas

247

for the Department of Special Education, you exercised poor judgment and demonstrated insensitivity toward a fellow colleague.

The remedy you offered as a solution to the problem is considered both unsatisfactory and unprofessional. In the future, please devise a plan of action and give due respect to the time on task in order to complete all given assignments.

Thank you in advance for your cooperation.

Sincerely,
Patricia Mary

<u>Ken Kassell 1/28/85</u>
I have received a copy of this letter.

1/29/85

Dear Ms. Mary:

I am in receipt of your letter dated 1/10/85 concerning your allegations: 1) failure to comply with a November 12th, 1984 memorandum from your office concerning mid-term preparation and planning, 2) your charge that it was "unfair" of me to "saddle" Mr. Prattler with the chore of completing my social studies and science exams.

My position on the above matters is in complete variance with yours. To begin with, I began planning for midterms shortly after I received your November 12th memo. Exams in 9th year social studies and 7th grade social studies were submitted for typing on or about November 19th. In fact, I expressed a concern to you during the 1st week of December relating to the problems of providing mid-

248

term tests for Mr. Broome's science classes and Ms. Biggs's science class. You may recall that at that time you suggested that I confer with Mr. Vallero for purposes of finding a possible alternative exam using the discipline of reading as a substitute medium for the science exams scheduled.

On or about December 10th, Mr. Prattler, in possession of the bulletin concerning the city-wide testing schedule pointed out to both of us the fact that 7th grade science was available in a city-wide uniform style. Your position was that the students would therefore take that exam. I protested on behalf of the pupils who were programmed to have Mr. Broome subjected to a situation in which they had no chance to experience success. You overruled my objection and further directed that I call Ms. Biggs to determine what subject matter she may have covered prior to her injury and subsequent absence. On January 2nd I submitted the following exams to Mr. Powers and Mr. Gax for duplication: 9th grade social studies, 8th grade social studies, and 8th grade science (Mr. Steadman only). It was understood that 7th grade social studies and 7th grade science could not be secured at that time, as they were scheduled to arrive at the D.O. on 1/4/85. The only unaccounted strategy concerned the question of what test to give in science for 8-202 and 8-204. On January 7th, 1985, Mr. Gittleman (in the presence of Mr. Prattler) proposed to me a plan whereby he would survey the experience 8-202 and 8-204 had in science with Ms. Biggs and then prepare a test for them. I gave that plan my approval.

As for your charge that I "saddled" Mr. Prattler unfairly with the chore of completing my social studies and science exams, I submit that on the contrary, I did everything possible to do all that I

249

Kenneth S. Karcinell

could in terms of preparing tests in various grade
levels. I had no control over the duplication process
concerning the exams. I had no control over the
January 7th arrival of citywide midterms from the
D.O.; actually, when I suggested to you that Mr.
Prattler had consented to work with me on some of
these problems, you gave your approval.

Finally, on January 8th, 1985 at 3:15 p.m. in your
office I stated that if need be I could be contacted at
home and would gladly come into school on a
weeknight and work on these midterms. During my
jury duty service from 1/9-1/25, I received no calls
from the school on any matters.

Sincerely,
Ken Kassell

Cc: Ms. M. Rios, Supt.

As if February's chilling cold wasn't enough, things at
John Paul Jones were even colder. By now Ms. Mary's
paranoia had reached epic proportions. No one was a friend;
and everyone was her enemy. She had lost all modicum of
professionalism and had resorted to haranguing people over
the public address system for every little thing. All rationale
was gone from the governance of the school. Veteran
teachers counseled the rookies to mind their business, do
their jobs, and don't make waves lest they be carried out by
the tide.

With each passing day Ms. Mary became more of a
recluse. She communicated with the staff either by PA
messaging or Main Office bulletin board announcements.
Imagine coming into work and upon checking the message
board, you find the following: "If you can't get here on
time, don't get here." Still, another said, "No personal
phone calls in-coming or out-going." While everyone

understood the admonition concerning personal out-going calls, no one could accept the admonition against in-coming calls. After all we all had families that were prone to having emergencies. How was one to know? Still, other staff members had outside interests that often required their immediate attention. Something had to happen. It was this last imperative that made me ascend to my second stint as "Acting Principal."

Chapter XXIX

Ms. Mary's Worst Nightmare

Thus, it came to pass on the fateful morning of 2/7/85 at 7:45 a.m. that a personal phone call for a certain Ms. Biggs came into the Main Office. None of the secretarial staff had arrived, leaving the task of answering the phone to Ms. Mary. At that exact moment, Ms. Biggs was "punching in." Doing so, she froze not quite believing her ears. "I'm sorry, Ms. Mary said speaking into the phone, I do not allow my staff to receive personal phone calls, Mr. Fallon. Ms. Biggs should have informed you of the fact." Approaching Ms. Mary, Ms. Biggs asked for the phone in a somewhat agitated tone. I'll do no such thing, replied Patricia Mary indignantly, placing the receiver back in its cradle. She then got up and retreated into her office closing the door behind her, leaving a shocked and angry Lila Biggs in her wake.

As the drama in the Main Office was unfolding, yours truly was in his second floor office partaking of my customary roll and butter, container of light coffee, a True Blue 100, and checking last night's sports scores in my morning NY Post. My "quiet time" was interrupted by a knock at my door. Looking up, I recognized the caller as one of the A.M. Office monitors. What is it, Thomas? Excitedly, Thomas stated, "You better come downstairs, Mr. K.—they're fighting." Look son, it's only 8:10, much too early for me to be breaking up student fights. Try to find out who is involved, and I'll get after them when school opens. In the meantime, reaching for my walkie-talkie I'll send officer Harrold to the yard. "But Mr. K, it's not the kids fighting Thomas said hesitantly,...it's Ms. Mary and Ms Biggs!" I half jumped out of my seat, and began a quick walk down the stairs to the Main Office. Arriving on the scene, my eyes beheld the following unbelievable yet somehow serene landscape:

Lying motionless on the floor straddling the doorway saddle between her office and the main office was Ms. Mary.. Seated in a nearby chair and rocking back and forth in the chair was Ms. Biggs. Ms. Gleason, the school secretary, was seated at her desk and was staring somewhat catatonically in Ms. Mary.'s direction.

Ms. Gleason, Ms. Gleason, I said in a soft voice. Yes, Mr. Kassell. Have you called the police or the ambulance? No, no I haven't. Let's begin with an ambulance. Then I want you to begin writing a report on whatever you saw and heard relative to what happened. Do you want me to write down what I saw, asked an excited Thomas? Certainly. I then called for Officer Harrold and asked that he seal off the office from arriving staff members and all others. I followed this up with calls to the local police precinct and the Superintendent.

You did the right thing, Ken. I'll be right over. Thank you Ms. Rios. Hanging the phone up, I surveyed the "Rockwell like scene." My eyes focused on Ms. Biggs. Slight of physical stature, she was well liked by the student body and her peers. Of late she had become somewhat preoccupied. I went over to where she was seated. Ms. Biggs, can I talk to you? She looked up and nodded in the affirmative. I asked Ms. Gleason and the office monitor Thomas to write down their accounts as to what happened here. Would you like to do the same? I can't; I'm not able to hold a pencil, she said while showing me a trembling hand. Would you like to tell me what happened, so I can record your version? Yes, yes, I would, Ms. Biggs tearfully replied. She went on to say that her son, a struggling young actor, had played a major supportive role in a recently released epic film. She further confided to me that in addition to her role as his mother and legal guardian, she was also his manager. As such, she explained, she had to be

253

constantly available to be contacted by public relations execs associated with the film's promotion. When she overheard Ms. Mary speaking to Walter Fallon, who was one of the public relations execs, she became frantic, as she had a scheduled meeting with him that same afternoon to plan for an up and coming public appearance for her son. That's when she approached Ms. Mary and demanded the phone. Maybe I shouldn't have used that tone, Mr. Kassell, but I was very upset at the fact that Ms. Mary was not going to let me speak with Mr. Fallon. What happened next? I prompted. Ms. Mary went into her office and closed the door. I lost it right there. I kicked and pounded my fists against the door. When she opened it, I punched her right in her face, and she fell down. Is that it, I asked? She nodded affirmatively. I'll be right back, I assured her.

The written statements retrieved from Ms. Gleason and Thomas more or less confirmed Ms. Biggs's story. Some added histrionics in both reports that Ms. Biggs had not mentioned. Apparently while pounding the closed office door with her fists and kicking it, Ms. Biggs uttered the words "open the door bitch." Ms. Mary, never known as one to turn down a challenge, did so immediately and said, "What." That's when Ms. Biggs "popped" her, said Thomas's report. "That's when it happened," stated Ms. Gleason's report. By now the police and EMS team had arrived. EMS had successfully revived Ms. Mary and was in the process of strapping her to a gurney preparatory to removing her to a local hospital's emergency room.

After reading the eyewitness accounts, I approached Ms. Biggs and disclosed to her that based on her own admission and the statements of the other witnesses, I had no choice but to ask the police to arrest her on the grounds that she had assaulted Ms. Mary. She had stopped trembling by now and had completely composed herself. She looked directly at me and said "Do whatever you have to, Mr. Kassell; the bitch got what she deserved."

Okayyy…Approaching the officer in charge, I informed him that the school wished to press charges against Ms. Biggs for assaulting Ms. Mary. The Officer approached Ms. Biggs read her her rights, and handcuffed her.

Strange, I thought, still no sign of Ms. Rios! By now the EMS team had begun the process of taking Ms. Mary. down the stairs to the outside waiting ambulance. I rushed to catch up with them. The police who had Ms. Biggs in tow followed me. Nearing Ms Mary., I leaned over and said, don't worry about a thing; I'll take care of everything. This was responded to by Ms. Mary. in a tirade of rantings and ravings to the effect that I had better not do anything. I don't want you in charge. You and that bitch planned this. At first I thought she was referring to Ms. Biggs, then I laughed realizing that she was referring to Ms. Rios Turning to go back into the school, my attention was diverted to the sound of a meek voice emanating from the throat of a young lady at the foot of the stairs. Excuse me, sir, I'm here to see the principal about the math vacancy position. Can you direct me? Pointing in the direction of the departing ambulance, I said, I'm afraid you just missed her. My God the young woman blurted. I'll have to discuss this with my husband. Suit yourself, I said turning to re-enter the school. Ken, Ken wait a minute. I turned to see the quick-stepping Clarke Lewis, Deputy Superintendent coming down the sidewalk. We entered the school together. Good timing, I said sarcastically. Ms. Rios felt that you were on top of the situation and asked me only a few minutes ago to check it out. I gave Mr. Lewis a photocopied set of all the written witness statements, saying that my own version would be dropped off later. You'll have to excuse me, now Mr. Lewis; I have to use the executive lounge. I'll be going, he called out. Later! I responded.

Several days passed when I received a phone call from Ms. Rios. I do not believe that Ms. Mary. will be returning any time soon, Ken. Therefore, I'm holding you accountable for the administration of the school. Are you kidding? I exclaimed. More than half of these people are in one way or another beholden to Ms. Mary for their jobs. I could not get their cooperation without another stripe. Done, she said. Anything else, asked Ms. Rios. I want it by 3 p.m. At that time, I shall hold an emergency faculty conference.

Good afternoon. I asked for this afternoon conference to debrief you on the state of affairs as they concern the governance of this school and our respective roles within that governance. To begin with, I am officially declaring the school to be operating under "emergency" conditions. Your union leaders will enlighten you as to what that means. Suffice it to say that all previous understandings are by the boards. When is Ms. Mary coming back called out one of her staunchest supporters? I'm told that she is still in the hospital and no definitive time for her return has been established. Are you taking over? he said. I think I can best answer that question by reading this letter to you that I received moments ago from Ms. Rios.

2/12/85

Dear Mr. Kassell:

For the period of Ms. Patricia Mary's absence, you are assigned as Interim Acting Principal of John Paul Jones JHS. You are expected to fulfill all of the duties and the responsibilities of the position during this period.

I look forward to the staff and your cooperation in maintaining school tone, discipline, and a high level of instruction.

Yours truly,
Lyn Rios

Community Superintendent

Any questions? There were none. Excellent. Be aware that within the week the entire school program will be reformatted. Again those of you who are affected are reminded of our emergency operational status and Ms. Rios's mandate to maintain a high level of instruction. Unless there are any other questions, we stand adjourned. Oh, Mr. Prattler, I'd like a moment if you don't mind. Jerry, I know how close you are to Ms. Mary. All I want to know is if I can count on you much in the same way she has while this crisis exists. I don't know, he said. I'll have to think about it. I admired his loyalty. His reaction was predictable; so much so that I had pretty much anticipated his response but did not want it said that I hadn't asked him for his support. Still, I said, not good enough. As of tomorrow, you will assume the special education math vacancy. I advise you to remove your things from the administrative assistant's office before you go home. I've already instructed the custodian to change the door lock this evening. Here's your program card. Good luck. I turned and left.

Arriving home I informed Ellen that once again I had been placed in the unenviable position of Acting Principal. When do you think Ms. Mary will return? she asked. No one seems to know. She is still in the hospital. I have a good idea, since it's almost Valentine's Day, why don't you pick up a box of Barriccini and go visit her? My respnse was, are you crazy? Did you not see the letters? It's the right thing to do, maintained Ellen. Don't let it be said that you have no compassion. The truth is I've been thinking about visiting her. Yet, a problem arises in that she sees me as a part of some diabolical conspiracy orchestrated by Ms. Rios to oust her. I don't think there's anything I can do to convince her otherwise. Then don't try to, Ellen said. Just visit and extend well wishes and leave. Ok, I'll do it tomorrow, I stated.

I arrived at St. Mary's Hospital by 3:30 the next afternoon. I inquired at the information desk as to Ms. Mary's room number. The stern middle aged "no nonsense" looking receptionist, removed a pencil from her hair bun and logged me in on the visitor's sheet, said it's room 333, you'll need this room pass. Thank you, I said. Remember fifteen minutes and no more. Yes, ma'am. I made my way to the elevator while contemplating my opening remark upon seeing Ms. Mary. I approached room 333 with caution, knocking ever so lightly on the doorframe while announcing my presence. Ms. Mary, I said in a "sotto voce." Is that you, Kassell? Her tone had its usual harsh bite to it. Yes, it is, Ms. Mary. May I come in? Proceed at your own risk, she replied. I've brought you this, I said, handing her the box of Barricinni chocolates. She then impatiently asked, what are you doing with my school? Ms. Mary, I don't think we should discuss business. I came here today to let you know that in spite of all our differences, I do care about you and hope that you get well soon. That's a crock, she said, becoming agitated. You and that bitch are out to get me. Ms. Mary, you're becoming upset; I'll be leaving now. As I exited the room, Ms. Mary continued to hurl expletives, referring to Ms. Rios alternately as bitch and witch. While I waited for the elevator, I began to second guess my decision to visit Ms. Mary. The elevator doors opened and who should emerge but none other than the aforementioned Ms. Rios. Oh, Ken, what a surprise! How is Ms. Mary? She's coming along fine, I said. In fact she was just talking about you. Room 333, enjoy!

Chapter XXX

Back on Task

The next morning, I held three consecutive grade assembly orientation programs. I informed the student body that until such time as Ms. Mary returned, that I would be in charge of the school. In each of the assemblies, I outlined a number of changes with regard to the school disciplinary code. Students I announced must have their program cards available at all times. Any adult in the school who asked to see their program card was to be cooperated with unhesitantly. If you lose or misplace your card, then you had better make getting a duplicate from your grade Deans your first priority today. Concerning the change of class routine, you will have four minutes to proceed from one class to another. Do not visit the toilets, permit yourself to be a monitor, or be distracted in any way from getting to your next class inside the four-minute interval. If you do, then you will be regarded as a Hall Walker, and I will suspend you. On suspensions, you need to know that if you are suspended and are seen lurking about the school, I will have the police pick you up. By the way, you are expected by 8:30 each morning. Lateness is not an entitlement. Each day the doors will be locked by 8:45. If you arrive late and you do not have an excuse note, you will be detained until your parent can be contacted. A word of caution: If you are late and don't really have a legitimate excuse, I advise you to have the courage to come in and be truthful about it. If you don't and instead loiter around the school, I will mistake you for intruders and call for a police car. When are these changes taking place, asked an eighth grader who was known to be a serious offender of most of the rules I'd just discussed. How long have you known me, Curtis? Two years, Mr. K. Then what's the one thing you know about me that you can count on? Your word, Mr. K. That's right, I said. If I say it, I'm gonna do it. These changes are in effect now. Unless there are any further questions, we have classes to go to. By tomorrow morning during lineup, each of your Deans will have letters for your parents outlining the changes we talked about today. They will also have nice new program cards for you. Have a productive day.

I would be remiss if I didn't mention the fact that for the period 2/12—2/19 I made several written requests to meet with the PTA. They went unanswered. I proceeded on a day-to-day basis, making changes where I felt I had to. One of the school's most glaring needs was for a seventh grade science teacher. As we were fast approaching the end of February, I held out no hope that the Board of Education would be sending such a person. I decided to resolve the problem through what can best be referred to as "creative programming." Mr. Prattler, the former Administrative Assistant, was as mentioned earlier dispatched to teach math in the special education department. Ms. Lendt, who had been the special education math teacher, and who had a license that allowed her to teach mainstream classes, had in fact taught science two years ago. I was her supervisor.

I called Deputy Clarke Lewis to run my plan past him. I don't see a problem, he said. Your rationale sounds fine. She'll grieve the assignment, but they don't have a leg to stand on. You have been charged with and are being held accountable for running that school. As you identify problems and offer solutions to those problems, then none of your decisions can be claimed to be capricious, which as you know is usually the basis for most grievances. Besides, if all else fails, you can always fall back on the fact that you declared the school to be operating under emergency conditions. Go for it, Ken. Thanks, Mr. Lewis, I will. Of course, Ms. Lendt filed a Step One grievance, she would later confide that she was pressured to do so. What follows is a transcript of the proceedings and the findings:

Grievance and Findings

Item 1—Ms. Lendt does possess a NYC issued license in Science.

Changes in routine and personnel affects the learning ability of those already classified "learning disabled" children. Maintaining structure for Special Education students is essential to improving their learning abilities."

Findings: Changes in routine and personnel affects all children. In this case, the careful selection of a veteran, guidance-oriented, and familiar teacher with a background in Social Studies and Special Education counseling was made to facilitate the maintenance of structure and continuity in the classes vacated as a result of Ms. Lendt's change in program.

Decision: Item 1—Denied

Item 2—"It is contractually illegal for a program change to be made so late in the year."

Finding: At a faculty conference held on February 15th, 1985, Mr. Kassell declared the school to be operating under emergency conditions. Program changes, which traditionally occur at Mid-Year (Feb.1st) and may have been contemplated, were not put into effect as a result of the injury on February 5th, 1985 and subsequent absence of the school principal. Therefore, in light of the fact that the change in Ms. Lendt's program is designed to promote a higher level of instruction for a greater number of pupils, the date of March 5th, 1985 is moot.

Decision: Item 2—Denied.

Item 3—Two vacancies in the Science Department are listed at the Board of Education and at the District Offices, thereby creating a jeopardy to my status.

Findings: The vacancies referred to have gone unfulfilled since October of 1984. The likelihood of a regularly appointed Science teacher (let alone two Science teachers) reporting for assignment is remote.

261

Decision: Item 3—Denied.

Item 4—"Each year I have received a split program. I have taught several subjects (requiring separate lesson planning). This year my program was entirely Social Studies; a change in my program is unfair and illegal. Additionally, the new program is split, calling for Science instruction in grades 7-9 and HC classes, thereby requiring separate lesson plans. The program includes Mock Court as well."

Findings: The fact that the teacher has taught split programs in previous years is irrelevant. As mentioned in Findings under item 2, the change in program is designed to promote a higher level of instruction for a group of 250 pupils who previously had no instruction in Science. Upon recollection, two years ago under Mr. Kassell's supervision, Ms. Lendt taught Science for a whole year and received ratings of Satisfactory on formal written observation reports and end of the year teacher's rating. Therefore, the assertion of unfairness is a matter for conjecture. Finally, the program being offered was prepared originally in September 1984 by the Principal, Ms. Mary, for a Science teacher, Mr. Broome. I must assume that the expertise of Ms. Mary was such that the preparation of this program was made in good faith to the UFT contractual agreement. The two periods per week of Mock Court are included in your program because of the Special training you and Mr. Kline received at the expense of the District office. Therefore, it would be inappropriate to assign these two periods to another teacher.

Decision: Item 4—Denied

Item 5—Request by Ms. Lendt to restore her original Social Studies program in Special Education.

Decision: Denied.

Sincerely,
Kenneth S. Kassell
Assistant Principal

Going home that night, I thought, well that's over. I wonder how they'll come at me next. It didn't take long to find out. The next morning I received a call from a Troy Brampton, who I recognized as the father of a child attending the school. He was, however, better known as a freeloading so called community activist, who had the habit of visiting schools in the latter part of the A.M. session and demanding a free lunch. Additionally, he had a track record of intimidation and baiting. Most recently, he had tried that with Fred Pickens, who responded to what he felt to be a threat by Brampton, by trying to choke the breath from Mr. Brampton during a D.O. meeting.

Good morning, I said cheerfully. What can I do for you, Mr. Brampton? You can get your white ass over here right away. What did you say? I said. You heard me. Bring your white ass here. Where is here? I replied. In the goddamned superintendent's office. Fine. You can tell the goddamned superintendent that I'll be right over. I couldn't get there fast enough. I walked into the district office and then stormed past the superintendent's secretary. Lyn Rios greeted me in her outer hallway. Why, Ken, you came over. That's great. Clarke is here, you're here, and Mr. Brampton is inside. Opening the door to her inner office, she led me in. As she attempted to define the purpose of the meeting, I said," Ms. Rios, none of that is necessary. Moving towards Brampton, I shouted at him. I'm here now. What do you want? You said something about my white ass. If you like my ass, I don't go that way. If you are threatening my ass, then I have to use Ms. Rios phone. I don't know what your talking about, responded Bramton, obviously shook-up at my demeanor. I'm talking about making arrangements to put you out of circulation for a while, scumbag.

Ah, Ken, interjected Clarke Lewis, we need to iron out the problem like adults. I'm in no mood for that. Get his kid out of the school or I'm out. I returned to the school and secluded myself in my office for the rest of the day. What's next? The next morning, I received in my letterbox the following letter. Alas, the returns of the paper trail.

2/14/85

Dear Ms. Rios,

Please be advised that this letter serves to notify you that it is <u>my desire</u> to <u>permit Mr. Prattler ONLY</u>, to serve as <u>my representative at all conferences, meetings, hearings, etc. germane to my general welfare, health, safety, and rights to due process during my absence</u> from service caused by an "<u>alleged accident</u>" in line of duty.

Sincerely,
Patricia Mary

February 21, 1985

Dear Ms. Mary,

I was delighted to learn yesterday of your discharge from hospital care. All professional differences aside, I was deeply concerned and remain so for your full recovery and return to work.

Among items being considered on a primary basis are the science vacancies previously assigned to Mr. Broome and Ms. Biggs. In as much as the classes assigned to these teachers have not received any meaningful or sustained science instruction for in excess of nine an a half months, I devoted a great deal of time and energy in trying to solve this problem from within our present school staff. Presently, I've developed the following concepts: all club periods would be dropped from Mr. Starks' program and picked up as group guidance instruction periods for Messrs. Lockharts and Adams. Mr. Starks would then pick up sixteen science periods from Ms. Biggs program. Mr. Prattler, who expressed a desire to return to the classroom, would take over Ms. Lendt's program of eighteen mathematics periods,(alas, he won't be able to attend the conferences you had asked Ms. Rios to allow for-the coverage costs would be prohibitive) plus four periods of remedial math. Ms. Lendt would take Mr. Broon's program in its entirety. Additionally, I've drawn up a plan wherein to facilitate more use of the Dean's office. Six periods of instruction will be removed from Mr. John's program and transferred to Mr. Manwaring.

As has always been the case, I should welcome any comments you would have concerning these items.

Best wishes for a speedy recovery.

Sincerely,
Ken Kassell

The letters and manipulations went on unceasingly. I could not bring closure to this chapter without this final anecdote.

Sometime around mid April, I began to receive phone calls from various district office staff coordinators complaining that I had failed to submit a report of some kind or other. My reply, of course, was that I had no idea what they were talking about, as I hadn't received any such report requests in my mail. During one such phone call, I was in the middle of a conference with a teacher with whom I had conducted a lesson observation. It didn't hurt that he was one of the few who openly supported my efforts since my ascension to the position of Acting Principal. After I hung up, he said, I'm not gonna mention any names but if you look out that window tomorrow morning at about 11, you'll find out why you're not getting your mail. You've got to be kidding I exclaimed—first, the grievance, then the paper maze, then an attempt at intimidation, and now MAIL THEFT!

Before I go any further, it is important to know that customarily throughout the school system, the mailman delivers school mail directly to the main office. At that point an office designee assumes responsibility for routing the mail to the addressees letterboxes. Items marked with the principal's name or Attention: Principal is usually placed on his secretary's desk for immediate attention.

The next morning at the appointed hour, with Polaroid in hand, I approached my office window. I couldn't believe the scene unfolding before my eyes. As usual the mailman was en route down the block in the direction of the school. As he got to the main entrance, he paused to remove the school mail from his pouch. I snapped a picture of him doing just that. Then to my great amazement, from the entrance vestibule appeared the rotund gnomish figure of Ms. Priddy, Patricia Mary's favorite gopher. She held out both hands as the mailman placed several large rubberbanded packets into them. I again "snapped" off several photos of the transaction. The mailman then entered the school with another bundle of mail. Perfect. All of the mail marked "Principal or Ms. Mary" was given over to Priddy, who was now entering her parked car and no doubt going off to meet Ms. Mary to "deliver the mail."

Hello, this is Mr. Kassell; it is urgent that you put me through to Ms. Rios or Mr. Lewis immediately. Good morning, Ken, nothing serious I hope. It depends on how you categorize mail theft, I quickly responded. Ah, Ken, I'm placing you on hold for a moment. Go right ahead; take your time. I knew she was hooking up the tape recorder. She was getting better at it, as she got back to me shortly. Ken, I have Clarke on the extension; I know you won't mind. I don't. I need both of you to stay put for five minutes. That's how long it will take me to get there to show you what I have. Show us? You'll see, five minutes. Bye.

You took these pictures, asked Clarke Lewis. Yes, I said. Was there anyone else present? No. Now you know why I haven't been filing various reports on time. Patricia Mary has them. What do you intend to do, Ken? asked Ms. Rios, tentatively. I'm going to call in the mailman's supervisor and request his reassignment. I intend to fire Priddy. Let's think this through, Ken. Remember, for every action there's a reaction. Our aim is to stabilize that school. The kids, parents, and staff have all indicated to me in various ways that you are doing a fine job accomplishing that task. Bringing Ms. Priddy up on charges for termination will detract from those efforts. I think you're wrong. I think that it will serve to reinforce those efforts. You know that the union will drag out the grievance process and, in so doing, Priddy will continue to work at the school. You will be portrayed as a bully, and I will not be able to help you, as she would be within her rights to continue work pending the outcome of perhaps a Step Three or Four grievance hearing. I see, I said. If I can interrupt, Mr. Lewis offered. If it were me, I would summon her to my office, present her with the photos, and make her "sweat." You know how to bluff as good as anyone I've ever seen. The game you ran on Brampton was a classic. You know, Mr. Lewis, you're right, I said. I'm gonna go now. Excellent, chimed in Ms. Rios. Then we are in accord, aren't we Ken? Absolutely, oh Mr. Lewis, the thing with Brampton. Yes. It wasn't a bluff!

In the final analysis, the next morning I summoned Ms. Priddy to my office. Yes, Mr. Kassell, you wanted to see me. I was standing at my office window when she entered.

You know, there's a wonderful view provided by this window—the large chestnut tree, the brownstones across the street, and the mailman. Come here and see for yourself; it's like a Rockwell, you agree? I'm not familiar with Rockwell. Doesn't matter; look closely at the scene. Do you see anything different than usual? No. You recognize everything? Yes. Good, look in that folder over there on my desk and tell me what you see. Oh, my God! Exactly. By the way, if you look out into the main office, you'll find that while we do have a mailman, he is not the one in the picture handing you the mail on the street. Mr. Kassell, you don't...spare me, Ms. Priddy. Shouldn't I have my union rep with me? Why? I responded. I haven't made up my mind as to whether I should have you arrested, in which case you'd need a lawyer not a union rep or if I'm just going to write you up on charges of larceny. By now Priddy was visibly perspiring. She had sat down and was just glaring at the floor. Of course, you know that mail theft is a federal offense; I went on. Oh Lord, not that, Mr. Kassell. I didn't mean any harm. You knew exactly what you were doing, I retorted. I'll tell you what; I'm prepared to keep all of this between us on one condition. Yes. When you see Ms. Mary, you tell her that you have retired from the mail carrier service. If I catch you in any such nonsense again I will hand over everything to the proper authorities. By the way, your mailman friend has been transferred to the South Bronx.

The outcome was such that word spread like wildfire as to my handling of the matter. That I did not have Priddy removed as I could have, warranted a certain respect from the entire staff. The rest of the year went pretty well. The staff, although not full of enthusiasm for my leadership, at least performed their duties in a rote yet professional manner, which in and of itself was a vast improvement from the time when I had taken over. Clarke Lewis' strategy was on the money!

Chapter XXXI

Hello, Elementary School!

As my stewardship of John Paul Jones continued through the spring term mercifully ending on June 30th, it was clear that Ms. Mary did not intend to divulge her plans for September. While it was known that she was recuperating at home, no one officially had heard from her. I closed down the school performing such obligatory tasks as "tentatively" programming the school for the fall and issuing "tentative" teacher program assignments. On July 1st I loaded up the station wagon and took the family to our retreat in the White Mountains of New Hampshire, some 350 miles from the city.

Over that summer respite, I had occasion to share my experiences of the past year with several friends, some of whom happened to be attorneys. When I described the details of Ms. Mary's assault, one remarked that it was "a ticket to ride." Explain, I asked. It's simple, as a civil servant, after having been disabled such as she was, any first-year lawyer would have no trouble establishing permanent disability. That means 100% benefits. It's like hitting the lottery, another remarked. She'd have to be crazy to come back. That's when I knew my goose was cooked.

About the middle of August, I received a telegram from Ms. Rios instructing me to report to her office on the day we were due back. Within the context of the message the phrase "DO NOT REPORT TO JOHN PAUL JONES JHS" was capitalized and underlined. I decided to get as much golf and swimming in as possible over the last two weeks of my vacation.

Good morning, Ken, how was your summer? Very relaxing and yours, Ms. Rios? I took some time to visit Greece, she said. Ms. Rios was going out of her way to be cheery. The last such time she greeted me in this way was on the Brampton business. I patiently waited for the other shoe to drop.

It's undeniable that by this particular period in my career I had developed a certain crust-laden veneer and an overall attitude that openly bespoke my contempt for the bureaucrats, both at the district and central headquarters. Over the course of these twenty-three years, I was hard-pressed to think of more than three or four individuals for whom I had any respect.

Tell me, Ken, how many years have you spent at the secondary school level? Twenty-three, I answered instantly. Did you ever consider getting experience at the elementary level? Not really, but now that you mention it, you've got my attention. Good. You know, Ms. Rios went on, it's the elementary school where our children either learn how to be lifelong learners or are turned off to learning for the rest of their lives. They are truly the formative years. I think a person like you could have a very positive impact at that level. As a further motivating factor, you need to know that Ms. Mary has fully recovered and exercised her prerogative to return as Principal of John Paul Jones JHS. She met with me accompanied by her union representative and demanded that you not return. Her exact words were "over my dead body."

Why am I not surprised? I said. I'm all ears Ms. Rios; what's your offer? May I remind you, Ken, you really don't have much to say in the matter. Ms. Rios was trying to reclaim her dictatorial style. I don't have much to say...you know better! As a supervisor who has been transferred within the same district on two occasions, I cannot be transferred again without my consent, I said. It's a contractual violation. In fact I'm thinking that I need to be back at John Paul Jones and unless your next statement makes more sense then, "I don't have much choice," that's exactly where I'm going when I leave this office. Placing her "pointer" finger on her intercom, she said, please have Mr. Lewis come to my office immediately.

No words passed between us until he arrived. Upon his arrival, Ms. Rios directed that Mr. Lewis contact Ms. Sarah Gilliam the Principal of the elementary school that shared the building with the superintendent and her district staff. Hi, Ken, how was your summer, asked a genuinely concerned Clarke Lewis. Fine, yours? I worked summer school; he was quick to say. Gentleman, interrupted Ms. Rios. Anticipating your request, a smiling Clarke Lewis said, I have Ms. Gilliam in the outer office. Excellent! Have her come in. Other than knowing her name and position, I knew little else of her. I assumed that she was effective, as it was a necessary prerequisite to serving as principal of a "D.O." school.

In the minutes that Mr. Lewis had gone to escort Ms. Gilliam to Ms. Rios office, Ms. Rios informed me that Ms. Gilliam had been without an Assistant Principal for the past two years and was very receptive to her idea of transferring me into her school. I see, I said. In the remaining moments, I searched my mind's data bank for any stored information on Sarah Gilliam. I drew a blank. Instantly the door was swung open by the ever courteous Clarke Lewis to allow the passage of a beaming Sarah Gilliam. Good morning, everyone. She wasn't at all what I'd expected. She was short and effervescent when I had expected her to be tall and overbearing. She had kept a good figure that served her very well as she gracefully entered the office. Her dress was an attractive floral print similar to those one might find on display at Loehmann's, and she wore her hair swept back and wrapped in a small tight bun. This style revealed a high forehead that according to Greek myth was a sign of inner and outer beauty, as well as high intelligence (ex., Helen of Troy). Sarah, allow me to introduce Mr. Ken Kassell, said Ms. Rios, in a somewhat "Sunday brunch like tone." I stood at my chair and while extending my hand announced, "It's a

271

pleasure." Shaking my hand, Sarah Gilliam said, "On the contrary, I've heard so many good things about you, the pleasure is mine."

She had me. First impressions are indeed lasting. Mr. Lewis, ever true to being the classy gentleman that he was, held a chair away from the conference table and said, "Sarah please be seated, we need to get started." Sarah Gilliam was not one to let grass grow under her feet. Do you mind if I call you, Ken? I would prefer it, Sarah, unless of course we are speaking in front of students, parents, or faculty. Works for me. Well then, tell me what you know about elementary school and its precepts? she asked. I wasn't sure as to what she meant by precepts, so I answered in this way:

According to my mother, I was excellent. Everyone laughed. Very good, said an obviously pleased Sarah Gilliam. And then in a coquettish-like tone, she said, "I prefer my men as inexperienced as possible." Well, that pretty much says it all, exclaimed Clarke Lewis, trying to sound as diplomatic as he could. Seriously, Ms. Gilliam stated, I know all I need to know about Mr. Kassell. His JHS successes are well known. His standards for excellence are likewise well known. To me, however, his major selling points are that he respects the teaching profession and that he likes children. The students learn that quickly about him and respond in kind. You can't teach those attributes. On the other hand, I can teach him elementary philosophy and work style. As she rose, Mr. Lewis quickly rushed to her side to hold her chair as she stepped off towards the office door. Come along, Ken, we have much to do; school starts the day after tomorrow. As an afterthought, she turned towards Ms. Rios and stated that she would have her secretary come over for my transfer papers later in the day. As you wish, Ms. Rios replied. Good luck to both of you. Turning to Mr. Lewis, Ms. Rios remarked, "a marriage made in heaven." She proved to be prophetic. Over the next four years I would learn as much as any student could learn from a mentor. Ms. Gilliam took great pride in referring to me as her protégé, and heir apparent. These years would be among the most enjoyable and productive years in my career.

Chapter XXXII

Elementary School and Its Precepts:
According to Sarah Gilliam

It was during my apprenticeship at the hands of Ms. Gilliam that I came to understand the meaning of the cliché, "excellence in leadership." Her biggest grace was her southern Virginian charm. She let you know that she was at all times a lady. You did not lean on a tabletop when speaking with her; you did not chew gum either. She would never admonish you verbally, preferring to stare in your direction until you corrected your own offending behavior. By way of example, I was always a very casual person, often resorting to leaning my backside against a desktop, while informally speaking with someone. Very often Ms. Gilliam, while observing me in such a mode, would simply stop dead in her tracks and stare at me. In the beginning, I reacted as if my fly was open, quickly turning and checking it with my hand.

Once I understood her look was a signal that something I was doing was offensive to her, my "open fly" anxiety attacks abated. The quality that made it all work, however, was the openness by which she administered the school. She encouraged the staff to actively participate in the decision-making process and conveyed her disappointment when they didn't. She often said that any success she enjoyed as a principal was a reflection on the teaching successes that they had. By the same token, when things were not good, they weren't good for her either. Her faith in everyone's ability and her belief that the teachers would do whatever it took to promote a successful learning experience for their students was a constant, repetitive theme, which she enforced with the word "colleagues." This consistence in style and manner worked. Even if you didn't see yourself as her colleague, you had every opportunity to truly be the best that you could be while serving under her.

In that first day of our meeting, Sarah Gilliam explained to me her frustration with the previous spring's declining reading and math scores. Because of those scores, the Chancellor had declared the school to be on review. This meant that most of the school's resources and endeavors had to be designed in some way to promote (guarantee) significant improvement in the aforementioned areas. Our aggregate reading score was 32%. This meant that out of 600 students, less than 200 were at grade level. Ms. Gilliam went on to lament the fact that she had plans for implementing a series of enrichment programs, which would now have to be put on the back burner. Only temporarily, I said.

I'm afraid you don't understand was her response. Once a school has been placed on review, that school must produce a plan of action identifying strategies and methods by which it will seek improvement. We must convene a staff committee with specific responsibilities, all of which will promote improvement. I must tell you that in addition to the obvious academic needs in math and reading, the Chancellor indicated that our school daily attendance average of 89% is unacceptable. We are obliged to submit a specific written plan of action on or before October 15th. Shouldn't be a problem, I said. Really, she replied. Well, in the meantime, we have a more immediate need to prepare the school's master prep schedule. I can't help you there, I said. Of course, I've done a lot of JHS programming, but I don't know the first thing about elementary school programming. I know that, Ms. Gilliam replied. Passing me a piece of notepaper, she said, "This is the name and address of an individual who retired as my Assistant Principal three years ago. He is a programming wizard and has eagerly volunteered to show you the programming ropes of an elementary prep schedule. You are expected for lunch.

Oh, and don't forget this, she said, handing me a small brown paper bag. Lunch? I speculated. Hardly, unless you're a beaver, she said. I looked inside the bag and discovered a rubber-banded bundle of #2 pencils. You better get going. See you tomorrow morning.

The trip to Peter Pratt's house afforded me the opportunity to reflect on my new surroundings. Ms. Gilliam was a true lady. She had wit, charm, personality, and knowhow. To find any of these traits present in the average NYC school principal was a rarity. To find all four qualities within an individual represented a discovery of immense proportion. At once I felt welcomed and wanted. I would reciprocate with loyalty and a renewed dedication to duty.

I spent five hours at Peter Pratt's house. I learned as many elementary school programming precepts as was possible. "Locked in scheduling," "common conference preps," "grade assembly programming," "cluster scheduling," "special education mainstreaming mandates," and "lunch duty assignments" had to be provided for in the overall programming scheme. I learned from Peter Pratt that staff identified as "chapter 1 reading and math teachers" could not be assigned to any duty schedule and could not be used for coverages. I learned that there were specific strategies for afternoon scheduling versus morning scheduling. I was taught the limitations of the use of paras and school aides with regards to their contract defined job descriptions.

Ms. Gilliam had few faults. Her one big one, however, was that she often would submit last minute requests for program changes. I accepted this annoyance as a prerogative of her position. In a way, I should have thanked her. It was because of her penchant for making last minute changes that I perfected my programming savvy. It wasn't long before my programs and schedules were used as models of perfection for others to follow.

I arrived the next morning at 8:30. As there was no one in yet, I went across the street to the neighborhood bodega, picked up a coffee, and buttered roll. A few minutes later I found myself savoring my buttered roll and very strong bodega coffee. Shortly, Ms. Gilliam arrived. How did your meeting go, she asked. As my mouth was filled with food, I pointed to a large stuffed manila folder. You'll find the class programs, cluster schedules, fire drill assignments, duty schedules, admittance and dismissal patrol schedules, yearlong assembly schedules, and hall bulletin board assignments in that folder. I'm impressed, she exclaimed. When you finish eating, come into my office; and we will review them all.

After having my True Blue 100, I joined Ms. Gilliam in her office. Peter called me last night. He told me that you were a fast learner. Not having your home phone number, I couldn't give you these changes, she said, handing me a piece of paper. Can you get them done by tomorrow morning? The teachers are due to report then, and I'd like to have their programs ready. No problem, I replied. Why don't we give each teacher a folder with copies of every schedule I've just given you? Great idea, she responded. I'll get Ms. Benton to start duplicating the materials. I'll also assign Ms. Diaz to collate the work and to prepare the folders. If you don't need me for anything for the next hour, I'll incorporate the program changes you wanted. Looking at me somewhat disbelievingly, Ms. Gilliam exclaimed, in an hour? Programming is nothing more than knowing the rules and juggling numbers, very much like handicapping something that I'm very good at. I don't understand. Anyway, see you in an hour.

Colleagues, I'd like to get started. Quickly the room came to order. I sat in the first row of the auditorium and observed the teachers as they filed in for the first full faculty meeting of the new year. Ms. Gilliam's opening salutation of "colleagues" would be one that would ring repeatedly in my ears for the next four years. I never heard her address them en masse via any other greeting. In short, she was saying that she expected as much from them as she did from herself. The result was that each person felt equal to the other. Colleagues as opposed to "ladies and gentlemen" were a singular term that did not allow for gender differentiation. What a wonderful word I thought to myself.

Colleagues, I hope you all had a wonderful and restful summer. We have lots of work to do this year. Before we get to our very lengthy agenda, I'd like to introduce you to our new Assistant Principal, Mr. Ken Kassell. I stood up at my seat, faced the audience, and gave a slight wave to them. To my great surprise, they applauded me. Thank you— thank you very much.

Later that morning, while I was handing out room keys, I was approached by an individual possessing a folded *New York Times* neatly tucked under his right armpit. His hair blown gerry curls reminiscent of the '60's. I'm Harold Sklar, the upper grade science cluster and school union rep. Immediately, I was reminded of Peter Pratt's warning…watch out for Sklar; he's very slick. I want you to know that I had you checked out. Not again, I mumbled. What did you say? Oh nothing, I was just thinking out loud. Elementary teachers are a unique breed. They require stroking and cajoling. You won't need to employ confrontation tactics here. I see, I responded. In the process of checking me out, your sources informed you of my penchant for the use of confrontation tactics? Yes, they did, a proud Sklar beemishly replied. You found it your duty to share these findings with the staff? Yes, I did. Then you've done me a great service. I should thank you. You see, it's not the threat of an act of confrontation with presumptuous, mealy-mouthed individuals like yourself that makes a difference; it's the knowing that gets it done. For instance, if you believed that by continuing to antagonize me as you have, that I might grab you by the shirt collar and slam you up against the wall, would you continue to so antagonize me? Of course not. Then don't. Here are your keys. Please sign the receipt on the space next to your printed name. Thank you. By the way I'll keep that stroking idea in mind for our next meeting, and don't forget to give my regards to Mr. Mittleman.

Later that afternoon Ms. Gilliam convened a meeting of her cabinet. The cabinet representatives broke down as follows: Ms. Lipscomb was tall and leggy. She served as the school's guidance counselor. Ms. Gilliam had publicly congratulated her on her impending marriage plans. Then there was Ms. Fundt, a member of the previous superintendent's staff but a victim of the spoils of war tradeoff with the new superintendent. She had a certain expertise in reading enhancement and staff development. More important was the fact that she was a friend to Ms. Gilliam. She was an AP wannabe and did not take well to criticism nor did she deal with change very easily. A real Ms. Know-It-All I thought to myself. Then there were two male teachers, one who served in Chapter 1 Reading and the other in Chapter 1 Math. Their physical appearance, when viewed in proximity to one another, reminded me of the image of Danny DeVito and Arnold Schwarzenegger in their movie "Twins." I would come to understand that both of these men were extremely competent at their jobs and could always be counted on to do their best. Truly, they would show me repeatedly that they were team players. Mel Mizell, Barney Sunderkind, and I would become good friends over the years, and I'm proud to say remain so today. The cabinet was rounded out by the presence of Mr. Sklar. His role was to inform Ms. Gilliam if he felt that any of the practices and policies under consideration might in some way cause the staff undue concern or stress, or more to the point—prove to be objectionable to the union.

By now you've all had the opportunity to exchange greetings with our new AP Ken Kassell. You know, she went on; in a way I'm pleased that he is inexperienced at the elementary level. I think that his views will be fresh and enlightening. I've already seen his capacity to adapting to our way of thinking. Every schedule in your opening day folders was prepared and authored by him and approved by me for release and implementation. It is my plan that Mr. Kassell be responsible for every administrative procedure we have. The staff will have to understand that Mr. Sklar, and they will have to address any concerns in those areas directly to him. In my chats with Mr. Kassell, I have found him to be a good listener and a man of reason. I'm sure they will share those sentiments after they interact with him.

Let's move on. As you will recall from my remarks at this morning's faculty conference, we are in trouble—and I don't like it. My goal for this meeting is to assign each of you to a specific "needs improvement area." You will then be charged with putting together a written "Plan of Action" for improvement in that area. Your plan should be formatted in terms of short and long-range goals. Ultimately, we will forge each plan into a master "School Improvement Plan." Two deadlines you need to keep in mind. October 1st is the due date for your individual plans. October 15th is the deadline for the submission of our overall School Improvement Plan to the Superintendent. The following areas have been identified by the state as being in need of immediate improvement: Reading and Math scores, Student attendance and punctuality, School discipline and building tone, Staff development and ongoing supervision, Early identification of "At Risk" students, Parental involvement, Enrichment and Remediation. Does this mean that we have to change our Mission Statement, asked Ms. Fundt. Nothing is sacred, Ms. Gilliam replied. We live in a world of change, and our survival is directly dependent on our ability to adjust to change. If we don't, then we fall victim to those who do. Ms. Fundt stared blankly at the floor, crushed by the rebuke.

Let's get down to cases. Mr. Kassell, which area or areas would you like to tackle? All of them. As your AP, I think it falls within my job description to coordinate all of the working sub-committees and remove any impediments to their success. Of course, I will assume personal responsibility for reading and math improvement, pupil attendance improvement, school tone and discipline, and staff development. Well, how did you decide upon these areas? Ms. Gilliam asked. All eyes riveted their focus on me anxiously awaiting my response to Ms. Gilliam's probe. I assume the bulk of the school's disciplinary problems emanate from within the upper grades. I have requested the supervisory responsibility for those grades. I can assure you that once those children become familiar with my codes of acceptable behavior versus unacceptable behavior that the frequency of maladjusted behavior will drop dramatically. There will be problems, but they will be isolated occurrences and not regular ones. Additionally, I look upon poor attendance and poor punctuality as discipline related. The upper grades will be at the 90% rate by Thanksgiving and 95% by the spring semester. In this area there is only one possible explanation—the parents. I will prepare a letter for Ms. Gilliam's signature for parental distribution, wherein we outline our standards and expectations for their child's attendance. We will make attendance improvement awards at our quarterly honors assembly programs. We don't have honors awards programs, offered Mr. Sklar. We will from now on, I replied. Finally, I view reading improvement as the logical outgrowth to a strategy conceived wherein every opportunity to seek reading improvement is examined. When, where and how are the key questions. Are we taking advantage of every opportunity we have to enhance reading instruction? If not, then why not? I look forward to working closely with Mr. Mizell and Mr. Sunderkind to find solutions to these questions. How do you expect to find solutions with your limited knowledge base asked Mr. Sklar. All problems have solutions Mr. Sklar. Do you wish to be a part of the solution or remain a part of the problem? It's rhetorical; you don't have to answer. Sklar stormed out of the room. Just to finish off, Ms. Libscomb will take the Student at Risk and Early Identification program; I will assume responsibility for Staff Development and Parental Involvement. Ms. Fundt will assist me. I will also supervise the lower grades. Unless there are any questions we will convene again one week hence. Mr. Kassell, a word if you don't mind. Once everyone left her office Ms. Gilliam said "I hope you haven't bitten off more than you can chew". You know that my greatest strength lies within the way I establish my rapport with my students. After a week you will see a marked difference in how they comport themselves not to mention their teachers. Yes, Mr. Sklar is very concerned about that. I can assure you, Ms. Gilliam, any teacher under my supervision who wants to teach shall teach. Any teacher who wants to improve their skill shall be afforded every opportunity to do so. Any teacher who wants to play "union" games is doomed to failure and ratings of unsatisfactory accompanied by all necessary documentation with recommendation for dismissal.

Do you think it was a good idea to ruffle Sklar's feathers? I can't help being who I am no more than Sklar can help being who he is. He knows the answers to the questions he asks before he asks them. For the most part they are self-serving and union driven. Don't get me wrong. I believe in unionism. I also believe that our children need more. I think the union probably feels the same. What about the reading problem? I don't know. I'll begin by looking closely at every facet of our present reading program. Which one do we use? How do we schedule it? How do we supervise it? Which reading programs are the more successful schools using? These are to me the obvious steps in assessing our needs. Of course, I want to hear what Mr.

Mizell has to say as well as Mr. Sunderkind. By this time next week I'll submit to you an outline of a plan which will address all of these concerns, and I'm sure many others. Then I won't keep you. You have a lot on your plate; keep me informed, added Ms. Gilliam. This school hasn't had a Principal/AP team in three years. I believe before it's all over we will do great things. Then, I'd better get started right away.

Chapter XXXIII

A Return to Routines

Ladies and gentleman, good afternoon. As soon as each of you has received an agenda we shall begin. Also, please sign the attendance sheet and pass it along. I'd like to begin by sharing with you my philosophy and background. To begin with, I don't like surprises. I'm very big on consistency, fairness, and predictability. As we apply these concepts in our own professional interactions, so do I expect that we shall apply them in dealing with our students. They have the right to expect us to be predictable in terms of our tolerances. "No" should mean "no" and not "maybe."

At that moment, attention was drawn to the fact that a late arrival had opened the door and was proceeding to her seat. Sensing that she had disturbed the meeting, she attempted to apologize. I'm sorry, I hope you don't mind, said the silver haired veteran. I'm afraid I do. People who are tardy I find are generally character flawed. You all might as well know, since we are talking about predictable behaviors, I abhor tardiness in any format. This business, in case you haven't noticed, pivots as deadlines are met. Throughout the year we will all have deadlines to meet and reports to submit, and meetings to attend. I shall regard tardiness in any of these areas as unprofessional. Pausing to make eye contact with each person, I asked...any questions? Good, let's move on.

You need to know that I set very high standards for those with whom I work and myself. I shall expect you to do the same with regard to your expectations from the little people. While your union contracy has guidelines for such things as lunch duty rotation, excessive paperwork tasks, hall bulletin board decorating, assembly programs, just to mention a few, the little people don't have a union to represent them when their rights are inadvertently abrogated by us. I warn you, negativity will be responded to negatively. Discipline, reward, and punishment are major components of what I'm about. I'm also about support, yours and theirs. I'm big on positive reinforcement. I believe the teaching and learning process should be a mutually gratifying one. Frequently you will hear me say to students and staff, "Did you have a good day? Did you have fun today? or some offshoot of the same theme. I don't believe that any of us has the right to behave in such a way towards one another as to spoil each other's day.

Let me give you an example of what I'm talking about. Last year, I found myself one morning in the outside yard just before morning lineup. I observed a youngster who hadn't been to school the previous four or five days. I called him over and told him how happy I was to see that he was back to school. He told me that he was happy and sad. When I asked why, he said that he was happy to be back with his friends and teachers but sad that his grandfather had died. I assured him that he was missed and that being sad was a natural and good thing. I invited him to have lunch with me later in the day. His face lit up like a Xmas tree. A few moments later the bell rang and all the kids scurried to get on line. By accident or fate, I located myself within a few feet of the class in which the boy was a member and this is what I heard. The teacher called him to the front of the line and said, "Alex where is your absence note?" The boy replied that he had forgotten to bring it. Get out of line, she wailed. Go to Mr. Kassell. Is there anyone in this room who would act similarly in such a scenario? Instantly every head nodded in the negative. Excellent!

Let's move along. I direct your attention to Item II on your agenda—Routines. Routines go to predictability. You will find that it shall be my routine to visit each of your classrooms every morning between 8:30 and 9 a.m. I will see no parents or schedule any conference during that time.

During the course of these routine visits, you will observe me walking about the room seemingly twisting my neck in every direction. What is he looking for you'll wonder? I'll be looking for the following: room decorations. Are they relevant and subject friendly? Rules and charts: Are they clear and precise? Pupil work displays: Are they current and corrected? Room tidiness: Does the teacher's desk serve as a model of organization or disorganization? The chalkboard: Is the school heading posted? Is there a specific area for the daily plan? Is there a fire drill procedure chart on display near the front door? Does the room have an American flag? Are the wardrobes closed and secure? Is the room "stuffy?" Is the aim or learning objective pre-posted? What exactly are the children doing? You will find that I consider myself first, last, and foremost to be a teacher. From time to time, I will sit myself down during a visit to listen and participate in the lesson. Please do not think of this behavior as a slight. Rather, think of it as a venture in team teaching. As time goes on and emergencies occur wherein your arrival is to be delayed, more often than not, I will cover your classes until you arrive. That is why you need to be very sure to get your lesson plans to me in a timely fashion every Monday morning. Pausing for effect, I asked, understood? Again, the head nods in the affirmative.

Attached to your agenda, you will find your bulletin board assignments, monthly bulletin board themes, and your assembly performance presentation schedules. If you work out any switches with one another, just send me a note to that effect. Of course, from time to time we will have "special assembly programs." One such event will occur on each marking period. Within a week either just preceding or immediately thereafter the report card issuance we will "highlight the positive" with an awards honors program. The next item on your agenda is perhaps the most important: First Day Routines. Every one of you is to report to the schoolyard with signs identifying your names and class. Lineup will begin promptly at 8:30. From the yard we shall proceed to the auditorium for an orientation assembly.

Excuse me, intoned the silver haired Ms. Brolly. Yes, what is it, I responded with an edge to my voice. I'd seen her type all too often; the veteran matriarch—all knowing, holier than thou, and regarded as an untouchable icon by her peers. You are deviating from Ms. Gilliam's pre-established routine of picking up our classes and reporting to our rooms for class orientation. Your comment is noted. I appreciate your concern. As I said, upon assembling your classes in the yard, please escort them to the auditorium. Before we break, let me say this. From here on out, I will view you in one of two ways, either as a problem-maker or a problem-solver. Makes no difference to me which is your leaning. Just be consistent. Thank you, for your attentiveness. I believe that Ms. Gilliam's plan for the remainder of the day calls for you to decorate your rooms, inventory your class records, secure the necessary texts from the book closets, and to prepare your first day routines. Did I get it right, Ms. Brolly? Everyone laughed. By the way does anyone know if the school has a bullhorn? Try Mr. Rankin in the gym, someone said. Thank you, and to whom am I obliged? I'm Ms. Bakerville, one of the sixth grade teachers. Thinking back to my meeting with Peter Pralt, I recalled his words,…"Bakerville the sixth grade bitch." In the years ahead, I would come to respect her as a truly gifted and remarkable teacher. We had a common background. Both of us spent significant time in the JHS. Both of us were strong disciplinarians. And both of us believed that our youngsters' talents and abilities were vast and that it was up to us to see that they realized those abilities and talents.

Later that morning, I got a call from Ms. Gilliam. I was well prepared for a summoning given my exchanges with Ms. Brolly. I was sure that Sklar's grapevine had made its reports and was demanding some form of retribution. You know, the staff lunches aren't being served until tomorrow, stated Ms. Gilliam. I'm planning to send out. Would you care to join me for lunch? Yes, yes I would. Good. What would you like? What do you have in mind, I countered—Chinese, Italian, or Kentucky Fried? I'll share a bucket if you're game. See you at noon, sharp, in my office.

This is very good chicken. Try the mashed potatoes and gravy. Tell me, Ms. Gilliam asked quizzically, how did your grade meeting go? Pretty good. There were several lively exchanges. That's putting it mildly, Ms. Gilliam said almost jovially. You do have a way with words. Seriously though, why do you want to have an assembly orientation meeting right from the yard? The fact that she asked this question rather than simply overrule my plan told me tons about her character. Aside from Open School Night, it will be the only time that we will have so many parents together. I think that it would serve them and us well to have them there for Q's and A's pertaining to our plans for the kids. Excellent, I applaud the idea, she said. It will also afford me the opportunity to speak to them, and to lay out our vision for the coming school year. That's great. More chicken I asked, passing the bucket in her direction.

That evening I was not able to fall asleep. I found myself visualizing the prep schedule and school program, looking for ways to improve the instructional delivery of our reading program. One of the tenets in life that I knew worked well was found in the axiom, "practice makes perfect." Oftentimes children and adults failed at tasks that they were confronted with either infrequently or for the first time. If you wanted better test results, I reasoned, we needed to teach the children how to take tests. Repetition, repetition, and more repetition. We needed to replicate test-taking conditions in every quiz, take-home assignment, class test, and all other reading formats. We would have to search for every possible block of time by which some aspect of reading enhancement could occur. Something Peter Pralt had said to me at his house kept ringing in my ear. The afternoons are pretty much non-academic, he said. The kids' attention spans are nil in the afternoon. Try to give them gym, art, or club activities. That's it...I knew what had to be done. Comforted by that thought, I drifted off.

Kenneth S. Karcinell

Chapter XXXIV

Two-Week Assessment...
What's Working, What's Not?

Let's come to order, Ms. Gilliam exclaimed. The deadline for submitting our rough draft comprehensive school improvement plan is quickly approaching. I'd like to know where we stand. Ken, I'd like to hear your report. If you don't mind, Ms. Gilliam, I'm going to defer to Mr. Mizell at this time. He and I have worked closely on several of the issues I undertook. Certainly, she said. Mr. Mizell, you have the floor. Mel Mizell slowly raised his 5'7" frame to an upright position, while lowering his eyeglasses from their "jacked up" position above his forehead. Because of the several consultatory meetings I'd had with him, I came to respect him as an individual who was dedicated and thorough. He was a diligent worker who truly had the best interests of the student body and his fellow teachers at heart. Consequently, he enjoyed a high standing among his peers, was well liked by his students, and greatly appreciated by their parents. When he spoke, people listened. His presentation this morning was deliberate and to the point. The fact that he was articulating a plan of action that we had collaborated on was tantamount to the fact that he endorsed it. The fact that I asked him to articulate it was a stroke of genius on my part. Whereas any plan put forth by myself might have met with some resistance, that same plan put forth by Mel Mizell would be well received by all. His honesty was refreshing.

In the years ahead, I would learn that he had attended law school and had indeed passed the bar exam. Given the choice of two professions, he chose teaching and we were all better for it. As an outgrowth of his legal training, one of Mel's favorite tactics was to play at "Devil's Advocate." In

290

a governing body, it is necessary to have at least one such "thinker" in the group. All too often, it's very tempting to take a "bandwagon" position. Without the input of the Devil's Advocate, the pitfalls of this type of thinking would raise up as a wrecking ball and lay waste the best-laid plans. The overall effect of Mel's thinking was to balance the sometimes over ambitious or over zealous sentiments of the "bandwagoneers" to be sure our present undertaking was not one that should in any way be vulnerable to the unforeseen. No "pie in the sky" fantasies. Every aspect of our program recommendations had to be well thought out and ready for instant implementation.

Mr. Kassell and I have met on three separate occasions since our last cabinet meeting. We decided that the conception of any "improved reading instructional format had to be geared to our students' needs and our teachers' abilities." We anticipated the fact that no matter what we did, teacher training was going to be necessary, and pupil target groups would have to be identified. Consequently, we divided our student body into three distinct groups: those reading above grade level, those reading at grade level, and those reading "slightly" below grade level.

What about those reading far below grade level? asked Ms. Fundt. If you'll allow me to finish, an indignant Mel Mizell responded. Now, where was I, the three distinct groups? I whispered. Yes,...it is our feeling that our resources and efforts as extended to the three aforementioned groups be minimum. We can "shore up" and enhance their reading activities through prep program scheduling changes and enrichment curricula, i.e. leisure reading and book review clubs, and additional library preps to name a few, are changes that can be accomplished with the stroke of a pen. It's the fourth group...I thought you only identified three groups, interrupted Ms. Fundt. We did for the purpose of separating them from all that remains, our fourth group or roughly 55% of our school. I think your math is off, asserted Ms. Gilliam. The figures show that only 32% of our children are at grade level. That leaves 68% below. You're correct, Ms. Gilliam. If you bear with me…I will, Mr. Mizell but I won't grin. Out of the 68% of students reading below grade level, 13% of them are one or two months or just "slightly below" their grade level.

In addition to what has been described as "stroke of the pen" remedies, we recommend some interclass transfers of these pupils to classes led by proven successful veterans, where we believe the necessary motivation to get these kids over the hump will be provided. That, therefore, brings us to our 55% figure. So you can see, already we have moved from a school reading at 32% on grade level to one that is reading at 45% We've improved by 13% in just 10 minutes. Think what we can do in a semester or whole year! Everyone laughed. I want to thank Mr. Mizell for working with me on this project and for his commitment to in his words, "do whatever is necessary to bring our scores up." When it comes to what's best for our kids and school, I'm a firm proponent of Malcolm's pronouncement "by any means necessary." I should now like to outline our plan of attack to improve reading in our fourth and most serious category, those children severely below grade level. If we don't, then by attrition in two years our entire school will be consisting of pupils mired in this fourth category. Everyone stiffened and looked directly at me. I then outlined a program of attack that left no stone unturned.

We recommend that three of the leading reading program publishers be contacted for purposes of having them make presentations to our staff as to their particular reading formats. We should then, immediately following their presentations, through fact-finding and consensus, come to a decision as to the adoption of one of those programs. This process should not take longer than two weeks to complete. Whichever program we adopt must have strong components for ongoing staff development, updating resources, on-site visitation, one-to-one teacher tutoring, and a willingness to pilot. This last component goes to getting "freebies." If we are going to lock in an entire school to one publisher's program, then that publisher better be willing to help us defer costs. Next, we believe that many of our students fail due to inexperience in taking tests. Accordingly, the administration shall mandate a policy of major subject area testing every third week, supported by a strong uniform mid-term testing schedule.

Isn't that a JHS approach, asked the relentless Ms. Fundt? Where is it written that elementary kids can't be tested in such a way? I'm reminded of an interview given by the principal of a Harlem elementary school last year, after she announced similar plans for her testing policy. When a novice reporter asked her the question you just asked, she said, "I'll stop testing when Harvard does the same." Every exam given, be it the monthly or the midterms are to be modeled after the standard uniform city and state tests. The questioning styles, the instructions, the point values, and the answer spaces are all to be exactly as they appear on the standardized exams.

Pausing for effect, I went on. Of course, Rome wasn't built in a day. Where does one get the time? Mr. Mizell and I believe that it is essential to provide an instructional test-taking skills lesson daily. The best time for this activity we believe is a twenty-minute segment following the pupil lunch periods. What about an instructional lunch hour format? asked Ms. Libscomb. As a guidance counselor, you should know that we would be doing our students and their teachers a terrible disservice if we take away their recess opportunities. I'm all for controlled and directed recess as a means of promoting such social skills as fair play, healthy competition, sharing, and tension relievers. Our kids are pretty much "controlled" all morning; if we continue that type of structuring during their recess opportunities, we will be doing more harm than good.

This is not to say, however, that we should overlook other options such as club activities in the library, science, computer, and chess. Of course, if you like, there is any number of guidance related activities that could also be pursued at that time as well. I'd be happy to discuss them with you privately, Ms. Libscomb. What about logistics— supplies, duplicating, materials, and grading, bellowed Mr. Sklar? I'm not sure I understand? You also need to know, Mr. Kassell, that our contract clearly defines "excessive paperwork," and I would submit that your proposal very likely would exceed those parameters. My teachers won't be happy campers. None of what I have presented thus far, is done with the idea that I am promoting happy campers. I appreciate your input regarding the excessive paperwork clause of your contract. I submit that the word "excessive" is subject to interpretation. After all, a man's excesses are intended to provide a certain degree of personal pleasure. That part of your question, concerning supplies, materials, and duplicating services deserves a more precise response. Mr. Mizell and Mr. Sunderkind assure me that the Title One closets for reading and math are amply stocked with materials, enough to carry us into the next decade. Recently, in our basement while orienting myself to its many storage bins, I came across a veritable vault of paper stock necessary for our duplicating needs. As we speak, that paper stock is being transferred to storage areas on the first floor. Concerning duplicating services, every one of our school aides and a corps of parent volunteers will be trained to use our duplicating machines. We will have such a machine available in the teacher's lounge, the principal's office, and my office. Teachers will receive a schedule of names and responsibility centers to whom they may submit their duplicating requests. All test-taking activities will be processed in such a way as to be graded by scanning. Any other question on this matter? Surveying the room and seeing that there were none, I proceeded.

Moving along, we want to re-philosophize the subject clusters that are assigned to our classes for prepping purposes. We intend to double the library preps for our fourth category of students. Previously they were doubled in Art and Music. Those subjects shall be reduced by one and extended to the upper grades as Liberal Arts Enrichment Classes. Re-programming to facilitate this philosophy is not a problem. I can knock it out in an hour or two. Our programming modifications will also provide for beginning each day with a locked-in SSR (Sustained Silent Reading) program, from 8:45-9 a.m. every class will do nothing but silent reading. The teachers will also model reading. There are to be no monitors, bathroom use, PA announcements, parent conferences, collegial chats, and latecomers. If there are latecomers, however, they will be detained by a corps of school aides and volunteers. After the SSR period, they will be escorted to your classrooms. Every latecomer will be logged in and given a letter reinforcing the fact that there is no "cushion or soft time" for tardy arrivals, emphasizing the fact that our instructional day begins promptly at 8:40 AM. You can be sure that staff members who have had a history of tardiness shall be similarly debriefed. Additionally, as part and parcel of our daily schedule, in the event of inclement weather, I will personally supervise the auditorium as a gathering point for our kids. From 8:20 until 8:35, they will be required to engage themselves in "leisure reading." They shall be informed (as will their parents) that we expect every student to have in his or her possession a leisure reader, which should never be kept in their desks. I would like to go back to our programming philosophy and instructional delivery procedure as concerns reading instruction. If I may interrupt Mr. Kassell, I think that now would be a good time for a break, do you agree? Of course Ms. Gilliam. Good, we'll reconvene in ten minutes everyone.

295

As folks departed for the lavatories and the smoking lounge, I made my way over to the coffee maker where Ms. Gilliam joined me. How are we doing so far? I asked. Not bad, not bad at all, she said. I just have one question. What's that? Tell me about the "paper vaults in the basement." Eminent Domain. I said. I don't get it, she said. The domain, although shared by the District Office, is ours. So too shall be its paper! As we speak, Darryl is moving it. He works for the district office. I assured him that for this favor, I could guarantee that his name would appear on our Xmas gift list. For confidential reasons, I don't want to hear anymore. We never had this discussion, I can assure you.

Let's come to order colleagues. Mr. Kassell, before the break you were about to discuss some aspect of our programming philosophy. Thank you, Ms. Gilliam. As a supervisor, I believe that if you undertake an initiative without providing for the supervision of that initiative, you've wasted your time. I think you'll all agree that anything worth investing time in bears watching and monitoring. Again, heads nodded in agreement. I think you'll all agree that the responsibility for watching and monitoring is specifically assigned to the administration. I, therefore, recommend that for purposes of uniformity and monitoring that our reading instruction be "locked in" during periods one and two in the morning. In the long run this will also facilitate on site visitations by the consultant.

Additionally, you have to appreciate the fact that administrators have any number of matters to tend to on a daily basis. It will help us immensely to know that since the improvement of reading instruction is our primary thrust, that we can monitor that thrust at specific regular times each day. I want everyone—parents, staff, superintendent, visitors—to feel that at our school the hours from 8:45 until 10 a.m. are sacrosanct, to be violated owing to only some type of catastrophe. To reinforce all that I said, I would ask Ms. Gilliam to announce to the staff that each of their formal observations this year will focus on their instructional delivery of our reading program.

In the final analysis, every facet of this presentation is doable. With the resources presently at our command, such menial tasks as: programming, supply requisitioning, and duplicating services are readily accomplished. Staff development will be provided as an ongoing component. What we have not provided for are naysayers and "doubting Thomases". I want to thank all of you for your attention. I also particularly want to thank Mel Mizell and Barney Sunderkind for their expertise and willingness to help. I echo those words, broke in Ms. Gilliam. Let me close by saying that until we select the reading format from among the three publishers alluded to by Mr. Kassell, we will continue to use the SRA program held over from last year. Last but not least, Mr. Kassell, how long will it take to incorporate your presentation this morning into the required format for our school improvement initiative, including the particulars as related to the multi-faceted lunch hour educational enrichment options? This time tomorrow. Thank you.

Next to speak was Barney Sunderkind, a big man with an equally big heart. I had briefly consulted with him concerning the Chapter 1 math curriculum to include that curriculum in the overall presentation scheduled for this morning. He was more than willing to contribute information to the presentation, but less than willing to make a presentation himself. I encouraged and assured him that he had no need to "sweat it."

In the months and years ahead, I would come to develop a close friendship with both Barney and Mel, trusting their counsel without equivocation, although not always following their advice. On more than one occasion when my initial reaction to an issue was to confront it a la my JHS style, their counsel led me to a more diplomatic solution. A leopard, however, cannot change his spots. Such was the case one fall morning which saw Barney and myself preparing the daily coverages for classes of absentee teachers. Suddenly a frantic parent who had come into the office from the outside yard interrupted us. Excitedly she proclaimed that there was fighting going on in the yard. When I asked her why the parent volunteers I had recruited and trained hadn't stepped in to separate the combative youngsters, she replied the parents seemed to be encouraging the fight. I leapt from my chair and proceeded bullhorn in hand to the yard. Barney followed closely behind.

As I arrived in the yard, my eyes and ears experienced the following scene: A grown woman was physically restraining a child, while verbally encouraging another child to render blows unto the restrained child. Hit him! Don't be afraid, hit him or I'll hit you, she threatened the reluctant combatant. In close proximity to the scene I saw a man dressed in NYC School Security garb who was smoking a cigarette and seemed to be amused by the goings on. I went over to him and asked why he hadn't intervened. You must be crazy, he retorted. This here (pointing to the reluctant combatant) is my kid; yesterday after school that boy took his candy. It's time for him to defend himself. Walking over to the woman who was still holding the one child while encouraging her child to hit the boy, I announced over the bullhorn, let the child go at once, or I will have you arrested for assault. Following behind me closely, the uniformed man yelled, who the fuck are you? I'm the Assistant Principal, and I don't allow fighting. School ain't started yet; you ain't got no jurisdiction. I turned and walked directly over to him, then got as close to his face as possible and said, put the fucking cigarette out, I don't want any burn marks on the bull horn when I crack you with it. By this time, Mr. Sunderkind had gotten all the classes lined up preparatory to entering the building with their official teachers. Unbeknownst to me, during my verbal exchange with the uniformed man, my finger had remained depressed on the bullhorn trigger. Thus, my words had been heard throughout the yard. As parents and teachers quickly assembled near the lined up classes, I heard one of them ask Barney, "What's going on?" Oh, nothing much, just Mr. Kassell making a new friend.

At that time, Ms. Gilliam entered the yard, went over to the uniformed school security guard and to the lady in question and after a few words escorted them into the school. As she passed in front of me, she paused and said, join us in my office as soon as you've finished your duties here. I nodded affirmatively. In her office, Ms. Gilliam informed both parents that the policy towards fighting at the school was one of no tolerance. She explained that the children are constantly reminded that every adult is available to listen to their complaints and to help them settle their differences peacefully. That's not how we 've trained our kid responded the uniformed father. I'm not comfortable with that response repied an angered Ms. Gilliam. Would you excuse me for a moment? She got up and went into the outer office. In a few moments, she returned with an envelope in hand and gave it to the man. What's this, he asked, sounding alarmed. Those are discharge papers. This school cannot service your child. We work in partnership with our parents. Anyone who would hold another person's child to allow their child to "get even" for some such nonsense as the two of you have described cannot be my partner. Have a good day; Mr. Kassell, will you show them out? Right this way. Passing me, the uniformed man said, this isn't over. You bet your ass it isn't. Later that morning, I called my good friend the director of school security and related the story of the morning's events with him. The gentleman in question was a veteran with seniority. In lieu of termination, he was suspended without pay for one month. I never saw him again.

Kenneth S. Karcinell

Getting back to Mr. Sunderkind's presentation, he made his remarks brief and to the point, and thankfully sat down. The next speaker was Ms. Fundt. As expected, Irma Fundt, wishing to project an aura of self- importance, proclaimed that as a result of her days as the district curriculum coordinator she was very familiar with the leading publishers of prominent reading instructional programs. She stated that she had arranged for a representative to come before us once a week for the next three weeks. We'll need to see them all next week, interjected Ms. Gilliam. We don't have the luxury of time. I don't know if I can arrange that with all three. That's not a problem, Ms. Gilliam answered, to whichever one that says they can't make it, tell them that your principal will simply evaluate the materials of those reps who do present. Ms. Lipscomb opened and concluded her report with the statement that, "Guidance would support all endeavors." I found her statement amusing.

Well, exclaimed Ms. Gilliam, I can't recall in recent years a more enthusiastic or more promising cabinet meeting. I endorse each of your reports. I do have some concerns, but they are mostly of a technical nature that I will address to you individually. I haven't given my report yet, she said. Please do, I urged. In addition to supporting all of your goals, I have an idea for an activity shared between our children and the community. I want us to have an anti-drug march through the neighborhood. Every class will design their own anti-drug use banner. We'll have cheerleaders, police escort, and refreshment stands along the way, with news media coverage and awards for the best class presentations. Also, we can stop at some of the community churches and our neighborhood high school, where those leaders can speak to our kids. What do you think? Allowing for the pregnant pause owing to the shocked expressions on the cabinet members' faces, Mel Mizell volunteered, "I'll video and edit the entire march."

Do I hear a motion for adjournment, Ms. Gilliam asked, with a hint of a smile?

For the next three years our anti-drug march became an attraction for such notables as local politicians and union officials from both the teachers' and supervisors' unions. The print and TV news media were eager to provide coverage. Private merchants offered to supply such items as fabric for our class displays; yards of felt for our school banners, food and drink along the way, and T-shirts displaying anti-drug use themes for every participant. By the third year, we did not have to solicit help or participation; we were solicited for participation.

The next three years saw our reading scores rise steadily, so that by the third year our school's aggregate reading score was such that 51% of our kids were at grade level, while an additional 11% were slightly below. Thus, with ingenuity, dedication, and pulling together staff and parents, we were successful. As a by-product worthy of note, during that three-year period, there was not a single incident of parent/teacher confrontation. The school had gained a certain air of respect within the community. It was not uncommon to see superintendents, local politicians, and neighborhood merchants in attendance at our report card honors assembly programs. They knew a "Kodak moment" when they saw one. It was truly a "Golden Era" for the school, its students, its staff, and its parent body.

Of course, we couldn't accomplish much of what we did without funds. For the most part our Board of Education Allocations did not provide for extra-curricula expenditure. We had to do some serious fundraising. There were regulations limiting pupil participating fundraising activities. After all, how many candy sales could one have in a year. We needed to strike like lightning—a one shot deal that would generate a large sum of money with a minimum outlay of costs. At our cabinet meeting, when the matter came up for discussion, Ms. Libscomb lamented that we were not a junior or senior high school. If we were, she offered, then we could do what they do in the suburbs. What's that, the cabinet asked in unison. They put on a spring play. They use their theater arts or English departments to produce the play. Expenses are deferred from vendor ads purchased and placed in the program. The show is usually put on for two or three days to packed houses. Many times the parents and family members of the players attend each of the nights. Why can't we do that here? I asked. Well, Mr. Kassell, we are after all an elementary school. Even more reason to try. If you don't think our parents and other family members of our kids won't come out to see their babies perform, you are underestimating their interests. Will you explore the idea further, Mr. Kassell, asked Ms. Gilliam? I'll report at our next cabinet meeting.

Of course you know it happened. Our sixth grade students under the leadership of Ms. Bakerville presented a hysterical version of "Arsenic and Old Lace." We sold out for three nights; ticket sales and refreshment sales netted us more than $3000. The learning experience for the kids and the adults was enormous. From my garage, I contributed an old Stanley Steamer trunk used by my aunt who immigrated to this country in 1919 from Russia. From the District Office, we commandeered an old oak wooden waiting bench used in most school general offices. Our parents provided carpentry expertise and worked alongside our art teacher in preparing our stage sets. Of course, the bookcases came directly from Ms. Gilliam's office. A local merchant donated an area Persian rug and two rocking chairs. PTA members provided make up and period clothing styles as well as some granny wigs. You had to be there. As for myself, I learned that there was something called a patent law that required that a fee be paid in order to use the script for our purposes. We gladly complied with this requirement and used the opportunity to educate our kids about patent law. As an outgrowth to this succees, all of our usual class play presentations were presented with the children having their parts memorized for presentation. Indeed the bar had been raised. The following year, the superintendent provided us with a grant of $5000 for theater arts development. Our kids performed "Cinderella" and "Snow White" to standing room only audiences. This was all accomplished under the joint direction of one of our teachers Ms. Sylvia Hurd, and a police detective from the local precinct Ms. Roberta Chaney. Our theatrical troupe made presentations at neighborhood senior citizen centers, some of the local churches, several private elementary schools, and several of the district's elementary schools. From all of this there are two observations that stand out more so than any I've mentioned thus far. The first is that over the course of the three years I've just described, only two teachers left the school. We had a non-turnover rate of 98%. Unheard of in schools located in the poorer areas of NYC. The second observation has to do with academics. Whenever our kids were involved in a performance, be it in our "Acting Troupe," or their own class plays, their testing results before during and immediately after the play production were heightened.

Chapter XXXV

And Then Like Magic, It Was All Gone!

The summer of '91 saw the city make its first early retirement buyout offers. This was a strategy designed to remove the expensive Tier I pedagogues from the city payroll and place them on the state's pension payroll. This process would go on for three years. It's important to understand that the strategy was at best an incomplete one. You see, as the Tier I people who by definition were the most experienced teachers were moved out; they were replaced at every level by novices, and in the long run many of these novices did not pan out and are no longer a part of the system. Of course, one could say "it would have been too much like right" to survey the various Teachers' colleges as to their numbers or to even survey their students as to whether or not they would be interested in teaching in NYC. At least the city could then have some idea of numbers in terms of an in-coming work force that fall.

The unions are not without blame in this matter, either. From '91 to the present, there have been two negotiated contracts. In both cases, they were "end" heavy, designed to pump up pension benefits of the retirees. Early entering teachers were expected to come and teach in NYC for a per annum salary of $29,000 that rose slightly to $32,000. Where were these kids going to live, eat, and enjoy life in NYC for that kind of money? Is there any wonder that there is such a shortage of teachers today? Is there any wonder that there is such a shortage of veteran supervisors to train the novices of today? In 1984, the state imposed its will on the city of New York and mandated that every elementary school provide for foreign language instruction. The city frantically examined its resources for meeting such a mandate and discovered that it couldn't do so internally. In an eleventh hour move, they recruited teachers from Puerto Rico and from foreign Spanish speaking countries to come to NYC. They housed them in YMCA's all around town. It wasn't long before several of them were mugged, assaulted, and otherwise accosted by the transients and perverts who often take residence in these domiciles. Shortly thereafter the new recruits returned form whence they had come. The city asked the state for an exemption for those schools who did not meet the foreign language instruction mandate. The state granted the request temporarily.

All too often the Board of Education talks about itself as a multi-million dollar operation. That's true. In the same breath, however, they assert that their management style is a "big business" one. That's not true. If it were, senior students in Teacher's College would be visited by a recruiter with promises of a base salary, augmented by moving expenses, rent allowances, and guarantees of on the job formalized training. Don't hold your breath.

Be that as it may, in the middle of the summer of '91, I received a telegram from Mrs. Banes, the new district superintendent. Banes was "old clubhouse." She and I were not strangers. I first encountered her when I arrived in the district. In her role as curriculum coordinator for the district, I had called upon her to advise and assist me in developing staff development activities for my departments. I found her to be a thorough planner and a willing partner. In short, she had my respect. The telegram's message was succinct. Ms. Gilliam had decided to take advantage of the pension sweetener and had submitted her papers for early retirement. The telegram went on to say that I was charged with the responsibility of having the school ready for its opening in September. I knew from its wording that I was not going to be the new principal. Such words and phrases as "acting principal," or "interim acting principal" were conspicuous by their absence. Who was she kidding? I angrily threw the note in the garbage. The school had been programmed and was ready to open tomorrow. I then went out and played the best round of golf I would play that summer. As I teed off on the first hole, I was also a bit miffed at the fact that Ms. Gilliam had not thought to call me concerning her decision. Of course, she was under no obligation to do so, but it would have been nice to hear it from her as opposed to the telegram I'd received that morning. No matter, I thought—back to the case at hand. Four!!!

When I returned to school in late August, several teachers and parents visited me to offer me congratulations. Their reasoning was that since I had worked hand-in-hand with Ms. Gilliam in revitalizing the school by authoring many of its programs that resulted in raised reading scores, the implementation of any number of special curricula thrusts, as well as any number of security and safety routines, therefore it logically followed that I would be chosen to inherit the throne. This was a classic case of illogical reasoning wherein valid premises lead to a faulty conclusion. If I have used the word "logical" anywhere in this text to describe the actions of a school board regarding the decision-making process with regard to the welfare of children, it has to be a "type-o,"—disregard it.

I went to the school on the designated date for reporting supervisors. For three days I fiddled around with the program and various and sundry administrative matters. Owing to the fact that the school program had been completed in June and there were no vacancies for which new hires had to be interviewed, there was very little to do other than some fine-tuning. I even found time to empty the five mail crates that had arrived during July and August. Finally on the fourth day, I was summoned to the superintendent's office.

Ken, I've known and respected you for a long time, she said. There is no easy way for me to say what I have to say to you at this time. There's no reason to offer for what I'm about to say that in any way will make it sound right to you. Then don't, I said laughingly. Just tell me who and when. I've been through this before, and I long ago abandoned my beliefs that people were recognized for their achievements. The chairperson of the school board thought that owing to the fact that the school community had become so accustomed to feminine rule (seventeen years under Ms. Gilliam) that it was wise to continue in that vein. Please, don't go on, I said. She continued. Upon further examination, it was found that one of our schools was grossly underpopulated and that it had a tenured female principal. I've decided to transfer this principal to your school. Please, spare me, I said. Knowing me as you do, you know it makes no difference to me personally as to who the principal is—male, female, straight, gay, it really doesn't matter. If they act right towards me, then I act right towards them. If they don't, then I won't, it's that simple. When is she reporting? I asked. This afternoon at one, she responded. Very well, if you don't mind I'd like to go back and take care of some matters in preparation for her arrival. I imagine she'll want to know all about our programs and planned activities for the new term. I couldn't have been more wrong about anything in my life. Of course, Ken. Oh, and Ken, you will always have my respect and support. Thank you, Ms. Banes, that's very comforting.

Chapter XXXVI

The New Sheriff

One o'clock came and went with no appearance from Beverlee Swoops. It would be two days hence before Ms. Swoops would make her appearance. It seemed that she had resisted Ms. Banes' efforts to transfer her into the school. After numerous meetings and consultations with the union, she reluctantly reported. She arrived with a chip on her shoulder bigger than the Empire State Building. In the two days that had passed, I learned that it was Ms. Banes' intention to closely monitor Ms. Swoops with an eye toward writing her up and out of the district. Just what I needed, to be in the middle of another good old-fashioned "cat fight." I was getting too old for this. First, there was Rios and Mary, and now Banes and Swoops. On day three, I reported to the school at 8:45 with my customary coffee and buttered roll. Upon entering the office, I was confronted by the shapely rear end of a tall woman possessed of shortcropped hair and a fan that she used in rapid side-to-side strokes to cool herself. As I entered the office, she turned to reveal a frontal view that was to say the least, well endowed. From her appearance and recognizing her from meetings I'd attended, I knew that the person before me was Principal Beverlee Swoops. I did not believe that she knew that I knew, so I decided to play.

Good morning, if you are waiting to register your child, we won't be doing that until the new principal arrives, I said. I am the new principal, replied Beverlee Swoops in a somewhat indignant tone, and you are? Ken Kassell, the AP. I'm pleased to make your acquaintance. Pointing to a stack of folders on one of the desks I said "I've taken the liberty to prepare these folders for your review". They contain profiles of most of our academic programs and copies of our prep and duty schedules. Without so much as a thank you, I heard her say, you were fifteen minutes late, and I don't allow snacks in the office. You're not quite right, I quickly responded. Really, and how is that, she asked incredulously? I'm a half-hour late, and now I'll find somewhere to finish my breakfast. Be back at nine or be absent, what is your pleasure Ms. Swoops? Nine will do fine she responded. Then I turned and left the office and made my way to my office where I completed the task of finishing my coffee and roll.

At precisely 9:00 I reported to the main office to engage once again Ms. Swoops. She didn't have a clue. Mr. Kassell, please see to it that the Coca Cola machine is moved from the room across the hall to the teacher's cafeteria. You must have me confused, I told her. I'm the AP not the APE. Quickly the chip she bore was joined by another. Ms. Swoops, as we will discover, was not one that suffered rejection very well. Little did she know, I hadn't even begun. Will there be anything else? As she did not reply, I left and spent the remainder of the day in my office, reading the *New York Post* and preparing a logbook to keep a day-to-day record of my dealings with Ms. Swoops. She had a reputation as being a big time unionist. I could see where this relationship was going. I would have to be at the top of my game to ward off the eventual paper path that our relationship would be bound to promote. I had spent the better part of thirty years in the school system. I'd learned my lessons well. I was ready for whatever Beverlee had in mind.

The next day, I reported at 8:30 promptly. Ms. Swoops was already there. Good morning, is there anything you'd like me to do, I asked. Yes, take an inventory of all books and equipment in our storage areas. That was done in June, I said. The inventory is amongst those papers I gave you yesterday. Well, those storage areas need tidying up, please see to it. Can't do it, I said. I'm ordering you to do it. It's excessive labor. Check the contract, I casually told her. Get out of this office, she screamed. I can do that, I said. I would find out later that as soon as I had left, Ms. Swoops had gone across to the superintendent's office and demanded my removal from the school. Ms. Banes denied her request. Later that afternoon, Ms. Swoops called me down to her office. I want you to know, I'm documenting everything that goes on between us. I should hope so, I said. Between what you are writing and what I'm writing, we could probably put together a good short story. Then I stared at her. I'm only going to tell you this once. If you like, this school can be a shining star. If you want to wage war with me, you will lose. If you think that you're good enough to "write me out," you're delusionary.

We didn't speak again for several days. During that time I made several phone calls; I had to know more about Beverlee Swoops My first call was to the supervisor's union. Hello, Kyle, Ken Kassell here. I need some info. Sure, Ken, name it. Kyle would forever be in my debt. Some years earlier, we had worked together in a Junior High School, which had had several of its staffers attacked after school as they were making it to their cars. On a particular winter afternoon, I was warming up my old Plymouth and noticed Kyle exiting the school. I also noticed a seedy looking subhuman emerge from the depths of a below street level vestibule in close pursuit of Kyle. I immediately blew my horn, rolled down my window, and called to him. Quickly, the seedy looking fellow turned around and commenced walking in the opposite direction.

Tell me about Berverlee Swoops. You're kidding, I heard him say. You know I'm not. Let's have it. The union knew that you were not going to get your shot at being principal, he said. The schoolboard chairwoman in your district is anti-white, and the superintendent while not necessarily being of the same persuasion, knows where her bread is buttered. We begged the superintendent not to put

the two of you together. Colonel Swoops, as she is referred
to, actually made a grievance when she got word of her
transfer. It was quickly heard and adjudicated. She lost. I
surmised as much, I said. You're not telling it all, Kyle.
She is a very strong feminist, he said in a low voice. Your
penchant for machismo makes this match the equivalent of
putting oil on a fire. She has already informed the union of
your behaviors and the things you've said to her the last two
days. We again asked the superintendent to transfer you.
Why can't the union find me an AP vacancy elsewhere in
the city? After all, I am competent and good at what I do.
We don't do that kind of thing anymore, he said. Don't or
won't? Let me see if I understand you, Kyle, I said. Here I
am at the hands of an egotistical feminist with no hope of
relief from either my superintendent or my union to whom I
pay $45 a month in dues. When we heard what had already
transpired between the two of you, the president himself
called the superintendent. Her reply was "excellent, I knew
Ken would be more than that witch could handle."

Sitting back I contemplated my situation. I was on the
proverbial limb. There would be no relief. I remember
thinking at the time that I must have in some way offended
God, that he had brought this pox on me. That's it, Kyle.
Not quite Ken. When Swoops finally moves against you,
and have no doubt, she will, respond to her in grievance
style. The district rep is well trained and will be at your
ready. Also, Ms. Banes has all but promised that you can't
lose at Step Two, which if you didn't know is adjudication
by her office. That's it, I'm supposed to feel good about
that. Let me ask you a question, Kyle. She's supposed to be
a strong unionist, right? Yes, so she says. Has anybody
suggested to her that she and I are union brothers, and union
brothers are not supposed to go after one another? It
wouldn't matter, Ken. She has a reputation for
vindictiveness. She is a viscious, calculating, and a
relentless individual. Where did she come from, I asked,

searching for some rational explanation? Two years ago, the then superintendent Lyn Rios who had worked with her in the Central Board Of Education quietly brought her into your district at that time. She was given a small underpopulated elementary school. So small, that it warranted no AP or Dean. Some members of the community who had been completely turned off by her, in an effort to get rid of her protested that the small population numbers (275 students) of the school did not warrant the assignment of a fully salaried principal. Their protests to Ms. Lyn Rios, of course, fell upon deaf ears. At least up until Ms. Banes forcefully transferred her to your school. Don't you see the play, Ken; it was masterful. You should know that many of the parents in your school asked the chancellor to reverse Swoops' transfer. He declined to interfere, saying that the matter was a local one to be resolved from within the district. The superintendent seeing the opportunity to avoid charges of racism let it be known that her transfer was a monetary issue. They wouldn't have had to pay me, the position of Acting Principal could be in place for six months. After that they first could have advertised it and gone thru the interviewing process without paying me for another two or three months. You were always an idealist, Ken. I gotta go now. Don't worry; we got your back. Like I had yours, right, Kyle? The phone connection was broken.

Sitting back, I mulled over everything Kyle had said. He more or less confirmed my darkest thoughts. I could forget about relief via transfer. I was indeed at the abyss. On the one hand, I would be at the mercy of an egomaniacal, self-indulging, and very angry woman. On the other hand, I was to be comforted in the knowledge that this same woman was loathed and despised by the superintendent, so much so that she had assured the union that when the inevitable "paper war" began, she would support my vollies. My greatest challenge yet. Would I be up to it? You have to know by now that not only would I be up to it, I'd relish it.

In retrospect, I often look back, and ask myself if I could have acted any differently that first day? The answer is always the same. No! Was I capable of acting differently? Certainly. Was I given the chance? No. My "life's code" demanded that I act in accordance with how people acted towards me. Turning the other cheek was not a dictum in that code. In the final analysis, it really didn't matter. Within a few weeks, Beverlee Swoops began to implement her own personal "chop shop" policy of non-tolerance for any pre-existing practices. Usually, a new principal has a certain degree of executive prerogative on their side when they go about the business of making changes. As they do so, they replace the thrown out "laundry" with their own brand. This was not the case insofar as anyone could see in Ms. Swoops' actions. She simply eliminated or shunned any practice, policy or initiative undertaken by the previous administration, with no replacement policies of her own. Let me amend that. She was preoccupied with the policy of "plausible deniability." There were to be no paper trails to her door. The outcome of her plummaging was such that teachers no longer had to put on class assembly programs, and they no longer were responsible for changing bulletin board decorations on a monthly basis. Uniform midterm testing would not be scheduled. The annual Anti-Drug march through the community was not to be scheduled. It's an excessively long walk, and it violates the teacher's contract, was Ms. Swoops' reason for discarding the walk. What it violated, I thought, was the fact that she couldn't get her 225 lbs. up and down those streets. There would be no need to "lock in" the reading program; the teachers could teach reading as they saw fit, maintained Ms. Swoops. No you can't have a lunchtime monitorial squad, Mr. Kassell nor can you have any gym equipment for the outside yard. You will provide an instructional lunch environment by

Kenneth S. Karcinell

reading to the children every day. This will be safer and cut down on the filing of accident reports. Don't hold your breath. Instructional lunch is a teaching assignment. Read aloud is a function of teaching. I am a supervisor. Find someone else. Unfazed by my comment, Ms. Swoops continued. There would be no more fundraising activities nor would there be a school "G.O. club." I simply won't have paper trails. Forget the senior trip. I refuse in any way to be held responsible for any "accident" that could occur on such an outing.

Not long after these "acts of abolition," the paper war began. Ms. Swoops sought to blame me for every untoward incident in and around the school. She went out of her way to undermine me at every opportunity. There was very little in the way of an academic thrust. About the only thing that got her attention were matters concerning special education. Her faculty meetings constantly focused on administrative matters. She dwelled upon "Chancellor" regulations governing corporal punishment, pupil rights, parent rights, special education referral procedures, and any number of drawl and mundane administrative matters ad infinitum. By the end of Ms. Swoops' first year at the helm, six teachers had transferred from the school and two other veterans had gone on record as saying that they would give her one more year to shape up. These same veterans told me that they were aware of the growing rift between Swoops and myself and understood my feelings, wondering if for the good of the school, would I mind if they tried to get Swoops and me to settle our differences over a conference table. My response was that while I appreciated their concern, I could not sit idly by while this lunatic tore down brick by brick the last three years of everyone's hard work. No child will suffer at my hand. Swoops, however, was another story. Stay out of it was my parting advice to these do gooders.

That spring the school reading scores declined dramatically. By the end of her second year at the helm,

314

declining math scores joined the downward spiraling reading scores. The school was accordingly placed under review, as its aggregate reading score had been halfed downwardly in less than two years. It would be another two years before the school would climb up over the minimum state reference point, which was twelve points below the aggregate reading score of the school when Ms. Swoops had been appointed as the Principal. The irony here is that the school was removed from "review" status, and Swoops received an Award for Excellence. It boggles the mind. A principal tears the heart and soul from a well above average functioning school. Scores in reading and math decline. Teachers are leaving in droves; those who remain are preoccupied with thoughts of transferring. What does the system do? It waits. Ultimately, it does what it does best—it awards mediocrity.

During the course of my years with Ms. Swoops, she had "written me up" on numerous occasions. Her favorite tactic was to give me such writeups at 3:30 Friday afternoon. Hoping of course to put a "damper" on my weekend. Very often it did! In every instance, however, through the grievance procedure, she was required to alter or remove the letters she had written. Our relationship had become legendary at the supervisory union office. They had become so desperate that they asked the superintendent to send over a mediator. Ms. Swoops and I agreed to this procedure. On the mediator's first and last visit, I was asked what I would like to see as an outcome to these proceedings. There isn't a night, I began, when I don't watch the 11 o'clock news with hope that I will hear her name as being the victim of a drive-by shooting in some bodega. I am fifty years old, I said to the mediator. Then I looked her squarely in the eye, and said...if I live to be 100 and something bad happens to this woman, pointing my finger in Swoops' direction, I want someone to come and tell me. The mediator got up, removed her coat from the closet, turned and left. Looking at Ms. Swoops, I asked, did you have anything?

In the spring, word had quickly spread that Ms. Banes had fallen out of favor with several board members. Her strength had always rested in the hands of the chairwoman who had recently lost her bout with cancer. The name that was being whispered as Ms. Banes' successor was that of Clarke Lewis. I counseled myself to be a good boy and see how things played out. I knew Mr. Lewis from past working experiences. I believed him to be a fair and decent individual. All I wanted was separation from Swoops.

Mr. Lewis took over during the summer. Significantly, he named as his Executive Assistant a certain Jack Pettiford with whom I'd had some history. Actually, Jack was heavily in my debt. Jack, you see, had been "removed" from his principalship by Ms. Banes and had been banished for "freshening up" purposes to one of the City University colleges. Jack, however, in protest had decided not to attend the required seminar. Bob Pritchard who had served as my union consultant and representative in my battles with Ms. Swoops called to ask me if I could take time to try to reason with Jack and if I could use any influences I might have "uptown" to see that Jack would receive proper treatment at the university. Always one to honor my obligations, I assured Bob that I'd do whatever I could. As it turned out, Pettiford was also a very close friend of Clarke Lewis. So much so that when Pettiford returned from his one-year exile, Lewis rewarded him with the Executive Assistant's job, instead of placing him back in his school as an unwanted principal.

Early in September I requested a meeting with Mr. Lewis. Surely you are aware of the situation between Ms. Swoops and myself, I stated. Everyone in Brooklyn is, he replied. Then when can I get out? I have a plan, replied Mr. Lewis, but I can't go into specifics with you now. Sit tight. That's it, I exclaimed; sit tight. I've been sitting tight for three years. I can't think of anyone who could have lasted in this situation as long as I could. Listen, Ken, I've known you for a long time. I know what you did for Jack. Have patience. It will happen soon. It took me one day to make it happen for Jack. You have a nice day, Mr. Lewis, I replied.

Chapter XXXVII

The Last Straw

Good morning, Ms. Swoops I have something to show you. Can't it wait? I'm afraid not. As a matter of fact you might even regard it as a bit of good news, you see I've been summoned for jury duty beginning tomorrow. I've taken the liberty to make a photocopy of the summons for you. I'm directing you to request a postponement for sometime during the Christmas, winter, spring, or summer vacation times. You can direct all you want. As you can see the summons clearly states, "no postponements unless owing to reasons of ill health may be requested." Please see my secretary when you come down for lunch. She will have a letter for you, wherein I shall request your postponement due to your presence being "essential" to the operation of the school. I will also indicate the specific dates of the various vacation days you will have during the year. Don't waste your time, Ms. Swoops, I won't be picking up your letter nor will I ask for a postponement. Jury Duty is a constitutional obligation that should not be shunted aside because it inconveniences you. Besides, how can you be so hypocritical as to refer to me as essential to the day-to-day operations of the school? You're pathetic. As I departed her office, I heard Ms. Swoops direct her secretary to come into her office and to bring her dictation pad. Quickly I returned to Ms. Swoops' doorway, when you dictate the letter requesting postponement you should also dictate a letter of insubordination. Today is Friday you know. Remember, I start Monday. I have duly notified the personnel secretary. At the minimum, I'll be away for five days, God willing, the rest of the year. You take care.

As it turned out, I served jury duty for ten days. Even though I had notified the payroll secretary of my absence in advance, I called in every morning and reported my continuing jury duty service. Unbeknownst to me, however, was the fact that Ms. Swoops had reported me as AWOL. She had gone so far as to return my paycheck as unclaimed. Certain colleagues at Central Headquarters made me aware of her actions. Enough was enough. The bitch was fucking with my livelihood. I considered any number of options. Finally, reasoning prevailed. I would do the right thing.

I parked my car directly outside the main entrance to the district office and waited for Clarke Lewis' arrival. Two True Blue 100's later, I picked him up walking down the sidewalk from his parked car. I got out of my car in enough time so that Mr. Lewis would not be startled but would have the opportunity to recognize me. Good morning, Mr. Lewis, would you mind if we just continued walking a bit before going inside? Not at all, it'll give me time to have a smoke. What's on your mind Ken? I then proceeded to describe in detail Ms. Swoops' latest antics. I closed by saying that I was strongly of the mind to have her arrested for theft. She wrongfully took possession of my paycheck and willfully deprived me of my wages unjustly. She knew full well that I was on jury duty. Can you prove it? he said. How long have you known me, Mr. Lewis? If I have to, I can prove it in a minute. When she returned my check to central, she stated that I no longer worked at the school and was in fact AWOL. The person she confided this to is on my bowling team. Added to that, the school payroll secretary will tell you that each and every day of the ten days I served jury duty, I called in to be listed on the daily absence record. Finally, I personally gave Ms. Swoops a photocopy of the jury duty summons and its effective date of service. Do you need more? No, no that won't be necessary, replied an all of a sudden pensive Clarke Lewis, as he lit up his second smoke. After a few moments of silence, during which time I had lit up my fourth cigarette, I said, do you know that it will take me at least two pay periods to recover my monies?

It will probably take a letter or two from you to re-establish my assignment to the school. Uh-huh, agreed Mr. Lewis. I gotta tell you, I considered any number of options. The one I decided upon, however, is based on my privileged knowledge of how the system works. I'm listening, he said. Tomorrow morning, I'm going to her office and am simply going to clear her desk of all its belongings. She will call you, of course, and you will direct that I report to your office immediately. Hell, you might even send the security staff over to escort me. For the next two years, you and I will get to know each other very well. It will take at least that long for the hearings into my conduct to reach closure. By then, I will submit my retirement papers, case closed. Clarke Lewis stared at me and then smiled. I believe you would. Let's go inside, Ken. His Executive Assistant, Jack Pettiford, met us at his office. Go ahead in, Ken, help yourself to some coffee; I want to speak with Jack for a second. Anything you say, Mr. Lewis. After about five minutes both Clarke Lewis and Jack Pettiford entered the superintendent's office. Clarke Lewis spoke first. Ken, we have a school in the district that has been evaluated by Central Headquarters as failing. The Principal has raised objections to that evaluation, maintaining that the reviewing committee purposely made no mention of any positive issues, highlighting only the negative. The Principal also alleges that the committee had conspired with his adversaries to paint him in a bad light, which would ultimately lead to his removal. I've been directed to appoint a committee to investigate both the principal's charges and the reviewing committee's findings. You shall head up that committee. Jack and I will round out the team. I'm placing you in the school as my special "fact-finder." You will investigate anything and everything. Any files that you wish to examine, any interviews that you wish to conduct are authorized with carte blanche approval by my office. The Principal for what it's worth, is aware of my plan, but not my choice of whom my ombudsman will be. Jack is going to call him over for a "working luncheon conference" in my office this afternoon. Jack will also notify Ms. Swoops as to my decision. My office will maintain your professional file and paychecks.

During the "working lunch," Mr. Lewis further enunciated my duties and his expectations. The Principal of the school was a gentleman who I had come to know over the years as a gentleman. Fairly even tempered, level headed, but clueless in my opinion as to curriculum and teaching methodology. He was instructed to provide me with an appropriate office, telephone, and typewriter. He was further informed that I was to receive no grade or department responsibilities. Turning to me, Mr. Lewis stated that each and every Friday, I was to report to Mr. Pettiford as to my activities that week. The Principal was informed that I was to be afforded total access to all files, records and materials I deemed necessary to my investigation. When the Principal balked at this dictum, Superintendent Lewis placed the Central Headquarters voluminous findings on the conference table and told him that I was his last hope in refuting the findings of the Central Board's committee. Very well, the gentleman replied. When will Mr. Kassell report? You and I will address your faculty in an emergency conference this afternoon. Have a 2:45 rapid dismissal fire drill to facilitate this conference, ordered Mr. Lewis. Ken will start tomorrow.

I waited for the room to empty. I don't know how to thank you, Mr. Lewis. Just then the superintendent's intercom buzzed. Laughingly, Mr. Lewis placed the phone receiver back in its cradle. Ms. Swoops just personally delivered your professional file. She left word that you can pick up your personal things at 3:30 this afternoon, and that you are to leave your keys with the custodian. Works for me, I quickly replied. Go home, Ken, and get a good night's enneth S. Karcinell

sleep; you have a lot of work ahead of you. Take this report home, pay particular attention to teacher absences, patterns of injury on the job claims by the same people, ethnic bias on the part of the Principal in promoting staff, unobserved teachers, and teacher literacy. There are seventy teachers in that school, some for more than five years, and yet there are more than half working under substitute license. How can they hold out high expectations for their students, if they can't pass a teaching test themselves?

Driving home, I couldn't contain myself. I put my favorite Smokey Robinson tape on and sang along with Smokey all the way home. The one recurring thought I had was for those good teachers I had to leave. After all, I was getting out and they couldn't.

As the school year ended, I was summoned to Superintendent Lewis' office for what I presumed would be a thank you for a job well done and a new assignment for the coming fall term. I was half right. I arrived at Clarke Lewis' office a little after 11:30 a.m. His secretary with a point of her index finger directed me straight in. Entering the office, I observed Mr. Lewis and his Executive Assistant Jack Pettiford seated at the large oak conference table. Good morning, Ken, come on over. What's your pleasure interrupted Jack Pettiford, wine or whiskey? To my great disappointment, Mr. Lewis informed me that he had received notification from the school board to the effect that his contract was not going to be renewed for the next school year. We had a good run, Ken. I tried my best, Mr. Lewis. Oh, I don't just mean this term, Ken. I mean the last twenty-five years. I have the highest regard for you, Ken. I have met only a few individuals who have had your resourcefulness, conviction, and courage to do what had to be done.

Here, here, Jack Pettiford chimed in, raising his glass. I lifted mine as well, and we all downed our drinks in unison. Immediately, we all went out to lunch and spent the time reminiscing and discussing our respective plans for retirement which we would be facing each of us in the near future. Listen, Ken, as my present contract doesn't expire until midnight on June 30th, I have authorized a transfer for you to our Talented & Gifted JHS to fill a previous vacancy in its administrative ranks. If I don't transfer you, whoever my successor is, will no doubt send you back to Ms. Swoops, as you were technically on loan from her school while you served as my special envoy. That no doubt would prove catastrophic for all concerned. I couldn't have that as my legacy. How can I ever thank you? I exclaimed. Pay for lunch, suggested Jack Pettiford laughingly. Done. One more thing, Ken. The Principal at the new school was not very pleased to hear of my decision. She had been holding out for the appointment of her own choice to the position. I'm sure you'll find a way to win her over, but be aware. By the way, did you know that I was that school's first principal? No, no I didn't, I replied. I won't let you down Mr. Lewis, and I won't ever forget you, I said, as I got up and extended my hand. We all parted company with an exchange of well wishes for a pleasant summer vacation.

Chapter XXXVIII

The Village of the Gifted...Valhalla!

In Viking folklore, the endless lifelong search is for Valhalla—that place of total harmony. Clarke Lewis already knew where that place was and had sent me there. Thus, unlike the Vikings, I would have the opportunity to experience Valhalla while still a part of this earthly world.

On the morning of June 20th, I cleaned out my special envoy's desk and reported directly to my new assignment. Entering the lobby area, I approached the front desk where a rather cheery school security officer greeted me, and a lady who seemed equally eager to make my acquaintance. I reached my hand into my back pocket to produce ID. Oh, that won't be necessary Mr. Kassell. Here at the Village of the Gifted, we don't require our AP's to sign in. Taking my arm, she went on to say "I'm Karen Backus, PTA President. Please allow me to escort you to our Principal's Office. Dr. Byrd is expecting you."

As we walked down the hall, the Karma was suddenly interrupted by the sound of a very pleasant and rich voice intoning morning greetings over the school's PA system. "Good morning Village. I am pleased to announce this morning that our Gifted Village is opening its welcome doors to our newly arrived Assistant Principal, Mr. Kenneth Kassell. I expect that every villager will do their best to make him feel welcome as you encounter him in the process of going about your business throughout the day." I simply stood frozen to my spot. Wow! I thought to myself. Talk about school culture and tone. Ms. Backus was tugging at my arm; Mr. Kassell shall we proceed? Yes, yes of course. I was completely overwhelmed. Even if I wasn't what the principal wanted for Christmas, she wasn't going to let her personal preferences change the school culture. Within five minutes of my arrival, I had been "schooled" as to what this school was all about. Look at the key words and phrases used by the principal in her greeting. Villagers...(taken to include everyone) not just students,...I expect...(leaves no room for doubt)...as you go about your business, reinforcing the idea that the process of getting an education and delivering educational instruction is a business. At once I was in awe and excited, a feeling I hadn't had in recent years. Odd I thought, I haven't even met her, and I felt like I knew her already.

As I sat in the outer office waiting for Dr. Byrd to conclude her morning announcements, my mind wandered back thirty years to a time when I had also sat in an outer office waiting to be processed. I recalled that I had mistakenly interpreted the fact that arriving teachers who did not even take the time to extend to one another such ordinary pleasantries as good morning, how are you, etc. etc. were dedicated and preoccupied with the challenge of their teaching assignments, when in reality they were thoroughly depressed and bitter about the day that was to come. As I gazed around my present surroundings, I was confronted with the reality I'd been searching for over my lifetime. Every individual who walked into the office had a smile on his or her face. Cheerily they removed their mail from their mailboxes and their room keys from the proverbial key rack (some things never change). They exchanged polite greetings with the school secretary and went off to their assignments. My observations were interrupted by the full rich melodious voice I'd heard moments ago over the PA system. Good morning, Ken, I've been expecting you. Looking up, I cast my eyes upon a very large woman. Later I would come to realize that an equally sized heart was contained within the body. This heart was full of simpatico and understanding for her fellow human beings. Her wisdom and temperance were sought after qualities by other principals, parents, and community leaders. I'll always remember her council to me repeated usually on the heels of my getting fired up over some inane board policy or some such other related matter. "Ken, this isn't a battle worth fighting," she would say, usually followed up with a facial expression that said, "move on," which I did.

Yesterday at about 2:30 p.m., Mr. Lewis informed our Parents' Association and me of his decision to transfer you to our village to fill our long-standing Assistant Principal's vacancy. I must confess I had some very serious concerns over that decision. Here at the Village, we have a special culture, and while I am somewhat aware of your accomplishments over the years in our district, its your reputation for confrontation which causes my concern. My reputation is well founded Dr. Byrd, and I would not insult your intelligence by denying it in any way. On the other hand, being as well informed as you are, you are no doubt to use your words somewhat aware of my high standing among the parents of the children I have supervised in the district. My reputation for confrontation should not be an issue. My reputation for fairness and child rights advocacy should. In a nutshell here's what that reputation says: If you are a teacher, be the best that you can be, do your job, know how to take constructive criticism, be nice to the children, and we will get along. If you are someone who "messes with my kids, you mess with me, and my reputation for confrontation." Bravo, broke in PTA President Backus. I shall tell you, Mr. Kassell that in those hours between Mr. Lewis' informing us of his decision to transfer you to our village and now, we were able to check you out in a hurry. Some parents spoke very highly of you, others less so, but all were united on the issue of your caring for our children, qualifying their opinion of you by saying that you had a way of getting the best out of them. I suspect that accomplishment has to do with your ability to communicate to them, and that you had high expectations for them. That quality is very important here. Smiling, Ms. Backus closed her remarks with the statement, "and we can work on that confrontation thing." Everyone laughed. Extending her hand, Dr. Byrd exclaimed welcome! Thank you—thank you both. It's very gratifying to know that after thirty years one can be found to have achieved one's goals as attested to by those he would serve. If I may ask, Ken, what are your plans? Well, I'm fifty-three, my daughter is about to graduate from Cornell, and my son will attend Cornell as a freshman this fall. I'm thinking retirement in four years, with as little fanfare and confrontation as possible. Again we all laughed. I've got two boys, Dr. Byrd volunteered. One attends Moorehouse, and the other is an eighth grader here. You're gonna love it here. Everyone is family. Come—let's take a tour of the school.

Ms. Backus and I followed Dr. Byrd's lead as we exited her office. Walking in the hall, we approached an elevator at which point I declared, now I know I'm gonna like it here. As we disembarked from the elevator on the third floor, my eyes beheld the following scenario: students were in the process of changing classes. Every student was "weighted down" with a stuffed bookbag. Each appeared to be dressed uniformly. Is there a school dress code? I asked Dr. Byrd. For students and staff, she quickly responded. They all know what is expected of them, she said. I further observed smiling teachers standing at their doorways supervising the traffic flow and urging students to hurry up to their next class. Looking at hall decorations, I was struck by the fact that not only was every bulletin board decorated but that most of the wall space as well was used for pupil work displays. This is our JHS village; you'll meet Ms. Casper, the AP in charge at lunch. By the way, in honor of your arrival, the PTA is providing us with a "special lunch" in my office at noon. That's great. I'll look forward to it. An approaching female student halted our walk, good morning, Dr. Byrd. Excuse me for interrupting you. Not at all, replied

Dr. Byrd. How is everything in our upper village this morning? Fine, answered the young lady, eagerly directing her attention to me. Are you Mr. Kassell, she asked, while taking out a notepad and a pen. Yes, I am. Would you mind spelling your name for me? I'm the senior activities officer. We want to send you an invitation to our commencement exercise next week, and we don't want to misspell your name. I stood motionless and speechless, reflecting on my first greeting with kids in other schools upon my first day arrival. Finally, I heard myself say Kassell, K-A-S-S-E-L-L. Thank you, Mr. Kassell. Do you have a mailbox? Not yet, interjected Dr. Byrd, but we will have one by this afternoon. Is that satisfactory, Etta? Yes, Dr. Byrd, the child replied sheepishly. I better get to class now. I'd say, affirmed Dr. Byrd.

Taking the elevator, we got off at the second floor. This will be your floor, Ken. You shall be in charge of grades 2, 3, 4, and 5. All of them are housed on this floor. As we got off the elevator, a pencil thin gentleman, whose heavy accent bespoke his West Indies heritage, greeted us. Good morning, Dr. Byrd, and with a glance in my direction he tacked on the word, sir. Good morning to you, Mr. Horn. I'd like you to meet out new AP Ken Kassell. Immediately, I stepped toward Mr. Horn and extended my hand. Extending his, Mr. Horn said, I'm very pleased to make your acquaintance. His firm and strong handshake impressed me. I'm going down to my office now. I'll leave you two to get acquainted. Do you have the master key, Mr. Horn? Yes, I do. I'll show the gentleman to his office and be as helpful as I can. I'm counting on it, said a departing Dr. Byrd as the elevator doors closed.

For the next three years, Mr. Horn would prove invaluable to me. His knowledge and understanding were a great resource. His council was wise. When I ran ideas by him, I knew his response would be an honest one.

For the most part, the rest of the morning was pretty much routine. There wasn't a teacher or child with whom I met that didn't go out of their way to extend kind wishes and welcoming greetings. The children, bless their hearts, even went so far as to inquire as to whether or not I liked it here.

At 11:45, I joined Dr. Byrd for lunch. Impressions, thoughts, questions? she asked. Many. Today is June 20th, just one week away from closing, yet every child had a full bookbag, and hall bulletin boards were all still decorated. Every classroom was academically engaged. All staff were professionally dressed. The children were adorned in their school uniforms. I even heard one teacher refer to the evening's homework assignment. What do you infer from those observations? Dr. Byrd asked, in much the same way as Lee Strausberg asked Al Pacino for his impression after Pacino recounted his observation of a cuban guerilla who blew himself up rather than get arrested by the police, in the "Godfather Part II." Pacino's answer was that he thought the rebels were dedicated to winning. Mimicking Pacino, I said, it occurs to me that everyone here is dedicated to the learning process. Looking at me, Dr. Byrd said, and therein lay the secret. From the first moment a student or teacher or as in your case an administrator arrives in our village, it is the job of everyone else to orient that person as to our culture—"The culture of teaching and learning." We stress the productive use of every minute of every hour of every day in our school calendar towards the end of maximizing our educational opportunities. Therefore, the teachers teach and the students learn. Learning has no calendar limitations; it is, as I'm sure you are aware, a lifelong process. That said, I want to put your mind at ease. We'll collect texts and secure our learning apparatus two days before the last school day. We will have our fun then. Can you barbecue, Ken? Hesitantly, I replied that I could. Excellent, I'll see to it that you receive an official school apron and I will inform

Mr. Demmick of your availability for our open school lunch barbecue. You'll have to supply your own hat.

Getting up from my chair, I walked over to where Dr. Byrd was seated and extending my hand. I said, "I want to thank you, Dr. Byrd." For what? she inquired. For your graciousness and for not prying. You mean about you and Beverlee? Listen we all carry baggage. None of us can afford to sit in judgment on things that are not our business. In this village, however, all that baggage is left at the door. By the way, what did you think of Mr. Horn? We got along great, I quickly replied. He's seventy-five years old. He is one of my parent volunteers. Every day he arrives at 7:30 a.m. with his grandson who is in our fifth grade. He supervises the breakfast program, the outside yard, and all three pupil lunch hours, not to mention a plethora of other duties I assign him. I think he and I are going to get along famously. It was a prophetic statement. Excellent, I'm going to assign him to you exclusively in the fall. The fact is you will be the administrator in charge of most of the programs of which Mr. Horn is already involved. I like your style Dr. Byrd. Thank you. There's just one more thing. Pointing at a small brown envelope, Dr. Byrd said, you'll find your office keys, master classroom and master closet key, as well as a Men's Room master in there. Also, you should have a yellow Board of Education dashboard placard for your car in there as well. Yes, it's all here, I said, examining the contents as Dr. Byrd was itemizing them. Good, I think that about does it. Just one thing, I asked. Yes…a typewriter. Is it possible for me to have a typewriter? I do all my own reports. This is the modern times, Ken; you will have a computer and word processor at the beginning of the next term. I'm afraid I'm not computer literate, Dr. Byrd. That will have to change, won't it? We both laughed and I departed her office feeling rejuvenated and very lucky. While driving home, it occurred to me that like the Vikings, I'd found Valhalla.

Chapter XXXIX

A Plague Descends Upon the Village

As I began my 32nd year, I found myself reflecting more often on the preceeding thirty-one years—a true sign that my mind was preparing for retirement. In each and every reflective pause, I managed to focus on any number of the myriad achievements I'd experienced in the face of the constant flow of impediments to them birthed by the system on a continuing basis. Coincidentally, I was beginning my second year at "The Village." This in and of itself was a most comforting thought. Over the course of my first year, I'd gained a great deal of respect for Dr. Byrd. I saw her as a great source of strength and an inspiration. I found her to be philosophically enlightening. She was frequently given to such "Byrdisms" as, "This is not a battle worth fighting," or "a rising tide lifts all ships." In many ways for me, she was a calming influence. So much so that I promised myself that I'd put in two more years and achieve my goal of thirty-five. Sadly, as you will see from the turn of events described in the pages ahead, this last personal goal would go unrealized.

August found me and the other district supervisors attending our annual superintendent's opening meeting. All too frequently (once every two years) this meeting was cynically referred to as the "New Superintendent's Imprint Meeting." So it was only appropriate that my second year at The Village would coincide with the arrival of a new superintendent to the district. For me Dr. Constance Jennings would be the nineteenth superintendent I would serve under over the course of my thirty-two-year career. There had been nine in eleven years in Harlem and ten in my thus far twenty-one years in Bed-Stuy. Is there a relationship between stability in leadership and learning?

331

You bet there is. Is there a relationship between local school boards and leadership instability? Absolutely. They thrive on it. In the short term school boards need to be redefined. Prerequisites for being a candidate for school board election must be revamped with a strong emphasis placed on academics and respect for the "Teaching: Learning Industry." You will not find coaches, managers, or CEO's running teams or companies whose products and goals are things with which they have no familiarity. On school boards in NYC, however, we discover all too frequently the presence of felons, illiterates, incompetents, bafoons, jokers and charlatans. These same individuals are placing superintendents and principals in their seats. Do you see a problem here?

So it was in this climate that Dr. Jennings began her remarks. In observing her "iron woman like style," it was easy to see why those with whom she had previously worked referred her to as General Jennings. Of course, I had checked her out. Walking directly over to where Dr. Byrd and the rest of us were seated and staring directly at her, I heard her speak these unthinkable words. "There will be no favoritism shown to any school under my governance. I do not believe in Talented and Gifted education. As a matter of fact, you will all see from your budget allocations that it is The Talented and Gifted school which has been cut the most." Mockingly, she offered as an afterthought, "after all they've been getting the most for years." My neck hairs perked up, and a chill ran down my spine. Dr. Byrd was motionless.

Immediately, I raised my hand to protest. Dr. Byrd placed hers over mine and gently pressed it down while ever so slightly shaking her head no. Whispering, she counseled, "The battle will be fought elsewhere." War had been declared, nevertheless. Shortly, Dr. Byrd got up and left the meeting. In a show of support I and the rest of the school cabinet followed her lead. In the car on the way back to the school, Dr. Byrd said we must circle the wagons. I will call an emergency meeting of our PTA executive board. They have a right to see what has been done to our school. Unfolding the allocation budget sheet, she announced that we had been cut one guidance counselor, one family assistant, one school aide, and one security guard. Prophetically, she stated, "I do believe that this is just the tip of the iceberg." She could not have taken these steps without the support of the school board or should I say the directive of its chairperson. They have, however, underestimated the resources of our PTA as well as our collective resolve that The Village remains at peace and thriving. Have no fear everyone; "this too shall pass". Little did she know that it would take the entire school year to do so and at great personal strife and loss to all of us.

Chapter XL

"Just When I Was Mellowing Out, They've Fired Me Up Again!

The morning of November 15, 1996 was particularly cold. It took several turns of the ignition to get my engine to turn over. Little did I realize that the day ahead would become gloomier by the hour. After dismissing the 4th, 5th, and 6th grade classes from our "leisure reading" morning assembly to the care of their official teachers, I made my way to the conference center for my second cup of coffee. Dr. Byrd met me there. Good morning, Ken, I'm glad I caught you; I just got a call from the Superintendent's secretary. I've been summoned to her office at once. Would you mind driving me there? Of course not. Thanks, Ken, I'll get my coat.

In the car I asked, what's going on? I wish I knew. For the remainder of the five-minute ride, no words were exchanged between us—both of us suspecting some unforeseen catastrophe. Upon arriving at the District Office, I told Dr. Byrd that I'd be waiting in my car for her, pointing at my *New York Post*. Thanks, Ken, I'll try not to be too long. After twenty minutes, I restarted my engine to heat up the interior of my car. Over the next hour, I repeated this process twice. After a wait of one hour and twenty minutes, I exited my car and entered the District Office. I approached the Superintendent's receptionist and asked as to whether or not Dr. Byrd was still in conference with the Superintendent. Please be seated, Mr. Kassell, commanded the superintendent's receptionist. Did this entire staff come from the military, I thought. My neck hairs stood straight up, a lifelong warning system that indicated danger. That won't be necessary, I'm just looking for Dr. Byrd. I repeat, came the calm but direct voice of the receptionist—be seated. As I did so, she depressed a button on the phone; I have Mr. Kassell out here. Very well. You can go in now, Mr. Kassell. The Superintendent is waiting. Entering the Superintendent's inner office, I was immediately drawn to the fact that she was on the telephone. With a wave of her finger, I was directed to a chair near the head of a large oval-shaped glass top table conference table, which had replaced the old oak table. I wondered where it had gone. It had been some time since I last had visited the Superintendent's office. The old motif of oak laden chairs and table had been replaced with contemporary state-of-the-art Macy's decor. I found the colors, a blend of variable purples and violets somewhat bordello-like. The carpet was a soft "cushiony" deep purple. The swivel chairs were likewise appointed with a purple leather cushion and backrest. Looking over at the Superintendent, one could not help but notice a "lot of leg." In doing so, I heard her say, I'll get back to you; he's here now." As she alighted from her console seat, I could see that Dr. Constance Jenning was a very well defined and endowed female. Her forties were being kind thus far. She stood about 5'5", her hair was short- cropped and had a red tinge that complemented her pale skin tone. Although not overly busty, it was worth resting one's gaze at that locale. Waistline and hip management was probably an ongoing concern at whatever health club she belonged to.

As she approached, I got up from my chair, just the way my mother had trained me. Dr. Jenning extended her hand saying, Mr. Kassell, I'm so very happy to make your acquaintance. Shaking hands, it was her next sentence that got my neck hairs to rise. I hope this is the beginning of a successful relationship. Superintendents didn't want successful relationships with Assistant Principals. They did not relate to Assistant Principals. It simply wasn't "hoyle." Excuse me, Dr. Jenning, I think there's been some misunderstanding. I'm looking for Dr. Byrd, who I had been led to believe was in conference with you. If you don't mind, I'll just go through the building until I find her. You won't have to do that, Mr. Kassell. You're right about one thing; Dr. Byrd and I did have a conference. The outcome of that conference is that she has been removed from her position as Principal. As senior Assistant Principal, you are assigned the responsibility of "Acting Principal." Slowly, I sat back down. I must have grown very pale, as I heard Dr. Jennings call on her intercom and order a cold bottle of Evian immediately. Why was she removed? I asked in a low voice. What was that, snapped Dr. Jennings? You heard me, why? Watch your tone, Mr. Kassell. You have no need to know the answer to that question. The Chancellor, the supervisor's union, and the school PA president have all been notified of my actions. Additionally, the school board voted in special session to approve of my removal of Dr. Byrd pending an investigation of charges. The Chancellor and Dr. Byrd have received a written list of those charges.

Where is she? I want to see her. That's out of the question. Are you saying I can't? I'm saying that you are to return to that school and assume its leadership now! By the way, you should look upon this opportunity as a career enhancing one. I look forward...as she spoke the words, I was halfway out of her office. At that juncture, I turned to face Dr. Jennings. Listen carefully, because I know that you're not the kind of person who likes to listen to others. I am fifty-three years old; my career speaks for itself. I understand the game plan all too well. Whoever has been advising you has marked your end. It will make no sense to anyone as to why a Superintendent in charge of a district with a seventy-five percent failure rating in pupil achievement in three quarters of its schools would declare war on a school that was functioning at a near ninety percent success rate in pupil achievement. You have miscalculated and indeed have misread the school, its parents, and the community support enjoyed by its principal. But most of all, you did not do your homework on me. For all of those reasons, your gambit shall fail.

Not waiting for a reply, I turned and left. Exiting the building, I ran into Douglass Tillerton, chairperson of the community school board who was lurking at the receptionist's desk. Then I knew. Here was the puppeteer waiting to see his puppet. What's up, Ken? You made a big fucking mistake, Doug. What? You'll see, you'll see, I repeated as I moved past him toward the street exit.

A year after I retired, I was providing mentoring services within the district. While walking to my car, I heard the familiar voice of Douglass Tillerton. Hey, Ken, how're you doing? Hi, Doug. Not bad, I'm retired and enjoying every minute. Yeah, I heard. So what are you doing here? I mentor a couple of days a week, plus I'm writing my memoirs. Really, I hope I got a page. You got two, Doug. Tell me was it really worth it? I mean after all, Dr. Byrd was fully reinstated, the school survives, and another Superintendent bit the dust. You have to understand, Ken, I got two boys there as you well know. Byrd was always messing over them. Finally when one of my kids was supposed to receive an honors award and didn't get it, that was the straw that broke the camel's back. Over the years, I was instrumental in making sure that school was left alone. But Byrd didn't understand loyalty or payback for that matter. In the meantime, I had a Superintendent who had literally sold her soul to the devil for the superintendency, me being the devil, of course. Of course I mimmicked. She had gone on public record as saying that she did not believe in Talented and Gifted education. A moronic point of view if ever there was one. Nevertheless, I had my stooge! This would be my opportunity to teach Byrd a lesson. I finally sold Jennings on the deal convincing her that with the little white guy at the helm, everything would come tumbling down soon enough. I reasoned that It would just be a matter of time before all hell broke loose, and then you'd be justified in having your staff take over the school—a move that would for sure be the school's death knell. This type of reasoning appealed to her racist nature, and she bought into the plot lock stock and barrel. Of course by now, she had also developed a strong dislike for Dr. Byrd who she saw as a potential threat to her superintendency.

Byrd being a neighborhood girl, Ph.D, principal of a successful school, and supported by the community, posed a serious threat to Jennings' tenure. She believed that all of these elements could be neutralized via Byrd's removal from the school. The fact that the charges for the most part would be unsubstantiated ones wouldn't matter. There would be so many that most supporters would have to back off. By the time the dust had settled, Byrd would be permanently damaged and no longer a threat. But she didn't know me I interjected. But I did, Ken, said Doug. Remember, I said that I never wanted that school to fold. The stupid bitch Jennings was so full of herself that she didn't bother to check you out, a cardinal sin as you know, Ken. I knew that you had twice served as Acting Principal. I knew that you could run any school in the district. I knew that the kids, parents, and staff would support you. In a way, you were my insurance policy. So I repeat, was it worth it Doug? My only regret, Ken, is that all the old warriors like yourself are gone or on the way out. Give my regards to your wife, Ken; I've got a meeting to go to. Regards to yours, Doug. Take care. He never did answer the question. But I knew the answer. For Doug it was the excitement of the game—manipulation, deception, daring, and ultimately status quo. Things indeed change and do stay the same, at least in public education in NYC they do.

Driving back to the school, I focused on the immediate meetings that would have to be convened. Of course, I anticipated that some word of today's events might have already leaked out. After all, this role was not new to me. I had been down this road before and pretty much knew the order of things. I would first call an emergency faculty conference for 3 p.m. that afternoon. I would then invite the PA Executive Board to a 3:30 meeting. In the interim, I would contact the supervisors' union to gain a clear understanding as to how to proceed. This was more or less a pro forma move. In situations such as this, the best thing one can do, indeed must do, is keep very good written records of actions taken, things said, and communiqués received, as well as responses thereto. Nevertheless, I would make the call. In so far as the day-to-day operations of the school were concerned, nothing would change. Calm and routine would be the governing catch words. This was a high profile school. I had to anticipate the arrival of the media, school board members, Chancellor's representatives, union officials, investigators, church and local civic groups, as well as our own parent body, all seeking to find out what was going on. It would be my goal to present to these "concerned" citizens an image of a school functioning at as high a level as was possible. Security would be instructed to bar all non-board of education personnel from the school. Finally, I would announce to the student body, that Dr. Byrd was on leave for health reasons. It was a well-known fact that she was an asthma sufferer. In the final analysis, I had no idea as to how it would all play out. I knew one thing; I was mad as hell. I held Jennings in personal contempt. She would pay dearly for her folly.

Chapter XLI

A Village Uprising!

Coups such as the one Jennings engineered were usually met with some resistance, that is, a few protests, a few cusses at some school board meetings, and then a petering out of resistance. Jennings had banked on this type of response when she made her move. She did not count on the fact that Gifted and Talented children have gifted and talented parents. She did not count on the fact that the removed Dr. Byrd would go outside the system, and retain the services of one of the city's high profile activist lawyers to present her case to the Chancellor. She did not count on the fact that the PA would on a weekly basis organize marches of protest and rallies on the school and district office steps. She did not count on the fact that both the teacher's and the supervisor's union would actively support the removed principal. She did not anticipate the degree by which all of these forces and the school community as well as myself would be bonded in an effort to thwart her objective as we saw it—namely the obliteration of the Village. It simply wasn't going to happen.

That Friday afternoon, I debriefed the PTA Executive Board as well as the entire Teaching staff and the custodial and Cafeteria support services staff as to the day's proceedings. I asked that the PTA use the weekend to plan a strategy as to how they wanted to proceed. I scheduled a Monday morning meeting with the PTA executive board at 9 a.m. I knew full well the limits that I could push in terms of my own resistance. Any hope for a reversal of fortune was rested in the power and conviction of the parents.

Over the weekend, I spent time reflecting on such questions as who to trust and whom not to trust. Jennings after all would not be fool enough to trust me. She'd need to have a way of knowing what was going on internally. We had no vacancies in any area, therefore I could rule out the arrival of some "rat" to fill such a position. In scenarios such as these, teachers usually minded their own business for fear of retribution. In this case the retribution might mean transfer from a school where they were safe and respected to one down the block where they would be subject to abuse on a daily basis. It was too early in the ballgame for any of the administrative staff to take sides. They would be watching, though. Rule them out. Who would it be? Quite possibly it could be a parent with his or her own agenda. I'd have to be careful and alert on Monday morning. Another question that came to mind was how to distance myself from any outward show of disobedience to Dr. Jennings' dictums. That wouldn't be a problem. I didn't get as far as I did by luck.

On Monday morning, as I monitored pupil lineups preparatory to their teacher supervised entry to the school, I was approached by six very well dressed and distinguished looking men and women. Their leader a tall man with dreadlocks asked if they could meet with me after I'd seen to the class dismissals. I recognized him as a certain Mr. Foxworthy one of my fourth grade parents. He had a reputation of always being there for the school. If we needed parent volunteers for trips, fundraising activities, or for advice, one could always count on Mr. Foxworthy. The fact that he was an attorney with connections in high places didn't hurt either. Of course I was quick to reply. I'll meet all of you at the conference center at 8:45. You'll find coffee and hot water for tea there—help yourselves. I had made up my mind to use the conference center as my first floor office. I would not glorify Jennings' folly by using the Principal's Office. As it turned out, however, over the weekend Jenning and several of her cronies had gained entrance into the school, had cordoned off all of Dr. Byrd's belongings, and sealed her office by changing the locks. In their eyes it was a done deal; Byrd was finished.

The conference hall was about fifty feet from the front entrance; and as I entered the school, I took note of the fact that several of the people with whom I had agreed to meet with had just entered the conference center. I also took note that one of our security guards was on the public phone, while the other was seated at the security desk. Casually, I said to the seated guard, please tell Martha that I said that she is still on duty. Her break time is 9 o'clock. I turned to leave and was frozen in my tracks when I heard, "That's not Martha, Mr. Kassell. She's still outside, that's a new guard sent here by the district office." When she's through, tell her I wish to speak with her in the conference center. Entering the center, I hung up my jacket and sat down at the conference table with my guests. If you don't mind, Mr. Kassell, began Mr. Foxworthy. Just a moment, please. I have to make this call. You may all remain; I want you to hear to whom I'm speaking. Good morning, this is Mr. Kassell; I need to speak to Dr. Jennings immediately. Is there something wrong? the receptionist replied. You're out of order, this call is for Dr. Jennings. One moment. Jennings' voice in a most condescending tone was next. Trouble in paradise? There will be if you don't pull out your spy, I responded. I didn't ask for a security guard add-on. We have no incidents which would warrant such an add-on. Finally, if you don't pull her out I will have her written up for dereliction of duty, negligence and post abandonment during the time she was reporting whatever she was reporting to your office. What a shame to ruin someone's career with just the stroke of one's pen. Don't you think? Jennings countered, my only interest was to maximize security at the school to ward off what might otherwise become a volatile climate. You may send her to the district office, but the responsibility for turning down my offer is yours solely. By the way, Mr. Kassell, I am holding you responsible for advising me as to any parental planned protests. You do realize that they may not use such school equipment as the photocopiers or telephones.

You have a good day, Dr. Jennings. Placing the phone back in its cradle, and facing the parents, just one more thing I have to tend to if you'll bare with me. I got up and opened the door to the newly assigned security guard. Disregarding the amenity of offering her a seat, I got right to it. I don't know your name nor do I care to. You are directed by Dr. Jennings to report to her office at once. By the way, if I were you, I'd refresh myself on role definition and job description quickly. Bye. Turning back to my guests, Mr. Foxworthy spoke first. You've answered our loyalty concerns, Mr. Kassell. We do want to hear your take on all that has gone on and the role you see yourself playing. Well, we've got plenty of coffee, and we can send out for more donuts.

Before you begin, Mr. Kassell, allow me to introduce the other members of our committee. We refer to ourselves as The Village Strategy Action Planning Committee. That won't be necessary, I said. In fact, this meeting has not taken place, and my best recollection of it will be that you all are just several of the many parents I will have spoken to during this long and no doubt tedious process. In that way I will have "plausible deniability" when and if the superintendent accuses me of conspiracy. That said, I will tell you that I believe that conspiracy is the operative word here. It was Foxworthy's turn. Mr. Kassell, we have had the weekend to try to understand what happened here that led to the removal of our principal. Nothing, I emphasized. Please let me go on. Of course, I'm sorry for the interruption.

Foxworthy continued. On the one hand while we are shocked at the turn of events, we are comforted in the knowledge that such a "war- tested veteran" as yourself is at the helm during this temporary sorry state of affairs. The operative word here being temporary. We will have Dr.

Byrd reinstalled as principal. Let there be no doubt as to that. Over the weekend we met with Dr. Byrd, and she shared the list of charges brought against her. Frankly we find them unbelievable. Our purpose in meeting with you is to get an understanding as to where you stand or see yourself in this matter. Judging by your actions we have already witnessed, you have reinforced in our minds that you don't take crap. Frankly there was some talk that you might have somehow been in collusion with the superintendent, but I can clearly see that that is not the case. Thank you, I said. Let me lay it out for you. I am fifty-three years old. I have been an Acting Principal on two previous occasions. I have answered the question for myself as to whether or not I could be a successful principal. Due to my many years of service, a longevity kicker boosts my salary, therefore my retirement allowance will be on a par with a principal's allowance. So I could not be enticed by promises of money. Was the offer made? interrupted Simon Foxworthy. It was alluded to as a reward for being a good boy. I regarded the offer as an insult. Let me tell you some of the things you need to know, if we are to function well. Earlier I referred to a conspiracy. In my view the conspiracy was not against Dr. Byrd—her removal, in my opinion was just a first step of a series of actions that are part of a larger conspiracy whose target is to bring the school down. Remember, this superintendent in her opening meeting with all of the district supervisors proclaimed that "she doesn't believe in Talented and Gifted education." Also, remember one other thing. A person like this isn't given a superintendent's contract unless the district chair and four other members feel the same; that is the conspiracy I speak of. So why take out the principal. It is the final piece of the "tearing down" process. First a guidance counselor's removal and then a family assistant, and then a security guard. Now the Principal Those moves in and of themselves, however, are not sufficient for a full hostile takeover.

Why not you, asked one of the female committee members? Another insult. I said. The superintendent believes that because I'm white and not community based that it will be just a matter of time before she is obligated to remove me and bring in her own forces to stabilize the school. At that point you will no longer have a school. So how do we avoid that? First you must get the word out to the parents that they must re-enforce in their children's mindset that there can be no incidents or arguments or perish the thought, fights at all. I am going to ask you to provide the school with parent volunteer patrols from 8 a.m. to 8:45 daily, as well as from 2:30 to 3:30 in the afternoon. Why do we need to take on the responsibility of perimeter security asked Foxworthy? Simple I replied. I believe that the parents are more apt to recognize the presence of potential troublemakers then my teaching staff. On a reciprocal basis, I believe that these troublemakers upon recognizing the parents many of whom would know their parents would be thusly discouraged. Having said this, then we can complete the equation by subtracting the possibility of having to call police in to intervene on our behalf. Therefore avoiding the possibility of being seen as a school in turmoil, and in need of takeover. Additionally, do not put yourself in a position of not obeying every school rule and regulation that governs parental conduct in a school. Upon visiting be sure to sign in. Do not be observed on any of the school telephones either downstairs or in someone's office. Do not encourage anyone to duplicate flyers on school machinery or on school duplicating paper. If there comes a time for flyer distribution, do so at dismissal as the students exit the various doors. Do not share your plans or strategies with me. Plausible deniability, Mr. Kassell? asked Simon Foxworthy. No, Mr. Foxworthy, just the voice of experience in such matters. Remember you are an ad hoc committee, not the PTA. Officially, the supervisors' union has advised me that my explanation to faculty, students, and to you for that matter, is that Dr. Byrd is out temporarily and is expected back soon. To that end all established routines will be maintained. All performance expectations remain high. In short all systems are go! By the way, I will not allow the press entree into the school. They will be directed to the superintendent. One more thing, do all of you have a child in this school? All heads nodded affirmatively.

At that point Mrs. Martin one of the school secretaries burst in and in an excited voice proclaimed, excuse me, Mr. Kassell, the superintendent is on the phone and demanded that I get you on the phone now. Calm down, Mrs. Martin, I'll take the call. Line 08, she said, exiting the conference room. Putting a finger to my lips I depressed the speaker button, sat back in my chair and extended the obligatory salutation. Good morning, Dr. Jennings. How can I help you? What did Simon Foxworthy and his group want. I'm glad your security guard made it back to you safely, I said. You're not answering the question. Nor will I. Understand, anyone with whom I speak is by my choice. The contents of those remarks are confidential and privileged, so far as you are concerned. How dare you speak to me in that manner, raged Jennings. Dares have never been an issue with me, Dr. Jennings. If there is anything you want to know concerning how I govern the school, I will certainly be responsive to those inquiries. Private conversations that I have will remain so. Is there anything else? Yes, she exclaimed. I'm removing you tomorrow.

Let me get this straight, I replied. You've already removed a guidance counselor, a family assistant, a security guard, the principal, cut back thousands of dollars from our school budget, stated openly that you were a non-proponent of Talented and Gifted education. Now after one day you are about to remove the assistant principal. The community, chancellor and supervisor's union are closely monitoring the situation, as by now are the media. Accusations are being made that you are negatively predisposed when it comes to this school. What do you think the impact of my removal will signify to those making such accusations? Then I said, will there be anything else, Dr. Jennings? The line went dead. Do you really think it's wise to provoke her? asked Mr. Foxworthy. Meet aggression, aggressively, I added. We'll be taking our leave now, Mr. Kassell. Our concerns as to where you stood in all of this have been answered. Is that a compliment or an endorsement? Neither, except to say that you are one less threat that the committee has to be concerned with. You do your part, Mr. Kassell, and we'll do ours. Have a good day, sir. You do the same! I asserted.

It was a week later during the weekly Superintedent's "Principal Conference" when Dr. Jennings and I jousted again. During this meeting she announced that I was to represent the district at a convention at Columbia University concerning low level achieving secondary schools. Your notes must be in error; my school is one of the leading overachievers in the city, let alone the district, I declared. You will attend, Mr. Kassell, or be charged with insubordination. You obviously never met my mother or wife. A hush came over the room. No, I haven't, Dr. Jenning responded curtly. And if I had? They would have warned you not to force or threaten me to do something I didn't want to do. Dismissing my remarks, Dr. Jenning suggested that the conference move to its next listed agenda item. Shortly, on the auspices that I wasn't feeling well, I left the conference and returned to the school. Upon arrival, I secured my *New York Post* and informed the secretary that I would be in the "executive lounge." After a short while there came a knock at the door. Yes, I bellowed. A very hesitant and nervous Mrs. Martin responded that she had been ordered by the superintendent to locate me. Did you tell her that I was indisposed? Yes, yes I did, Mr. Kassell;

but she ordered that I get you to the phone now. What shall I tell her? Tell her, tell her that I said I'll be there when I'm done wiping.

A week later I found myself getting out of bed at the ungodly hour of 5:30 a.m., so as to beat the traffic from Long Island to Columbia University as per Dr. Jennings' directive. As there was no street parking in the immediate area, I allowed myself to be gouged by one of the high priced parking lots which dot the landscape on the upper west side of Manhattan. Arriving at the conference center, I recognized no one among what had to be a throng of at least 100 individuals. This pleased me much. Immediately, I took a coffee and danish then seated myself in the very last seat in the last row of the auditorium, whereupon I commenced to enjoy the respite while perusing my *Post*. The tranquility of the moment was interrupted by Dr. Jennings' voice. Good morning, Mr. Kassell, I'm so disappointed to see you; I was looking forward to writing you up for insubordination. The day is just beginning, Dr. Jennings. I'll try to make it a memorable one for you.

Shortly thereafter the meeting commenced with the appearance of a gentleman who identified himself as the author of a proposal designed to improve underachieving secondary schools. He went on to say that he had spent his entire professional life reaching his conclusions. I had no trouble accepting that statement, as I judged from his grey eighteen inch ponytail that he had to be among the last of the '60's liberals in education. We're going to begin, he said, by having everyone in this room stand and introduce themselves stating the position they hold in their schools and their purpose for being here. My god, I thought—one hundred people identifying themselves and why they're here. We'll be here for dinner! An hour later after I had made several trips to the bathroom, I heard the MC say, "What about our friend in the back row? We haven't heard from you, yet." He's talking about you, Mr. Kassell, prompted Dr. Jennings between clenched teeth. Standing up, I proclaimed, "Ken Kassell," Acting Principal, The Talented and Gifted Village School. Other than the fact that she (pointing my finger in Jennings' direction) ordered me here, I don't know why I'm here.

On that note responded the MC, we'll adjourn to our workshop room on the second floor. Please check the chalkboard for your table assignment. Our first exercise will be designed to promote Team Building, an activity that may serve to enlighten our bewildered friend from the last row. Jennings smiled widely at the rebuke. If I were in his place why would I want to provoke someone who so clearly seems to be a bit off. He's fucking with me was the only answer I could come up with. I'll let well enough alone. I said what I had to say; there was nothing to be gained from continued confrontational behavior.

It was almost 10:30 when we all assembled in the workshop room. The tables had been arranged much like a Bar Mitzvah reception. There were ten tables with fifteen place settings. Each table had a centerpiece identifying the schools and school districts assigned to it. Alongside of the centerpiece there was a basket containing such sundries as: Elmer's glue, scotch tape, popsicle sticks, paper clips, and a deck of 3x5 index cards. My new liberal friend stated that the opening activity was designed to promote "Team Building." The challenge was for each table to function as a team. The task before the team was to use the materials in the basket to construct a castle or pyramid. Each person was expected to contribute to the process. The team was to be leaderless. Individuals could only communicate by sign language using either hand gestures or facial expressions to do so. I don't know about you, but my thoughts about leaderless groups are similar to my thoughts about a rowboat without oars. What good are they? At any event I participated as best I could, albeit not enthusiastically. After about ten minutes our fearless MC stopped the activity. He then announced that he was now going to survey each group as to their experience. He asked that each table appoint a "reporter" to give the feedback. This activity will take us up to lunch, which we have had catered by "Footlong Heroes." Things were looking up, I thought. At least the lunch sounded promising.

After an hour of hearing the reporters from each table proclaim such feedback as: having accomplished something in a way I didn't think possible, how exciting it was to feel so integral to a common purpose. On the negative side one table reporter asked "where would one employ such a tactic in a school"? In my school, the staff doesn't listen when spoken to—how can I expect them to function via sign language? Let's move to our friend in the rear who doesn't know why he is here stated the MC. He wants you to speak, Mr. Kassell, urged Dr. Jennings. I didn't know I was the reporter for the group, Dr. Jennings. You are now, she said. Standing at my place, I paused momentarily allowing for everyone to focus on me. We're waiting prompted the MC. Only one word comes to my mind and (looking directly at Dr. Jennings) I think you'll agree with me, Dr. Jennings One word asked the MC. I don't think I've ever had a one-word response before. Softly, I said the word. Sensual. What was that? the MC asked. In a louder tone I exclaimed, SENSUAL while looking directly at Dr. Jennings. I went on...don't deny it, Dr. Jenning, I saw your skin get goose bumps when we touched while I reached for the Elmer's. I sensed that same emotion at that moment of touching. How dare you, Dr. Jennings screeched. I think we'll break for lunch now, declared our MC. I want to speak to you immediately, Mr. Kassell. Sorry, nature calls, Dr. Jennings. Be back in ten minutes. Knowing that I had to speak with her and also knowing how she had once declared at a meeting that she was allergic to cigarette smoking and therefore would not allow it at her meetings, I used the the time to smoke two Pall Malls and then went to speak with her.

I have never been so embarrassed, she began. No less than three people came over to me to inquire as to your state of mind. Only three from all of these people. I'm flattered. Who are they? I'll personally explain my state of mind to each of them on an individual or small group basis. Never mind, Mr. Kassell. Aschew! Bless you. I need to know if you will be able to behave during the afternoon workshops, or I'm sending you back to the school. Listen carefully, Dr. Jennings. I told you I didn't want to attend this conference; it had no relevancy to my situation. You ordered me to attend, and I have complied. There is a contingency plan in place for the governance of the school during my absence for all of today. A few moments ago during the break I called the school and learned that all was normal. Therefore, if you would prefer that I leave the meeting, I shall. Where I go, however, is a matter of personal choice. Actually, if that is your final feeling on the matter, I wish you'd let me know; I still have time to get to Aqueduct for the double. I'll instruct the secretary to mark me absent for a half day. As far as behaving myself, we threw all of that out the window at our first meeting. You should have done your homework. Stay or leave, Dr. Jennings, I'm waiting. She turned to leave, saying do whatever you like. I'm finished. A most prophetic statement. A couple of months later, the chancellor called her downtown and according to whispers, harangued her bitterly with such terms as "horse's ass," imbecile, and fool. He ordered that the school board terminate her contract forthwith. He suspended the school board pending a full investigation as to their culpability in the entire fiasco. He further ordered that Dr. Byrd be reinstated immediately.

Kenneth S. Karcinell

Epilogue

For me, it was my last great battle. I believe that while I fought it well, it depleted whatever reserves I might have had. My goal to reach thirty five years of service would go unfulfilled. Going away for summer vacation, I confided to Dr. Byrd that I would be giving serious thought about retiring in the fall. You know that you're welcome here as long as you like, Ken. Retirement is a very personal choice. Do it for the right reasons, is all I can tell you. Make sure the money is right and the future is bright! Another Byrdism I thought as I pecked her on the cheek and left for summer vacation.

Kenneth S. Karcinell

About the Author

On November 1, 1997, after thirty-two years of service to the NYC school system, Kenneth Karcinell retired. It was time. The fact is that at age fifty-five, he was in a place that most in the profession can only dream of, a Talented and Gifted PreK-8 school. Although the school was located in one of Brooklyn's high crime neighborhoods, his school was relatively free from incident. He served there as Assistant Principal and as Acting Principal for the three years leading up to his retirement. During his tenure there, he enjoyed a very positive relationship with pupils, teachers and parents. It was just time to go!

Ken Karcinell was born and raised in NYC. He is a product of its public school system, graduating from DeWitt Clinton HS in the Bronx in 1960. After acquiring his BS degree from Rider College in Lawrenceville, New Jersey, Ken was undecided as to a profession. He knew that he had to make a living while he contemplated his future. He had done some truck driving while in college, so he resumed this line of work. In 1965 Ken passed the NYC substitute teacher's exam and thus began a thirty-two year career in the education field. Early in his career Ken received a Master of Arts degree from Hebrew University of NY in School Administration and Supervision.

Presently, he is an Adjunct Professor in the School of Education, Graduate Studies Department, CCNY. He is also a Consultant to the Teaching Fellows Program for the NYC Board of Education. In his spare time, he serves as a mentor to novice teachers in a public school in Brooklyn, New York.

Ken and his wife of thirty years Ellen are the proud parents of a son Joey who attends Cornell University and their recently married daughter Sarah Fried of Manhattan. Ken and Ellen reside in Hewlett New York, but escape to their "campsite" in the White Mountains of New Hampshire whenever they can.

Printed in the United States
1416500001B/40-135